MW00803685

"William Cornell is among our most brilliant a
of psychotherapy integration and to clinical practice. In this new book, he provides a collection of essays that bring to bear a dazzling range of therapeutic and analytic schools of thought. He builds a richly imaginative yet critical integration, infused with his own deeply personal idiom, so that the reader is drawn into an intimate engagement with Cornell's mind. We see how these complex ideas and systems are filtered through one's own unique subjectivity and character and how they may be utilized to benefit the growth and healing of our patients."

Lewis Aron, PhD, Director, New York University Postdoctoral
Program in Psychotherapy & Psychoanalysis, USA

"William Cornell claims Transactional Analysis as his 'home team' and what a privilege it is to have him playing for us. He has long been a key TA theoretician and practitioner but also critic and challenger. His dual role has been, first to ensure that TA did not become parochial, to keep it lively, and secondly, to let people outside our community know that 'TA is still very much alive'.

This collection charts the process of how he has consistently challenged even the key tenets of TA theory such as ego states and script, both in terms of the inherent contradictions within TA, and by introducing TA to the broader context of modern psychoanalytic thinking, neuroscience and body work. This has been enriching for our own community and allowed people from other disciplines to begin to hear and appreciate TA in a language that is familiar to them. Cornell is not only a good communicator but also a superb translator.

However, I think it is in his accounts of his clinical work that Cornell gives of his best. He clearly enjoys his work and his deep love and respect for even the most challenging client is palpable. He never ceases to examine his own thinking and practice and is constantly seeking and learning. We are the fortunate recipients of this journey with his clients. Although many TA therapists may work differently from him they will, I think, readily identify with his commitment to what drew many of us to TA… Berne's radical, egalitarian and practical view that people are ultimately in charge of their own process of change and have what it takes to make that change. It is up to us to find how we can be useful (or in Cornell's terms) used in that process."

Diane Salters, ITAA President

"In the complex, intense, sometimes murky world of the psychotherapy session, at moments when theory and training prove insufficient, Bill Cornell offers an alternate, powerful source of guidance, within the therapist's own self. His new book connects his theoretical roots in transactional analysis, neo-Reichian body therapy, and psychoanalysis, with his evolving focus on the therapist's use of one's self as a source of understanding of the patient and an instrument of therapeutic change. The theoretical ideas are presented as they play out in the session; as his readers already know, Bill has the gift of story-telling. The case descriptions, including the many ways that impasses can occur, are transparent; the reader can see and feel into the room and inside of Bill himself. As in Freud's stories of Anna O., Frau Emmy von N., Fraulein Elisabeth von R., and Dora, the reader can experience the worlds of Alessia, Kurt, Simone, Ben, Charlie and Abby, the tripartite interaction with Lara and Emily, and the painful failure in the treatment of Samantha. The stories also go beyond most case reports in incorporating the struggles of each participant in the treatment and the growth in each of them.

Bill's stories and his explorations provide a rich source of ideas and observations, not only for clinicians but also for psychotherapy researchers who are seeking to understand the therapeutic process in new ways. In several papers, Bill finds and explores conceptual connections among the script theory of transactional analysis, the psychoanalytic ideas of Bollas, and the theory of multiple coding and the referential process. From my perspective, these connections help to build a new general theory of therapeutic change, incorporating subsymbolic bodily and emotional experience along with symbolic forms, and applicable across treatment types.

A major take-away for me from this collection of papers is the idea of a 'vital base' rather than a secure one, arising from Bill's acute recognition of the difficulty for all of us - the person in the role of client, the person in the role of mental health professional, the citizens of our country and our world today - to accept the destructive forces, the feelings of hatred, terror, loss and shame that we share. Bill writes about the effects of these feelings, and the damage done by avoiding them, in the context of ideas concerning group psychology and social responsibility that emerged in the writings and work of Freud following WWI, and Berne in the 1960s. It seems necessary to think about these broader ideas and let ourselves confront such feelings as we struggle, in our varying roles and states, with the events of our times."

Wilma Bucci, PhD

At the Interface of Transactional Analysis, Psychoanalysis, and Body Psychotherapy

At the Interface of Transactional Analysis, Psychoanalysis, and Body Psychotherapy revolves around two intertwined themes: that of the critique and expansion of the theory and practice of transactional analysis and that of the generative richness discovered at the intersection of transactional analysis, psychoanalysis, and somatic psychotherapy.

William F. Cornell explores the work of psychotherapists and counsellors through the lenses of clinical theory, practice, supervision, and ethics. The reader is thus invited into a more vivid experience of being engaged and touched by this work's often deep, and at times difficult, intimacy. The book is grounded in the approaches of contemporary transactional analysis and psychoanalysis, using detailed case discussions to convey the flesh of these professional, and yet all too human, working relationships. Attention is paid to the force and richness of the transferential and countertransferential tensions that pervade and enliven the therapeutic process. Unconscious processes are viewed as fundamentally creative and life-seeking, with the vital functions of fantasy, imagination, and play brought into the foreground.

In the era of short-term, cognitive-behavioural, solution-focused, and evidence-based models of counselling and psychotherapy, *At the Interface of Transactional Analysis, Psychoanalysis, and Body Psychotherapy* seeks to demonstrate the power and creativity of longer-term, dynamically oriented work.

William F. Cornell maintains an independent private practice of psychotherapy and consultation in Pittsburgh, PA. He has devoted more than 40 years to the study and integration of transactional analysis, psychoanalysis, and somatic psychotherapy. He is a Training and Supervising Transactional Analyst and has established an international reputation for his teaching and consultation.

At the Interface of Transactional Analysis, Psychoanalysis, and Body Psychotherapy

Clinical and Theoretical Perspectives

William F. Cornell

Routledge
Taylor & Francis Group

LONDON AND NEW YORK

First published 2019
by Routledge
2 Park Square, Milton Park, Abingdon, Oxon OX14 4RN

and by Routledge
711 Third Avenue, New York, NY 10017

Routledge is an imprint of the Taylor & Francis Group, an informa business

© 2019 William F. Cornell

The right of William F. Cornell to be identified as author of this work has been asserted by him in accordance with sections 77 and 78 of the Copyright, Designs and Patents Act 1988.

All rights reserved. No part of this book may be reprinted or reproduced or utilised in any form or by any electronic, mechanical, or other means, now known or hereafter invented, including photocopying and recording, or in any information storage or retrieval system, without permission in writing from the publishers.

Trademark notice: Product or corporate names may be trademarks or registered trademarks, and are used only for identification and explanation without intent to infringe.

British Library Cataloguing in Publication Data
A catalogue record for this book is available from the British Library

Library of Congress Cataloging in Publication Data
Names: Cornell, William F., author.
Title: At the interface of transactional analysis, psychoanalysis, and body psychotherapy : clinical and theoretical perspectives / William F. Cornell.
Description: New York, NY : Routledge, 2019. | Includes bibliographical references and index.
Identifiers: LCCN 2018015594 (print) | LCCN 2018016996 (ebook) | ISBN 9780429464430 (Master) | ISBN 9780429875625 (Web PDF) | ISBN 9780429875618 (ePub) | ISBN 9780429875601 (Mobipocket/Kindle) | ISBN 9781138607873 (hbk : alk. paper) | ISBN 9781782205852 (pbk. : alk. paper) | ISBN 9780429464430 (ebk)
Subjects: | MESH: Transactional Analysis | Psychoanalytic Therapy | Psychoanalytic Theory
Classification: LCC RC480 (ebook) | LCC RC480 (print) | NLM WM 460.5. T7 | DDC 616.89/14--dc23
LC record available at https://lccn.loc.gov/2018015594

ISBN: 978-1-138-60787-3 (hbk)
ISBN: 978-1-782-20585-2 (pbk)
ISBN: 978-0-429-46443-0 (ebk)

Typeset in Times New Roman
by Integra Software Service Pvt. Ltd.

Contents

Figures

Acknowledgments

In acknowledgment and appreciation—Keeping Our Work Alive

Over the course of 45 years of learning and practice, many people have come to challenge, provoke, and enrich my thinking. It is a daunting task to name but a few here.

The spirit of this book has been grounded in an 18-year-long seminar series created by a group of colleagues here in Pittsburgh called "Keeping Our Work Alive" (KOWA). A self-sustaining group of 25 psychotherapists and psychoanalysts from diverse models, meeting six times a year, we organized these seminars to keep us constantly involved in clinical and research perspectives that will help our thinking stay fresh. The spirit of these seminars infuses the writings that are gathered in this volume. During this same period of time, I have also had the exceptionally good fortune to meet weekly in a lively study and consultation group with several analytically oriented colleagues. Our commitment to one another has provided a "vital base" that has supported much of the clinical thinking I have brought to these chapters. My thanks, also, go to Stan Perelman and Jim McLaughlin whose mentoring and friendship here in Pittsburgh over many years have been the foundation of my professional maturation.

Throughout my career, my colleagues in the International Transactional Analysis Association (ITAA) have been my home team. The practicality of transactional analysis (TA) always appealed to my working-class roots. The chapters in this book, written as papers over 30 years, all start with TA as the base. The TA community has welcomed my efforts to challenge and expand TA theory and practice through encounters with other models. In 2010, the ITAA awarded me the Eric Berne Memorial Award, the Association's highest honor, for that endeavor—an enterprise not always welcomed in other theoretical models. The three papers chosen for the award are included in this volume. Among my many TA colleagues, I must single out Robin Fryer, the managing editor of the *Transactional Analysis Journal* (*TAJ*), where I have served as an editor for the past 15 years. It has been through my editorial partnership with

Robin that I have learned to write. In recent years, I have also had the pleasure and satisfaction of working with my current *TAJ* co-editors—Jo Stuthridge in New Zealand, Diana Deaconu in Romania, and Sylvie Monin in Switzerland—a wonderful team committed to creative thinking and to expanding the reach of transactional analysis.

Within the body psychotherapy world, Mark Ludwig has been my partner in crime for four decades. Mark brings one of the most inquisitive minds to the fields of somatic work, being relentless in his efforts to enliven the field through his teaching, conferences, and conversations.

Within the psychoanalytic world, the influence of many will be evident in the papers collected here. I have had the good fortune not only to read many referenced here but also to meet and talk with them (often courtesy of KOWA). It is particularly difficult to single out individuals for acknowledgment here, and yet there are some to whom I owe a great deal of thanks. Through many years of consultation and conversation, Christopher Bollas first brought contemporary psychoanalysis alive for me. His writing has given me a profound model for courageous, creative clinical thinking. I first met Kit at the time when the analytic world was largely closed off to those who hadn't drunk the Kool-Aid— Kit's consultation groups, in contrast, were open to anyone who wanted to think and deepen their work with clients. Muriel Dimen's fearless and provocative writings on sexuality brought a depth of understanding to my own thinking and clinical work that stands as a true gift, as did our rich and challenging friendship over the years. The multiple code theory developed by Wilma Bucci opened crucial doors for me as a way of bridging psychoanalytic and somatic orientations—a gap that had seemed impossible to bridge until I discovered her work. Our interchanges as authors and friends have been and continue to be precious to me. Lew Aron's boundless exuberance for ideas has underscored a friendship and intellectual partnership for which I will be forever grateful. It was Lew's support that enabled me to bring my work from the somatic domain, including the practice of touching clients, into the psychoanalytic literature.

Particular thanks go to Rod Tweedy, the Karnac editor who first took on my manuscript, to Charles Bath, who has seen it to completion, and to Alyson Silverwood, who has skillfully, thoughtfully added the final polishing of the text.

The voices of so many others are reflected in the chapters that follow. My heart-felt thanks to all.

Permissions

The following chapters are reprinted by permission of Taylor & Francis, LLC:

Chapter 1 was first published as "Opening to the vitality of unconscious experience," in *Transactional Analysis in Contemporary Psychotherapy*, edited by Richard Erskine. London: Karnac, 2016, pp. 79–98.

Chapter 3 first appeared as "Fostering freedom for play, imagination, and uncertainty in professional learning environments," in *Relational Transactional Analysis: Principles in Practice*, edited by Heather Fowlie and Charlotte Sills. London: Karnac, 2011, pp. 337–343.

Chapter 4 first appeared as "The intricate intimacies of psychotherapy and questions of self-disclosure," *European Journal of Psychotherapy and Counselling*, 9, 2007: 51–62.

The following chapters first appeared in *Explorations in Transactional Analysis: The Meech Lake Papers* (2008) and are reprinted by permission of the TA Press:

Chapter 7 first appeared as "Babies, brains, and bodies: Somatic foundations of the child ego state," in *Explorations in Transactional Analysis: The Meech Lake Papers*, TA Press, 2008, pp. 141–158.

Chapter 8 first appeared as "'My body is unhappy': Somatic foundations of script and script protocol," in *Explorations in Transactional Analysis: The Meech Lake Papers*, TA Press, 2008, pp. 159–170.

The following chapters first featured in the *Transactional Analysis Journal* and are reprinted by kind permission of SAGE Publications Ltd:

Chapter 2 first appeared as "Play at your own risk: Games, play, and intimacy," *Transactional Analysis Journal*, 45, 2015: 79–90.

Chapter 5 first appeared as "Failing to do the job: When the client pays the price for the therapist's countertransference," *Transactional Analysis Journal*, 46, 2016: 1–11.

Chapter 6 first appeared as "Life script: A critical review from a developmental perspective," *Transactional Analysis Journal*, 18, 1988: 270–282.

Chapter 9 first appeared as "Aspiration or adaptation?: An unresolved tension in Eric Berne's basic beliefs," *Transactional Analysis Journal*, 40, 2010: 243–253.

Chapter 10 first appeared as "What do you say if you don't say unconscious?: Dilemmas created for transactional analysis by Berne's shift away from the language of unconscious experience," *Transactional Analysis Journal*, 38, 2008: 93–100.

Chapter 11 first appeared as "Impasse and intimacy: Applying Berne's concept of script protocol," *Transactional Analysis Journal*, 36, 2006: 196–213.

Chapter 12 first appeared as "Nonconscious processes and self development: Key concepts from Eric Berne and Christopher Bollas," *Transactional Analysis Journal*, 38, 2008: 200–217.

Chapter 13 first appeared as "The Old Stone House: Eric Berne's memories and mourning for his father's life and death," *Transactional Analysis Journal*, 40, 2010: 305–307.

Chapter 14 first appeared as "Grief, mourning, and meaning: In a personal voice," *Transactional Analysis Journal*, 44, 2014: 302–310.

Chapter 15 first appeared as "The inevitability of uncertainty, the necessity of doubt, and the development of trust," *Transactional Analysis Journal*, 37, 2007: 8–16.

Chapter 16 first appeared as "In conflict and community: A century of turbulence working and living in groups," *Transactional Analysis Journal*, 46, 2016: 136–148.

Deepening our capacities for therapeutic work

Part I

Deepening our capacities
for therapeutic work

Chapter 1

Opening to the vitality of unconscious experience

> My view is that the analyst's technique is his attitude actualized, and that what matters most is the passionate curiosity tamed in the service of the patient's self inquiry, the analyst knowing a bit about how analytic work unfolds, not about how the patient should live his life.
>
> (Poland, personal communication)

I trained simultaneously during the 1970s in transactional analysis (TA) and Radix, neo-Reichian body education, becoming a trainer in each modality. At the surface, these two methodologies were rather strange bedfellows, in that TA was profoundly cognitive and rational, with a strict rule against touching clients, while Radix was, to an equal and opposite extent, profoundly emotional, with touch and bodily expression at the core of the neo-Reichian techniques (Kelley, 1988, 2004). However, what these two modalities held in common was a positioning of the therapist on the *outside* of the therapeutic process as the one who assessed the client's difficulties from a specific theoretical frame of reference and then *acted upon* the client's way of being so as to promote change. It was the task of the TA therapist to identify games and scripts so as "cure" the client. It was the task of the Radix practitioner to confront the interpersonal and bodily character defenses so as to promote emotional catharsis and ultimately establish "orgastic potency." This active, knowing positioning of the therapist had great appeal to me as a young, rather frightened, and overly responsible psychotherapist. It served me well, but I gradually began to see that it did not always serve my clients so well. I took my questions and clinical concerns to my TA and Radix supervisors. The supervisory responses were uncannily similar: the problems were rooted in the depths of my clients' resistances and character defenses. I was doing fine; I was simply to do more of the same—longer, harder. I did as I was told, and some of my clients got worse. I decided to look elsewhere for consultation. I knew the fundamental difficulties were in my working style, not in the resistances of my clients. I sought supervision outside of transactional analysis and the Reichian worlds, and I began to read, searching for an understanding of the problems I was finding in my clinical work.

I began supervision with a Kleinian therapist, whose style was unlike anything I had ever known. I hated the process, and I hated her, but I knew she was up to something important. We worked from session transcripts. She said nothing about my clients—no diagnoses, no interpretations. She made no technical suggestions, nor did she challenge what I was doing. She essentially asked one question in seemingly endless variations, "What was going on inside of you that you chose to speak right then? Why did you feel the need to do something just then?" Gradually, reluctantly, I began to see how often my interventions—be they verbal, bodily, supportive, or confronting—were precipitated by my own anxiety and my need to *do something*. I also began to recognize that my affinity for these active methodologies was an enactment of my script. In my family of origin, I was the doer, the caretaker, and the problem-solver, so here I was again playing out these roles in my professional work, whether or not they suited the needs of my clients.

I then sought supervision from a Jungian analyst, in spite of my stereotype that Jungians were all overly intellectual and spent their time diagnosing archetypes and drawing mandalas with their clients. This man proved to be a gift to my professional development. He gave me my first lessons in listening rather than doing. He taught me to manage my anxiety and to soften my style. Most importantly, he listened for the more grow-oriented impulses of my clients, helping me to shift out of my habitual game/character/defense listening mode.

During this period of time, I suspended most of my Reichian-style therapy and invited several of my body-therapy clients to meet and read with me to see if we could figure out what was wrong with the way we had been working. It was our reading of the Vietnam-related literature on post-traumatic stress disorder (PTSD) that gave us our first insights into the impact of trauma and to distinguish dissociative defenses from those of the more classical repressive sort that both Berne and Reich emphasized. The result was an evolution in my understanding of working with body process, about which I've written extensively over the years (Cornell & Olio, 1992, 1993; Cornell, 2007, 2008, 2011, 2015).

Without my busy, allegedly empathic, "useful," "good parent" therapist-self in high gear, I often fell into a muted, rather empty silence. I needed not only to learn how to listen differently, I needed to learn how to speak differently. I returned to the psychoanalytic literature, now exploring contemporary analysts. The discovery of the work of D.W. Winnicott (1960, 1971), Christopher Bollas (1987, 1989, 1999), James McLaughlin (2005), and Warren Poland (1996, 2012) was like a revelation to me. Here were accounts of the force and vitality of unconscious experience that stood in stark contrast to the classical psychoanalytic theories of the unconscious that Berne had rejected in his development of TA. Here were analysts who, each in their own way, described how to listen, to welcome and to tolerate uncertainty, and to spend long periods in attentive quiet. It was a fundamental task in classical psychoanalysis to render the unconscious conscious. For Bollas, the thrill of psychoanalytic explorations was that of enriching conscious experience with the depth, mystery, and vitality of unconscious experience.

My immersion in their writings, and my good fortune to work closely with both McLaughlin and Bollas, provided the basis for much of the work I will describe in this chapter. Jim McLaughlin and I were never in supervision or therapy together, our working relationship was around his writing and mine. As he became familiar with my writing, he made a pointed and unforgettable interpretation, "It seems to me that the closer something is to your heart, the quieter you become. It is as though you imagine that silence can best protect what you cherish." In supervision with Christopher Bollas during this same period of time, he made the comment that I seemed to be afraid of the unconscious—of my own as well as that of my client. These were transformative interpretations.

My discovery a few years later of the writings of Muriel Dimen (2003, 2005) and Ruth Stein (1998a, 1998b) radically transformed my understanding of the meanings and functions of sexuality, returning attention to sexuality in my clinical work. My reading and meeting with these analysts made fundamental changes in my understanding of my work through the 1990s and the first decade of this century. The impact of these analytic perspectives on my work will be the focus of this chapter.

This chapter is based in my evolution as a psychotherapist. However, the force and vitality of unconscious realms are present whenever we work as professionals involved in facilitating psychological change, regardless of our particular field of application.

A brief pause with Eric Berne

Reading Winnicott and Bollas opened new ways of reading and understanding Berne, which led to a series of papers exploring both the richness and the limits of Berne's writing (Cornell, 2000, 2005, 2006; Cornell & Landaiche, 2008). In re-reading Berne with a fresh perspective, I began to see a depth and an often conflicted wisdom in his work that had not been apparent to me in my initial study of his books or in the rendering of Berne that had been in my TA training.

I found in re-reading Berne a concept that proved to be a key in my unraveling the clinical dilemmas I was trying to find my way through. In his theory of games, Berne (1964, p. 64) made distinctions between what he called "first, second, and third degree" games, which I have further extended to the understanding and differentiations of script. By "first degree," Berne was describing levels of intrapsychic and interpersonal defenses that were reasonably available to conscious awareness and change through cognitive interventions and understandings. Berne saw games at the first degree level as serving a "social" function, which is to say, to make relationships more predictable.

"Second-degree" games and scripts serve defensive purposes that operate outside of conscious awareness and control. At the second degree, Berne saw a split between the conscious level of communication and another, which is more psychologically significant, that represents more unconscious motivations. "Second-degree" games are understood as serving a more fundamental psychological function—i.e., maintaining script—rather than a social function. Defenses operating at this level are not so readily amenable to change through cognitive interventions. Berne (1966) developed his model of group treatment primarily as a means of helping clients identify and alter their second-degree games.

Berne characterized "third-degree" games and scripts as held and lived at the "tissue" level, by which he meant at the level of the body rather than the mind. Berne saw defenses at this third level as being extremely resistant to change and ultimately destructive. As I read Winnicott and Bollas, I came to see Berne's pessimism for successful treatment of third-degree (and sometimes second-degree) defenses was a direct consequence of his turning away from maintaining a place for working with unconscious experience and motivation in transactional analysis.

My emphasis here is on the use of Berne's differentiation of the "degrees" of games as an indication of intrapsychic organization. Stuthridge and Sills (2016) offer a further elaboration of Berne's model, emphasizing the interpersonal implications and impacts of the degree of the game. It is important to recognize that while Berne framed his differentiations of the degrees of games in terms of levels of defense, these variations of psychic organization are not in and of themselves defensive or pathological. The fact, for example, that aspects of one's experience are organized and experienced primarily at nonverbal body ("tissue") level does not make them pathological.

When writing about script theory, Berne (1963) introduced the concepts of protocol and palimpsest:

> A protocol or palimpsest is of such a crude nature that it is quite unsuitable as a program for grown-up relationships. It becomes largely forgotten (unconscious) and is replaced by a more civilized version, the script proper....
>
> (p. 167)

In this way, he described a level of unconscious, somatic organization without the attribution of defense and pathology that attended third-degree games (Cornell & Landaiche, 2006).

In the fifty years since Berne's death, the study of attachment patterns, implicit memory processes, the subsymbolic mode of organization, transference/countertransference, and neuropsychological research have radically shifted our understanding of these somatic, and often unconscious, realms of experience. Protocol and palimpsest are not inherently pathological, but are grounded what we might call "the good, the bad, and the ugly" of our earliest experience that lives on within us in what we would now call implicit, procedural memory. At the "third-degree" level, *living the experience* with our clients precedes and informs whatever comes to be analyzed and spoken.

Berne's differentiations helped me see that I needed to develop a much more varied approach to psychotherapy. I could see that while my more active, interpretive interventions, be they in the more cognitive style of TA or the more somatic interventions of the neo-Riechian modes, were often sufficient for clients whose defenses were organized primarily at the first and second degree levels, for other clients and the deeper, more troubled phases of treatment, there needed to be fundamental changes in my customary ways of working. I did not need to trash everything that I had been doing, but it was abundantly clear that I needed to expand my ways of working.

Two-person, separate

It was a painful period of learning in which I gradually shed my manic, overly active, relentlessly useful style of psychotherapy. In my personal psychoanalysis I was able to painfully face the defensive functions of my manic need for action and efficacy. Here was the mother's presence in the unconscious motivations for my manic overdoing. My father's absence underlay my dread of silence and separateness, which I felt to be the equivalent of neglect and isolation.

My consultants gently, but persistently, pointed out how often my apparent "empathy" for my clients served the needs of my self-image more than the needs of my clients. Bollas repeatedly spoke to how an over-investment in "empathy" foreclosed the experience of the client, taking away their right to self-exploration. McLaughlin argued, "Here I emphasize the working of two separate minds so that I can make clear that the central focus on the patient's reality view does not mean seeking unbroken agreement and oneness in the dyad" (2005, p. 207). Poland (2012) emphasizes the fundamental separateness of the subjectivities of the therapist and client:

> Whatever the analyst then says, from the most trivial clarification to the most profound interpretation, whatever the content of the words, a crucial message buried deep in the structure of the very making of the statement is one that states, "**No**, I am **not** you, nor am I one of your ghosts, but as separate people we can speak of what is involved. No, I am not part of your dream, but as a person who cares for what you are doing but who is separate, I can help you find the words to say it.
>
> (p. 947; emphasis in original)

The willingness of the therapist to respect that essential separateness gives the client the space and freedom of self-discovery and self-definition. I came to see how a therapist's self-disclosure or the valorization of mutuality further risks an impingement on the client's psychic realities and struggles.

Gradually I learned to be *informed* by my countertransferences, and for the most part to keep them to myself, so as to allow my clients to inhabit their own intrapsychic wishes and struggles:

> Psychoanalysis takes place between two people yet feels as if it lives within the deepest recesses of my private life.
>
> ... For every encounter with a patient sends me deeply into myself, to an area of essential aloneness processed by voiceless laws of dense mental complexity.
>
> ... the analyst and his patient are in a curiously autobiographical state, moving between two histories, one privileged (the patient) and the other recessed (the analyst), in the interests of creating generative absence, so that the patient may create himself out of [these] two materials....
>
> (Bollas, 1999, p. 11)

Bollas' position often seemed frightening and alien to me as a therapist who habitually used his work with clients to escape himself. His sense of a "generative absence" was a startling and liberating contrast to the meanings of absence that I had internalized with my father.

Deeply depressed during her graduate school years, Catherine was desperate to have a place where she could figure out her life and her sense of self. She had lived her life being seen only through the demanding and judgmental eyes of those around her. It was with Catherine that I learned with particular poignancy the importance of keeping our histories separate and of tolerating my countertransference.

We had been working for four years when her mother was diagnosed with a recurrence of an earlier cancer that had metastasized to her bones and brain. During that same period of time, my sister was terminally ill with massively metastasized cancers. My sister died while Catherine's mother was still undergoing treatment. Many times, as I listened to her, I thought of my sister, who was the same age as Catherine's mother, and of my niece's, my nephews' anguish. At times I found it nearly unbearable to listen to her as I anticipated what lay ahead for her and her mother. I said nothing to her of my sister's plight or the impact that listening to her had upon me. I could not, in the sessions themselves, sort out which of my reactions had to do with Catherine and which were mine—they were too immediate and intense. Her father was as emotionally self-absorbed and oblivious to his children as was my sister's husband, so my countertransference was intense and risked being intrusive. I kept it to myself and worked it through with myself, so as to remain open to her experience.

Catherine's parents were each in their own way so profoundly self-involved that there was no room for her struggles or needs as she faced her mother's illness. She needed a space with me that was entirely hers. Her relationship with her mother had been turbulent and deeply conflictual but also loving and intimate. She felt an intense need to avoid conflict as her mother grew more ill. Catherine often said, "if my mother dies," which I never corrected. However, when I spoke of her mother's illness, I always said, "When your mother dies." She asked me one day why I said "when." I told her that her mother's cancer was terminal, and that her mother undoubtedly knew that. When Catherine, her father, or other family said, "if," they were lying. "It is a lie intended to comfort," I said, "but it is a lie nonetheless. Perhaps it is a lie that comforts your father and family, but it signals to your mother that there are things that cannot be spoken, cannot be faced together and that she may be facing her death alone. I'm not willing to participate in the lie with you. You may make a different choice with your family." In time, Catherine learned to speak freely to her mother, and her mother was able to respond in kind, and, fortunately, they did not lose their capacity to argue with each other. Catherine found her way to accompany her dying Mom. They could speak the truth to one another.

As her mother approached death, Catherine was often told that she was too emotional and that her feelings would upset her mother. As her mother became less and less able to communicate verbally, Catherine wanted desperately to hear from her mother her beliefs and feelings about dying. Catherine wanted to say goodbye, to tell her Mom how much she would miss her, and how angry she was at the cancer. But Catherine was rendered mute by her family, who insisted that her mother needed to be "protected" from the fact that she was dying. I was silently furious with her family and frightened that she would lose this precious opportunity with her mother. I felt certain that her mother knew she was dying and did not need to be "protected" from that reality. I had to make a decision about how and whether to speak to what I was thinking and feeling. I was not at all certain what to say, or whether to say anything at all.

Self-disclosure is not a casual decision, and I didn't want to speak just to alleviate my own distress (Aron, 1996; Maroda, 1999; McLaughlin, 2005; Jacobs, 2013; Cornell; 2014). I did not want to be another person telling Catherine what to think and feel, intruding my feelings upon her. I finally decided to speak to her directly about my own experience with my sister and her family. "You may remember last summer when I took some time off from work. My sister died last summer of cancers very much like your Mom's. I took time off to be with her and her children. I learned some painful but important things with my sister in her illness and dying that I would like to share with you, if you think that would be helpful. It is different from what you are hearing from your family." She agreed, and I talked with her about how important it was for my sister and her children to stop pretending there would be a miraculous recovery, to give up hope together, and to speak openly about her impending death. These conversations gave my sister some final peace and intimacy before dying.

The conversations with Catherine about my sister and her family, typically very brief, continued after her mother died. My focus was on my sister, her children, and their needs, not my own experience. Catherine never asked me what it was like for me—she knew that was not the point. The stories from my sister's dying gave Catherine the courage and freedom to go against the pressures of her family and speak with her mother as she needed to. Her mother welcomed the opportunity.

Catherine is now a mother herself with a baby girl. Our sessions have been a place in which she can grieve her mother's absence during this very precious period of life. Her mother is never mentioned in her family.

The therapist as an unconscious object in the evolving psyche of the client

I have been reading Winnicott for more than two decades. His way of writing, as well as his way of working as an analyst, was highly idiosyncratic. His ways of writing and working have required years of study to understand. His way of thinking about the psychotherapeutic process has deeply informed and transformed my understanding of psychotherapy. At the heart of Winnicott's understanding of human development, be it within the parent–child or analyst–patient dyad, is the necessity of aggression, ruthlessness, and object usage (1960, 1971). Winnicott (1984), through his work with children and adolescents as well as his adult patients, came to understand that the expression of aggression and destruction was an effort to force the external environment to respond to internal needs. Winnicott saw aggression as a manifestation of hope that the object (other) will survive one's projections and demands, thereby facilitating the differentiation of self and other.

In ego development and the elaboration of the "true self" of a child or a patient (Winnicott, 1960), the unconscious intention in the use of the object is not the destruction of the object but the discovery of the self. My long-standing wish to be a *useful* therapist foreclosed the possibility of my clients to *use* me in their own ways in the discovery and elaboration of themselves. They did not have the freedom or space to find themselves, because I was always there first. My reading of Winnicott and consultations with Bollas began to show me ways to get out of the way of my clients to open a different kind of therapeutic space, so as to be available to be *used by* my clients rather than be *useful to* them. Bollas (1989) eloquently represents this core thesis of Winnicott:

> The issue Winnicott addresses can only be understood if we grasp that he does not assume we all "live" a life. We may construct a semblance of such and certainly the false self attests to this. But to live a life, to come alive, a person must be able to use objects in a way that assumes such objects survive hate and do not require undue reparative work.
>
> (p. 26)

I learned the true meaning of object usage through my work with Alessia. She first burst into my office like a storm cloud, a dark and broiling presence that filled the room. She commanded attention, and she immediately had mine. A graduate student in her late 20s, she seemed simultaneously a lost girl and a powerful, self-possessed woman. She was married but was fed up with her husband and contemplating leaving him. "Oh," I thought to myself in that initial session, "a simple job—helping her to make a decision about her marriage." That was not to be the case at all.

Alessia's parents were both prominent medical professionals who had related to their daughter as the identified patient, since probably from about the time she had learned to walk. Barely into elementary school, she had been sent off for psychotherapy. I was, perhaps, her eighth or ninth psychotherapist (she'd lost precise count). As she described the range of diagnoses she'd been given over the course of her relatively young life, I had the fantasy that the DSM would require continual revision so as to afford her parents new opportunities to assign diagnoses.

While her parents were relentlessly concerned with the psychopathology of their daughter, they paid little attention to her actual life. As a young teenager, Alessia had fashioned a secret life, completely outside the awareness of her very busy and preoccupied parents. Her secret life was full of sexual exploration and encounters. In her sexuality, she felt herself most fully alive. By her college years, she had married. Her marriage was a polyamorous arrangement, accompanied by multiple lovers of both genders. What more, I wondered as I heard her stories, could a young person ask for? I found myself envious. During those formative years of my life, while my sexual fantasies had been closer to the life Alessia was actually living, I had limited myself to the safety of a single, heterosexual relationship. Alessia, on the other hand, seemed to devour lovers and other intense experiences as food and fodder for her life.

For the first five years of our work, any comment, observation, reflection, or interpretation I offered was dismissed out of hand. Most of the time, I was left with the sense that what I said was simply unheard as irrelevant, but there were times when Alessia's response to my interventions was to make it abundantly clear that what I said was quite dumb and unwarranted. I couldn't have explained why at the time, but I did have the very clear sense that the only thing that would have been even dumber than what I'd already been saying would have been something like, "Have you noticed that you reject everything I say? I wonder if we could talk about that." Or worse yet, "I think you are putting your father's face on me."

My countertransference was intensely mixed up. I always looked forward to seeing her, being rather thrilled by her passionate and aggressive nature. At the same time, I felt reduced to an audience watching some kind of one-woman theatrical performance. My negative countertransference found relief through diagnoses that could situate the problem squarely within her way of being. I could fall back on my Reichian characterology and declare her (to myself silently) as a hysteric, perhaps even a psychopath. From my TA frame of reference, I could fill a short lexicon of games: "If it weren't for you"; "Now I've got you, you son of a bitch"; "Corner"; "Uproar"; "Ain't it awful"; the list could go on. It was interesting, and not accidental, that she never asked me for anything, except for a diagnosis, which she asked for repeatedly! Here I had the tact to quietly reply each time something like, "You've had a lifetime of diagnoses. I can't possibly see the use of another. I want to get to know you, not diagnose you." But anything else I offered would be immediately rejected. Had I been working with her a few years earlier, I would most likely have destroyed the therapy through some form of confrontation rather than tolerate and learn through my countertransference.

Alessia never stopped talking. We had no "contract" in the TA sense of an explicit purpose or goal for our work. She came to sessions; she spoke; I listened. That seemed to be the deal. As the months passed, I felt like a therapist without a job, certainly not the job I typically cast for myself. Although I felt like I had no personal importance to her whatsoever, the sessions were clearly important. She was never late. She never missed a session. When she traveled (which she did for her work rather often), she always arranged a phone session. Strangely, I did not feel irritated with her. Quite the contrary, I felt a growing paternal countertransference of admiration and protectiveness toward her. I didn't know what was going on, but I "knew"—in the Bollas sense of the unthought known (or perhaps "unthinkable known" was closer to the truth)—that something important was going on.

Although she never said so, I was reasonably sure that my admiration of her registered somewhere inside of her. It was, perhaps, most important that I never called into question her sexual activities, which by conventional standards would only be seen as perverse. It was clear to me that her sex life was an essential platform for her wellbeing. At the same time, I feared that it left her open to being exploited. She would often express surprise and/or outrage when some sexual partnership collapsed or exploded. I had the distinct impression that she was also hurt, but I kept my observations to myself. I grew more comfortable with the erotic aspects of my countertransference. I could sit with Alessia and feel my growing affections for her, relishing her passionate sexuality.

Fortunately for both of us, by the time Alessia came to see me I was working with McLaughlin and Bollas, each of whom, in their own way, was teaching me how to live in and with my countertransference, rather than acting it out through confrontation, interpretation, or "sharing" it in self-disclosure. Bollas writes of the necessity of "countertransference receptivity," which he describes as "a capacity to receive life and bear a not knowing about what is taking place even though a profound mulling over and playing is the medium of such reception" (1999, p. 44). What became clearer to me was that my willingness, indeed the necessity, to keep a distance was serving an essential function. I began to get the sense of my paternal presence being that of a father who cared but could stay out of the way.

Her automatic dismissals of my comments in the early months of the therapy were deeply instructive. Seen through the lens of Berne's degrees of games, it was clear that we would not be working at the level of cognitive insight and/or transferential projections and relations. Our work together was not to be at first or second degree levels. We were not together to *solve* a problem. We were together to *live* the problem together. Our work was at the third degree level. Years passed. If I was traveling, a request for phone contact was never made. She never asked where I was going. She had never asked a single question about my life or work. After about five years, she asked at the end of a session, "So what do you think?" I was startled. Why now, I wondered. I no longer recall what she'd been talking about or how I answered her question. I do recall her response, "Well, I don't know how the hell you came up with *that*." Oh well. Maybe there would be another time when she would ask again.

As is so often the case for me when I'm working with a client during periods of not-knowing and uncertainty, various bits and pieces of things I've read come to mind as objects to be used. Thrashing my way through difficult authors is one of my favorite and most productive forms of object usage. The first bit that began to press itself into my consciousness was Berne's (1972) account of script forming a wall around the child's "secret garden" to protect their most precious wishes and fantasies from the intrusion and harm of others. I thought about how Alessia had managed to keep so much of her life secret from her parents. I found new meaning in Alessia's honesty with me; she did not seem to need to keep any secrets from me. Some sort of understanding was taking shape as another association to hiding and privacy came to my mind, this one from Jim McLaughlin:

> It is this private self that provides inner stability and nourishment. Yet it is also a hiding place for those most unwanted and troublesome aspects of what we fear and wish we were not. It is this aggregate that we zealously protect, keep mostly hidden, and cling to as our essence. It is what we bring to the other when we engage in the analytic dyad.
>
> (1995, pp. 434–435)

I found new understanding and regard for the careful, attentive distance I was maintaining. I continued to "consult" with various authors as I sat in session.

Winnicott also "visited" me during several sessions. Something from him nudged the edge of my consciousness, but I couldn't quite catch hold of it. At the time Alessia had started working with me, she had pretty much cut off all contact with her parents, especially her father, whom she found to be boorish and "way too full of himself." Over the course of our work, she was feeling more settled in herself, so she felt confident enough to begin re-establishing more contact with her parents. Her father rapidly returned to his intrusive and opinionated self. She was telling me, angrily, of her most recent phone conversation with her father that ended with her shouting at him, "It's none of your damned business." As I listened to this latest encounter with her father, Winnicott returned to the room.

Now I knew what "Winnicott" had been trying to tell me, and that evening I found the piece I needed to read. Winnicott was writing about the early roots of the capacity for aggression, in which he is describing the young child's "motility" through which "the environment is constantly discovered and redis-covered" (1950, p. 211). "Motility" is the word he used to characterize the infant's and young child's sensorimotor explorations of the world around her. He describes three patterns of the environmental (usually parental) response to the child's bodily explorations: 1) freedom to explore and experience, 2) the environment "*impinges*," thereby restricting the child's freedom to form their own experience, and 3) a persistent and extreme pattern of impingement. The result of such "persistent and extreme" impingements is that:

> There is not even a resting place for individual experience.... The "indivi-
> dual" then develops as an extension of the shell rather than of the core....
> What is left of the core is hidden away and is difficult to find even in the
> most far-reaching analysis. The individual then *exists by not being found.*
> (p. 212, emphasis in the original)

I developed a keener and keener sense of Alessia's vulnerabilities—which I *sensed* but never *spoke*. Neither did I. I also felt a growing recognition of my identification with her manic energy. As I allowed her energy and that of my own to register more and more intensely in my body, I began to find a way forward, a way of creating a slightly different space with her. I knew I had to find a way to speak past her relentless energy and activity.

From the accumulation of now more than five years of working together, I knew I could not speak to her directly. I could not say something like, "You got mad at your father, but it must have also been quite painful." I had to speak in the third person, "Fathers can be so infuriating." "Yeah, tell me something I don't already know." "And they can be so disappointing." This time her reply was in a soft voice, "Yeah, they sure can." A new space opened between us. I could find ways to begin to speak to (or for) her vulnerability, sadness, uncertainty—qualities I knew from my own experience can be so deeply hidden under manic defenses. I learned to speak to her (and for her) in the third person: "Sex would be so much easier if there didn't have to be someone else there." To this, she replied, "Yeah, well *that* can certainly be arranged. Half the people on the planet have their best sex by themselves. The porn industry makes billions. But it is kind of empty that way." There were, of course, many variations in my third-person reflections: "Partners can be so clueless"; "People often don't recognize that starting a business is like having a child—it's very precious"; "Sometimes the words that come out of someone's mouth are not what they are actually feeling"; "Anger is so often only part of the picture"; "It's hard enough to bear disappointment—it's nearly impossible to speak it";

"It's a mystery how people ever come to understand one another." Gradually, she began to speak from and for these places within herself. She began to ask me, "So what do you think?" and mean the question. Our sessions became increasingly and more reliably conversational.

Winnicott makes an important distinction toward the end of his discussion of object usage, "I wish to conclude with a note on using. By 'use' I do not mean 'exploitation'" (1971, p. 94). To the contrary, he argues, "it is the greatest compliment we may receive if we are both found and used" (1989, p. 233). He placed great emphasis on a child's or patient's *right* to *find* the object reliable. The therapist does not simply *provide* a supportive atmosphere that the grateful patient can lap up. The therapeutic environment needs to be *used*, tested, and sometimes attacked, so as to be found to be reliable. It is a process that is simultaneously impersonal and intimate. Winnicott goes on to suggest, "Along side this we see many treatments which are an infinite extension of non-use, kept going indefinitely by the fear of confrontation with the trouble itself— which is an inability to use and be used" (1989, p. 235). For years, Alessia had held me as an object to be used for her own intrapsychic development, an object that was present and interested but un-intrusive, undemanding. I had been found to be reliable, and now we could move gradually to confront "the trouble itself."

Sexuality and eros in psychotherapy

Sexuality can be a wonderful contributor to our erotic capacities, but sex can also be deadening, numbing, distracting. There are very few clients with whom discussions of sexuality do not become a part of our work together. Alessia's sexuality was always very apparent, but its multiplicity of meanings—and, perhaps, of "trouble itself"—remained to be explored. Levine's (2003) reflections on the nature of sexual desire captures the work that was to unfold in Alessia's time with me:

> Sexual desire, therefore, educates us throughout our lives. It often reflects our longing for something that we do not currently have. Since almost all of our lives are periodically unsatisfying, our new sexual desires inform us about our felt deficiencies in ourselves and our relationships and how they might be improved.
>
> (p. 284)

Alessia's day-to-day life was filled with overt sexual activity. Here, together, we had slowly, quietly fashioned a different kind of erotic space, a space for the erotics of thought. I can imagine that this may strike some readers as a rather bizarre pairing—eros and thinking—especially from a writer often known for his body-centered approach to psychotherapy. The force of the erotic is about coming more fully into life, the establishment of the capacity for deeper and more robust vitality with which to meet life, be it body-to-body or mind-to-mind. Thinking together can be a wonderfully erotic experience.

Ours was a vitally necessary psychic space allowing each of us a very particular kind of solitude. The underlying eros of our working couple became more apparent. In a brilliant essay on the erotics of transference, Jessica Benjamin observes:

> In the solitude provided by the other the subject has a space to become absorbed with internal rhythms rather than reacting to the outside. .... This experience in the transference has its countertransference correlate, in which the analyst imagines her- or himself sharing with the patient a similar state of intense absorption and receptivity, immersed in a flow of material without the need to actively interpret or inject her- or himself.
>
> (1995, p. 141)

It is perhaps most fully and persistently in our sexual relations that we encounter "object usage," both as the user and the used. Sex carries the same paradox that Winnicott attributes to the use of the object—it is at one and the same time the possibility of being profoundly impersonal and gratifyingly intimate. Human sexuality simultaneously forces us toward the other and into ourselves.

Contemporary models of psychotherapy and psychoanalysis have seemed either to ignore or domesticate sexuality (Green, 1996; Cornell, 2003, 2015). As Muriel Dimen has rather cuttingly noted, "Sexuality has become a relation, not a force" (2003, p. 157). Over the past couple of decades, contemporary analysts such as Benjamin (1995), Davies (1994, 1998), Dimen (2003, 2005, 2011), Slavin (2003, 2007), and Stein (1998a, 1998b, 2008) have been articulating anew the *force* of sexuality and erotic life. Stein, for example, argued that it is in the very nature of "the excess of sexuality that shatters psychic structures... so as to enable new ones to evolve" (2008, p. 43). It was only through the more contemporary psychoanalytic literature that I found meaningful and provocative clinical discussions of sexuality that informed my clinical practice (Cornell, 2003, 2009a, 2009b, 2015).

With many of my clients, our work involves fostering a capacity for more aggression and object usage in their sexual relations. But for Alessia, her sexuality needed to become not only a force, but also a relation. Sexuality had long provided an essential function—and I stress *function*, in contrast to defense —of knowing through sensation and action that she could manage and contain the intensities and potential intrusiveness of others' sexual desires and practices. The vigor of her sexual relations needed to expand to make room for her longing and vulnerability.

My speaking in the third person about loss, sadness, vulnerability, uncertainty, and disappointment could resonate within her without defining her personal experience. The space created by the third person allowed me to speak and allowed Alessia the freedom to consider, consciously and unconsciously, the relevance for her of what I was saying. She began to look for different emotional qualities and capacities in her partners and friends. Her sex life has remained as robust as ever.

I have never engaged in transference interpretations or reflections with Alessia. The nature of our relationship has been lived and *experienced* rather than discussed and analyzed. I have no doubt that my quietly, respectfully attentive ways of being with her created at an unconscious level a sense of new possibilities for relatedness. She began to look for more consistent and attentive relationships in her life. She seems to have managed to coach her mother to be a better listening and receptive parent. Her father remains problematic.

What I hope I have illustrated with this account of our work together is that it was not the content of Alessia's talking that informed me, it was *how* she spoke and related to me. This is the core of unconscious experience organized at the third degree (or protocol): it is in one's very way of being. Many clients, of course, can and do make use of much more frequent verbal (and somatic) observations and interventions. This was not the case for Alessia. The relentless intrusions of her parents were like the air she breathed—for a very long time. Our sessions needed to provide a very different atmosphere—for a very long time—and I needed to bring my attention and care to her in a very different way from what she had always experienced. I was to be shaped by her, rather than the other way around. The consistency and reliability of my non-intrusive interest gradually allowed her the freedom to relate to me and to herself differently.

In closing

I have been in practice for over forty years now. Through all those years, I have had the very good fortune to learn from a remarkable, challenging, and inspiring group of consultants and mentors. Ours is a profession rich with the opportunity, the necessity really, to constantly think anew.

I was first drawn to transactional analysis by Berne's deep regard for his patients. My academic training had been in phenomenology, a foundation that has afforded the best possible base for the psychotherapeutic endeavor. I saw in Berne the beginnings of an integration of the phenomenological perspective with psychoanalysis. At the time of my initial training what was most important to me was that TA gave me a structure for thinking and some idea what to actually *do* with the people when they were in my office. That was such a rich gift to a nervous, novice therapist.

Phenomenology and transactional analysis have been my ground. For the past twenty years, my readings of and studies with contemporary psycho-analysts have carried me "under" that ground into the rich domains of uncon-scious experience and communication. In recent years, my learning has been particularly enriched by studies with Maurice Apprey (2006), a classically trained psychoanalyst who is also deeply versed in phenomenology and is bringing these two disciplines into an exquisite dialogue. With Apprey I have found a deepening integration of these two modes of psychological investigation that I first saw as a possibility reading Berne.

As I look ahead, I also continue to learn how to create space for the emergence of the unconscious domains in my work with groups. I've long been much more at ease in dyads, and as a group leader have found much security in the typical structure of a TA treatment or training group. But in recent years, I have grown more tolerant, sometimes even eager, for the discomfort, unpredictability, and depth offered through the models of analytic and process-oriented groups (Nitsun, 1996; Landaiche, 2012, 2013; van Beekum, 2012). Herein is the leading edge of my ongoing learning.

Chapter 2

Play at your own risk: Games, play, and intimacy

Eric Berne (1964) placed games within the overall context of his theory of structuring time through patterns of social contact. He argued that while "the solitary individual can structure time in two ways: activities and fantasy" (p. 18), a person as a member of "a social aggregation" (p. 18) has several options for structuring time: withdrawal, rituals, activities, pastimes, games, and intimacy. He listed these patterns of time structuring in the order of increasing complexity, risk, and satisfaction. For Berne, the human need for social contact was essential for the maintenance of "somatic and psychic equilibrium" (p. 19), which he saw as providing "(1) the relief of tension (2) the avoidance of noxious situations (3) the procurement of stroking and (4) the maintenance of an established equilibrium" (p. 19). He saw games and intimacy as the most gratifying forms of social contact but thought "prolonged intimacy is rare ... [so] significant social discourse most commonly takes the form of games" (pp. 19–20). Berne devoted far more of his writing to considering games, their meanings, and their treatment than he did to discussing intimacy.

By the time of Berne's death, a lexicon of more than 40 games had been identified in the transactional analysis literature (Stuntz, 1971). In treatment, games were dealt with transactionally, with the therapist in the driver's seat choosing to play the game, ignore the game, diagram and analyze the game, confront the game, switch to a less destructive game (as determined by the therapist), switch to a different role in the drama triangle, or shift to a lesser degree of the game. Games were understood to be primary forms of emotional and interpersonal defense and were dealt with accordingly. In classical transactional analysis theory, the therapist's interventions were conscious and intentional, aimed primarily at promoting change at cognitive and behavioral levels. There were, however, times when the identification and analysis of a game could elicit the experience of the less conscious (dare we say "unconscious"?) conflicts, motivations, losses, or trauma that underlay the game.

In the more contemporary transactional analysis literature, games have been reconceptualized as periods of mutual impasse (Cornell & Landaiche, 2008) or as unconscious enactments (Gowling & Agar, 2011; Hargaden & Sills, 2002; Shadbolt, 2012; Stuthridge, 2012). Seen from these perspectives, the professional partner in the "working couple" (Cornell & Landaiche, 2008, pp. 27–29) in a game process is a participant/observer:

> The therapist was required to *play* the game ... and not to confront it at this stage of the therapy. ... When the therapist allows himself to be moulded by the interpersonal pressure, and if he is able to observe the changes, this is a rich source of data about the patient's internal world.
>
> (Hargaden & Sills, 2002, p. 80)

Seen in this way, games are meaningful, and the professional's willingness to experience the impact—the pull and molding—of the game is deeply informative to both participants. In framing games in terms of transactional analysis impasse theory or the more psychoanalytically based theories of enactment, the place of unconscious disturbances and communication comes to the foreground. At the point of impasse or enactment, for both the professional partner and the client, something is entering an arena of unconscious trouble that cannot yet be spoken. Conscious, cognitive reflection is not readily available. From the perspective of enactments, the working couple must do—that is, enact—something together before being able to speak and reflect about it.

Play as a time structure

Laura Cowles-Boyd and Harry Boyd (1980a, 1980b) addressed what they saw as a significant gap between games and intimacy, wondering if there might not be another form of social interaction that provided a transition between them. They argued that the nature of interpersonal games is antithetical to the essence of intimacy, so how does one make the leap from games to intimacy? They proposed *play* as a time structure that fosters an intermediary function between games and intimacy and offered a formal definition of the characteristics of play:

> In transactional analysis terms, we give the formal definition and characteristics of play as: 1) as series of ongoing transactions, 2) which has no concealed motivation, 3) in which a predominantly continuous positive stroke value is maintained, 4) which pays off in positive feelings, 5) is carried out by the Free Child, and 6) which occurs in Adult awareness with P_2 permission.
>
> (1980a, p. 6)

They further compared and contrasted the structure and functions of play to those of games. For example, whereas games are seen as confirming script and archaic worldviews in enacting the belief systems internalized as the primitive Parent introject within the Child ego state, play is seen as allowing experimentation with new options and the development of new Parent ego state belief systems that facilitate change. Playing a game is held in contrast to actual play.

The game/play shift

In an accompanying article, Cowles-Boyd and Boyd outlined the technique of the "game/play shift" (1980b, p. 8) through which "the game is more gently and pleasantly brought into the patient's awareness" (pp. 8–9) via a series of playful, typically unexpected transactions that knock the predictable unfolding of the game off course. Games, in Berne's accounting, were structured and predictable (rather like playing a board game or a sport) and followed unconsciously derived rules. Cowles-Boyd and Boyd suggested that in shifting to play, an element of unpredictability is introduced, thus creating interactions that are closer to the spontaneity of intimacy. In the game/play shift, the therapist matches the psychological energy typically brought to a game and seeks to foster intellectual and emotional insight with a positive feeling payoff. They stressed that "safe play presupposes the presence of an appropriate limit-setting Parent" (p. 8) and that the therapist must intervene "*before* the patient takes the negative-stroke payoff"(p. 9).

The shift to play is an effort to capture the intensity and stroke value of the game while introducing a positive interaction in place of a negative payoff. Cowles-Boyd and Boyd described exaggeration, imitation, derailing, and mirroring as interventions that shifted games into play. Viewed through a more contemporary lens, these interventions can be seen to likely trigger shame, but the authors stressed that play always needs to come from an OK/OK position. The game/play shift seems to capture Berne's (1964) own observation: "Experience has shown that it is more useful and enlightening to investigate social transactions from the point of view of the advantages gained than to treat them as defensive operations" (p. 19). In *Principles of Group Treatment*, Berne (1966) discussed the place of humor in psychotherapy and characterized the "Adult laugh" as "the laugh of insight ... [which] arises from the absurdity of circumstantial predicament and the even greater absurdity of self-deception" (p. 288).

Game/play vignette

It was our first session, and Kurt was not happy about seeing me. Referred by his wife's psychotherapist, Kurt was cuttingly skeptical about the usefulness of psychotherapy. Head of a major law firm in the city, he let it be known that he was accustomed to being in the leadership role. As he spoke about the relentless misery of his marriage, I wondered aloud if he had some sense of how it was that his leadership skills fell short at home. Although I thought I was opening up an interesting line of inquiry, Kurt did not follow my lead. He quickly took back the lead in a move that I thought heralded the future of our relationship. As he described the state of his marriage, it struck me that the relationship had involved a decade of mutual character assassination. I found myself silently relieved that they had not had children, each of them being too career-driven to have made space for kids. My standard first session inquiries into his childhood or the nature of his parents' relationship were dismissed as irrelevant. As the session neared its end, Kurt asked me my fee, and when I told him, he said it was absurdly low, adding, "I hope you don't have a family to support with fees like that." My head was full of a catalogue of the "games" from the old TA lexicon (Berne, 1964) and the power plays that I imagined looming in our therapeutic future. At the same time, I found myself quite liking Kurt and looking forward to working together. I enjoyed his aggressiveness and found an opportunity to join it as our first session came to a close.

When I asked if he would like to schedule another session, he said he would think about it and asked for a business card.

> "I don't have cards," I replied.
> "What kind of a therapist doesn't have cards?" he asked with an edge in his voice.
> "The kind who doesn't have cards," I replied.
> "What a way to run a business," he replied. "So just send me a statement, and I'll send you a check for today."
> "I don't send statements."
> "What the fuck kind of therapist doesn't send statements?"
> "The kind of therapist who doesn't send statements."
> "How do you get paid?"
> "By check most often. People pay me when they come to sessions. I expect them to keep track of their own bills. Are you telling me that you are the head of a major law firm, and you can't keep track of a simple bill? If we work together, this will be a personal relationship, not a business relationship."
> (Long pause)
> "Well, fuck it, let's schedule another appointment," he said with a slight grin. This was, perhaps, what Berne would have considered an Adult smile of recognition. Of understanding what had just transpired between us.

Our closing interactions are an example of the game/play shift. This first session introduced a wealth of possible games: "Now I've Got You, You Son of a Bitch," "Blemish," "Corner," "Courtroom," and "Let's You and Him Fight," all games first named by Berne (1964). If Kurt were to continue working with me, I was already imagining ongoing power plays for leadership and authority between us, as well as his repeated discounting of my competence. In this initial session, it seemed to me essential that I demonstrate my capacity to match Kurt's directness and energy and introduce some pleasure in a vigorous give and take. I shifted from the edge of the incipient games that ran throughout our first session into a playful, and rather provocative mode of holding on to my own way of doing things, which seemed to engage Kurt's curiosity and garner a bit of respect.

My replies to Kurt were quite conscious and focused in intent. He did continue the therapy, and I have, in fact, come to send him statements on a highly irregular basis.

Winnicott's *Playing and Reality*

I (Cornell, 2000) took up the Cowles-Boyd and Boyd articles on play and linked them to Winnicott's thesis that "play was crucial to emotional development and to the creative and ongoing unfolding of life's learning" (1971, p. 274). Cowles-Boyd and Boyd situated the function of play squarely within the interpersonal realms that are at the heart of Berne's theory of structuring time, defining play in transactional terms, that is, in terms of the actual, specific interactions between participants. Winnicott's theory of play is more complex; he viewed play first and foremost as a means by which we develop creativity, subjectivity, and selfhood, and only secondarily in terms of its interpersonal and communicative functions. Games can be seen as the arena for mutual enactment; play, as described by Winnicott, is the terrain of mutual exploration and unconscious communication.

The capacity to play, for Winnicott, was a developmental accomplishment whereby the young child begins to realize that it is possible to discover one's own mind and imagination through experimentation and manipulation of the surrounding physical and human environments. It is interesting to note that Freud (1908) foreshadowed Winnicott's understanding of play when he observed the following:

> Might we not say that every child at play behaves like a creative writer in that he creates a world of his own, or, rather, rearranges things of his world in a way which pleases him? It would be wrong to think that he does not take that world seriously; on the contrary, he takes his play very seriously and he expends large amounts of emotion on it. The opposite of play is not what is serious but what is real. In spite of all the emotion with which he cathects his world of play, the child distinguishes it quite well from reality.
>
> (pp. 143–144)

While there is in everyday parlance a nearly automatic association of play with fun, what Freud and Winnicott conveyed in their understandings of play is something else, as Winnicott (1971) made explicit:

> Playing involves the body: (I) because of the manipulation of objects; (ii) because certain types of intense interest are associated with certain aspects of bodily excitement. ... Playing is inherently exciting and precarious. This characteristic derives *not* from instinctual arousal but from the precariousness that belongs to the interplay in the child's mind of that which is subjective (near-hallucination) and that which is objectively perceived (actual, or shared reality).
>
> (p. 52)

Although Freud never seemed to link his observations about the importance of play to his analytic work with adult patients, Winnicott certainly did: "Whatever I say about children playing really applies to adults as well, only the matter is more difficult to describe when the patient's material appears mainly in terms of verbal communication" (1971, p. 40). In his work with babies and children, Winnicott devised the spatula (1941) and squiggle (1968) games to provide nonverbal, sensorimotor ways of offering exploratory spaces to his young patients. While much of his work was deeply informed by his pediatric and educative work with children and their mothers, his writing in this area often offered metaphors for his work with adult patients. His reflections on mothers and babies and analysts and their patients regularly appeared in the same articles, sometimes in the same paragraphs. Winnicott gave attention to the importance of play from his earliest work as a pediatrician and then throughout the course of his work, culminating in *Playing and Reality* (1971).

When viewed in the context of Berne's theory of time structure, as Cowles-Boyd and Boyd did, the understanding of play is in the interpersonal and communicative realms. For Winnicott, the primary function of play was in the child's exploration of his or her relationship to his or her own mind by pushing reality, both internal and external, around into different shapes and possibilities.

Play, reality, and intimacy

On the surface, the word *play* suggests something pleasant, fun, a childhood phenomenon with a quality of playfulness that is put forth in the articles by Cowles-Boyd and Boyd. Play permeates not only childhood but our adult lives as well. However, as understood by Winnicott (1971), play is not necessarily pleasant or reliable because it involves interplay, which makes it inherently precarious:

> The thing about playing is always the precariousness of the interplay of personal psychic reality and the experience of the control of actual objects. This is the precariousness of magic itself, magic that arises in intimacy, in a relationship that is being found to be reliable.
>
>   (p. 47)

These two sentences evoke worlds in terms of the possibilities and risks engendered through play. In Winnicott's words, we can sense the gap between games and intimacy that Cowles-Boyd and Boyd (1980a) filled with the idea of play, which they deemed an expression of the "Free Child" (p. 6). But play is not all fun (and games). While Berne (1964) suggested that, since intimacy was so hard to sustain, "significant social discourse most commonly takes the form of games" (pp. 19–20), Winnicott linked play and intimacy. The "actual objects" to which he referred are both concrete realities in the physical environment, which afford varied malleability, and objects as other people who have minds of their own, which also afford varying degrees of malleability. Although Winnicott's primary focus was on the function of play in the discovery of the self, he also recognized the gradual unfolding of the self in relation to others. Play plays out over the course of a lifetime, and in so doing, there is a constant interplay and replay between self and other. Berne stressed the predictability of games in human relations in contrast to the unpredictability and risks of intimacy, and it is the precariousness of play that situates it quite naturally between games and intimacy. In fact, it is this precariousness that gave rise to the title of this article: "Play at your own risk."

For Winnicott, play was not simply about pleasant childhood activities but a way of potential being that permeates all aspects of our lives, conscious and unconscious, a place/space for experimentation and imagination. A quick look through an English-language dictionary (1982) illustrates the complex and multiple meanings of play, which go well beyond the Bernean conceptualization of playing psychological games:

- "child's play," suggesting something easy and perhaps a bit foolish
- play a game, as in a board game or sport, following shared rules
- play up, to emphasize, publicize
- play down, to minimize or dismiss
- play a joke
- play with an idea so as to explore its possibilities
- play at, that is, pretend, deceive
- play with someone as a form of engagement
- play a role
- the plays of theatrical performances
- play music
- the interplay of one thing with another, one person with another
- played out, as in exhausted
- play it by ear, improvise
- play with fire, court danger
- play for keeps (as Berne suggested was true of third-degree games)

And, of course, there is sex play, foreplay, playboy, playing with yourself, being a player, making a play for, playing around, and playing the field. As one sees in these common phrases, sex is not inherently loving, tender, or intimate; it can be an impersonal or tricky pursuit. Remarkably, in his article "Aggression in relation to emotional development," Winnicott (1950) offered a rare comment on sexuality, emphasizing the fusion of aggression with sexuality:

> In adult and mature sexual intercourse, it is perhaps true that it is not the purely erotic satisfactions that need a specific object. It is the aggressive or destructive

element in the fused impulse that fixes the object and determines the need that
is felt for the partner's actual presence, satisfaction, and survival.

(p. 218)

In the many variations of the meanings of play, it is abundantly clear that
play is not only playful, fun, and constructive but can be deceptive, impersonal,
and/or destructive. The borders between games, play, and intimacy are perme-
able ones.

Play in psychotherapy

Winnicott (1984) had a fundamental confidence in the hope patients brought to
treatment, seeing even problematic symptoms as unconscious expressions of
hope if what they were seeking to communicate could be heard rather than
"cured." There is also a sense of hopefulness in the game/play shift described
by Cowles-Boyd and Boyd, and it is possible that embeddedness in games may
be the result of the blunting of hope. Winnicott (1968) felt strongly that "a
patient—child or parent—will bring to the first interview a certain amount of
capacity to *believe* in getting help and to trust the one who offers help" (p. 299).
It is incumbent on the helper to provide a "strictly professional setting in which
the patient is free to explore the exceptional opportunity that the consultation
provides for communication" (p. 299).

For Winnicott (1971), play was the primary form of unconscious communication. He identified psychoanalysis as "a highly specialized form of playing in the
service of communication with oneself and others" (p. 41). The phrase "in a
relation that is being found to be reliable" (p. 47), which he used later in the same
book, is crucial for understanding the nature of play in our professional work.
Winnicott called attention to the constant, shifting tensions between the precarious and the reliable. He did not suggest that the therapist provides a reliable
relationship but rather that he or she affords patients the space and time within
which to find the therapeutic relationship to be reliable. Agency is thus returned to
the patient. Play is an aggressive act, the effort to discover, to find out by doing.
As Winnicott wrote, "To control what is outside one has to do things, not simply
to think or to wish, and doing things takes time. Playing is doing" (p. 41).

Embedded in much of Winnicott's writing was a critique of the heavily
interpretive and analytic techniques of classical and Kleinian psychoanalyses, a
critique that I find highly relevant for the practice of transactional analysis as
well. While rarely directly questioning the work of his mentors, Winnicott (1971)
shifted attention away from interpretive/cognitive interventions to those that are
more exploratory and experiential. In *Playing and Reality*, he stated explicitly:

> Interpretation outside the ripeness of the material is indoctrination and
> produces compliance. …. Interpretation when the patient has no capacity
> to play is simply not useful, or causes confusion. When there is mutual

playing, then interpretation according to the accepted psychoanalytic principles can carry the therapeutic work forward. *This playing has to be spontaneous, and not compliant or acquiescent,* if psychotherapy is to be done.

(p. 51)

He went on to write, "*Psychotherapy is done in the overlap of the two play areas, that of the patient and that of the therapist*" (p. 54; italics in original).

For imaginative and exploratory space to open up, it is essential that the analyst not be an intrusive presence in the psychotherapy. Reading Winnicott, I was able to begin to play with and challenge some of the core tenets of my training as a transactional analysis psychotherapist and group therapist. Seen from the perspective of Berne's (1964, p. 64) conceptualization of the degrees of games, Winnicott's work described a mode of listening and relating that opens a space for the exploration of fantasies, wishes, absences, trauma, and intrapsychic conflicts that often foster second- and third-degree levels of defense. He sought to provide a therapeutic space "to afford opportunity for formless experience, and creative impulses, motor and sensory, which are the stuff of playing" (Winnicott, 1971, p. 64). He saw as essential to the therapeutic process an openness to the unintegrated experiences that underlie second- and third-degree games and scripts. It is the defensive function of games and scripts to defend against these realms of fragmentation and uncertainty so as to enforce more predictable patterns of living, even if such patterns end up ultimately become deadening and unsatisfying. Winnicott argued that only by welcoming and accompanying (and not interfering with) the unintegrated areas of the personality does one discover one's creativity and true self.

At the core of play is the search for the self. For this search to be alive and deeply creative for a child, a client, a student, or a group, the facilitating professional needs to be reliable, curious, and quietly receptive. Winnicott cautioned his fellow analysts not to move too quickly to make sense of nonsense, arguing that the fields of nonsense, no-sense, and uncertainty are rich with the potential discovery of glimmerings of an emergent self. His accounting of the responsively receptive and unintrusive attention of the therapist has been accepted as vital by other contemporary psychoanalysts (Bollas, 1999; Davis & Wallbridge, 1990; McLaughlin, 2005; Milner, 1987; Ogden, 2009). (Although it is outside the scope of this chapter to explore the ideas of these authors on this subject, interested readers will find much of value in their books.)

Winnicott (1971) argued that the therapeutic setting—which he interestingly described as "analytic, psychotherapeutic, social work, architectural, etc." (p. 55)—must provide an atmosphere in which it becomes possible for the patient to speak nonsense without having to organize it into some form of sense for the benefit of the therapist. It is incumbent on the professional listener to allow space for nonsense to be spoken by professional and client alike. Winnicott bemoaned the fact that all too often "the therapist has, without knowing it, abandoned the professional role, and has done so by bending over backwards to be a clever analyst, and to see order in the chaos" (p. 56). His audience, of course, was his psychoanalytic peers, for whom interpretation was the primary mode of intervention. Likewise, in classical transactional analysis, the predominantly interpretive/analytic approach to the treatment of games and script risks a complete foreclosure of the potential space for play. It is important to note that therapeutic styles overly invested in empathy and the provision of corrective experiences also may foreclose the freedom of the therapeutic play space.

Winnicott's language was rarely proscriptive or literal (Abram, 1997), and his use of words was often idiosyncratic. It is intentionally vague, evocative, and elusive so as to leave the reader to wonder, "What is he talking about? Now what does he mean?" Over years of reading Winnicott, I have come to understand that, in fact, he does not want the reader to know exactly what he means but rather to wonder what the reader means, that is, what meaning and possibility the reader makes out of a text. In Winnicott the writer there is a glimpse of Winnicott the therapist creating a play space between his mind and that of the reader. For example, in the introduction to *Playing and Reality*, he wrote that he was reluctant to provide clinical examples for fear that they "can start to pin down specimens and begin a process of classification of an unusual and arbitrary kind" (Winnicott, 1971, p. xii). When I first read this statement, I found it both startling and enlivening. It stood in such stark contrast to our tendency in transactional analysis to categorize, label, and enumerate, thereby creating an illusion of predictability and knowingness that, in fact, defies the realities of human life and relating.

In his theory of play, Winnicott's language was filled with notions of intermediate areas of experience, environments that hold and facilitate, transitional spaces, potential spaces. It was as though he were trying out different phrases and concepts to find one (or several) that best conveyed what he was trying to communicate. He was not offering his patients a relationship so much as a space, an environment, within which they could begin to find and articulate themselves. The therapeutic dyad, the classroom, the group, or the training program can provide a working environment as an area of experience between the individual and the world around him or her, a space in which the individual can both join with and separate from others.

This is delicate terrain. Writing about the child's world, Winnicott (1971) observed that "in favourable circumstances the potential space becomes filled with the products of the baby's own creative imagination" (p. 102), which is not overly encumbered with the needs, anxieties, or pressures of the external environment. Then, as was so often the case in his writing, in the next paragraph he is writing about the analyst and patient:

Analysts need to be aware lest they create a feeling of confidence and an intermediate area in which play can take place and then inject into this area or inflate it with interpretations which in effect are from their own creative imaginations [rather than those of the patient].

(p. 102)

Be it in empathy or interpretation, we need to be cautious in our languaging of clients' games and scripts. Seen through the lens of Berne's description of the degrees of games, those individuals for whom their games (and scripts) are organized predominantly at the first-degree level will have a rather ready capacity to keep and use their own minds in cooperation with or contrast to the professional's. At the level of second- and third-degree games and scripts, people are less likely to have the psychic strength or personal freedom to play with or reject the interpretations and other interventions offered by the professional. As I read, reread, and gradually incorporated aspects of Winnicott's style into my own work, I saw repeatedly how often my haste to make game or script interpretations closed off the potential space between myself and the client or group. I imposed my understanding and imagination (in the guise of a competent and confident knowing of my client's mind) on my client. Playground closed.

At play in psychotherapy: A case vignette

André Green (2005), while deeply influenced by and respectful of Winnicott's work, argued that the latter's view that play and transitional phenomena were all rooted in the mother/child relationship was "mad" (p. 9), that Winnicott could not free himself from his pediatrician's viewpoint in working with his adult patients. Green (2005) challenged Winnicott's systematic lack of attention to the centrality of sexuality in the maturation of the adult psyche and his tendency to valorize health over the realities of human sickness and violence.

I am afraid that on this occasion, as on many others, we meet Winnicott's idealization and his refusal to consider play as part of sickness. ... But what I am sure of is that it is not enough to incarnate the good-mother to cure a patient, to vanish when she acts out her destructivity, or to accept passively with the patient's destroying the setting. Sometimes the analyst cheats, lies, acts out violently. In none of these instances is play absent; it is in fact provocative.

(p. 11)

Green's appreciation and critique of Winnicott came to mind as I decided which vignette from my clinical work to present as an example of therapeutic play.

Simone told me in our first session that she had spent every day since her adolescence wishing to be dead. I believed her. As I sat with her, I thought to myself, "Her wish has come true. She is far more dead than alive." And I felt a nearly unbearable deadness between us.

Simone, who was in her thirties, had been told by her psychiatrist that she needed to be in therapy. She said that she had been referred to me by her mother, who after some inquiries had been told that I would not be unnerved by the depth of Simone's suicidality. Normally, I do, in fact, feel quite at ease and engaged by suicidal wishes. For the most part, I think few of us get through life without occasionally wishing to be dead or wishing someone else dead. But something else seemed to be happening with Simone that I found hard to bear. I was not channeling Winnicott. André Green's (1977) powerful essay "The dead mother" ran through my mind; perhaps "dead mother, dead child"? The session was marked by long periods of silence, which I experienced as deadening and deadly.

But I had a job to do, so I said, "I am trying to imagine what might have happened to a young girl such that by 13 she would rather have been dead. Did something happen to you?" Simone had not yet made eye contact with me, but as I asked the question, she lifted her face, looked me "dead" in the eye, and replied, "I started to think." Great. I could not think. I really, really do not like not being able to think. I wanted her gone: "Who the hell are you to wander in here and disturb me so?" Not a good start. Playground closed? Or maybe this was to be our playground. And maybe Kurt was right after all—my fee is too fucking low for all of this.

In my mind I fled into a decidedly anti-Winnicottian reaction: It was time for a diagnosis, a category—diagnosis is a form of thinking, after all—as I sought a cognitive bail-out of my discomfort. I knew even as I tried it that this was a desperate and irrelevant form of thinking. Sometimes, as Green observed, the analyst cheats, lies, or acts out violently. In the face of my anxiety and bewilderment, I was about to cheat, to exit the picture, so to speak, and to act violently by dehumanizing Simone with a diagnosis of a character defense. By the end of our first session, I had no doubt that Simone's games and script were in the realm of the third degree and that the work we were embarking on was deadly serious. Was she consciously playing a game with me? Most certainly not. She was bringing herself to me in the only way she knew how, although in that way of being she was profoundly defensive and distancing. I, in turn, felt pressure to distance myself from her, as had so many others. If we moved in that direction, we would begin a deadening, and possibly deadly, game.

In the work with Kurt described earlier, I could think. I knew, more or less, what I was doing during those closing comments and challenges of the game/play shift. I spoke with a quiet sense of strength, warmth toward him, and humor. In contrast, with Simone I could not think in any meaningful way until after the session. I had the vague sense, as I sat with my reactions after she left my office, that there was something dangerous and informative in my impulses to create distance, and, perhaps, there was something important in my association to André Green and the dead mother.

I (mistakenly, in retrospect) started the second session with an effort to establish some sort of narrative history. She could recall no events of any significance to explain how she felt. I asked if she enjoyed her work. "No." So I asked her why she did it. "Because that's what adults do. They go to work. But I don't know anybody who enjoys their work." She first sought therapy in college because her suicidal thoughts were so intense that she could not concentrate. The therapist had her see a psychiatrist, who placed her on medication. When I asked if it had helped, she said, "No," and after a pause, added, "I think they wanted me to have a different mind." "And do you want a different mind?" I asked. "No," was her one-word reply. Her answer struck me as an important communication, that as much as she was suffering, she was not about to give up her mind, to turn it over to someone else to repair or change. That was the first clue to my job description, and a bit of space opened up for me.

Simone then told me that she had had a series of therapists, none of whom she had found useful. When I asked her how she understood the problem with her previous therapists, she replied simply, "They were stupid." Her last therapist had "fired her," and when I inquired as to why, Simone replied, with a slight smile, "I guess she wasn't comfortable with silence." Our second session, like the first, was marked by no eye contact and long periods of silence. I then asked why she was willing to see yet another therapist. She explained that she did not want her mother to worry so much, and her mother had sought me out. After another long period of silence, as the session neared its end, Simone asked me, "What kind of therapist do you think I need?" I sat with my experience of our first session and how it was to be with her in the second. After a while, I replied, "Someone who finds pleasure and meaning in the work of being a psychotherapist, someone smart, someone who doesn't particularly care if you're dead or alive but who wants simply to get to know you, and someone who is comfortable with having his thoughts shredded, dissembled, and discarded as soon as they leave his mouth." There was a long silence. Finally, Simone said, "Well, you've got smart down for sure, maybe a couple of the others on the list, too." We scheduled another appointment.

Now we had a contract of sorts, and I felt some space to breathe and think. I had an inkling of the terrain in which we would need to play and work. My reply to Simone opened our field of play, a field in which we would be living for many months to come. In my answer to Simone's question, she could see that I had been listening carefully and could make some meaning of what had happened between us. It is important to note here—and this is characteristic of what Winnicott means to convey in his understanding of play—that the meaning I found and articulated in my list was not based primarily on what was said between us (which was actually very little). My list brought meaning to how we had been together in the first two sessions, what Simone had been showing me in her way of being. This was what fostered sufficient understanding for me that I could provide a description of the "kind of therapist" she needed. My list made it clear that I did not expect Simone to be or do anything different from how she was already being and what she was already doing. It was my job to listen, to be receptive (consciously and unconsciously) to the impact of her ways of being with herself and me, to hold on to my own mind and imagination, and to stay alive—to not become yet another "stupid" or dead therapist. It has not been easy for either of us.

In closing

How do I come to a closing in writing something that is intended to create an opening? It is my hope that this chapter will encourage readers to incorporate Cowles-Boyd and Boyd's ideas about the role play can have in the theory of time structuring and relationships within the transactional analysis lexicon. I also hope that it will raise more questions than provide answers. And it is my hope that, although the concept of games as Berne originally presented it is rarely used in transactional analysis today, transactional analysts will continue to evolve their understanding on this fundamental, problematic aspect of human relating, which Berne first sought to articulate and render meaningful.

Chapter 3

Fostering freedom for play, imagination, and uncertainty in professional learning environments

Transactional analysis, as developed by Eric Berne, was predominantly a theory and system for identifying and changing patterns of psychological and inter-personal defense, which he called games and script. Berne's emphasis was on the therapist as an outside observer of the patient's internal and interpersonal dynamics. Believing that the thinking capacities of the Adult ego state were the primary mechanisms of the treatment, Berne's use of group treatment, game theory, and the diagramming of transactions and scripts provided a set of predominantly cognitive tools for clients to develop insight and self-observation skills to foster change.

In his theory of games, Berne (1964, p. 64) distinguished between three levels (or "degrees") of defense in a progression that he understood as increas-ingly destructive and difficult to change: 1) first degree, social; 2) second degree, psychological; and third degree, "tissue," that is, held in the body and the most pathological and resistant to change. In differentiating these levels of defense, he invited transactional analysts to notice how defenses are organized and expressed. But he never differentiated which styles and levels of interven-tion might be needed to work effectively with these different levels of defense. While Berne articulated these distinctions within a theory of defenses, we can apply these levels of psychic organization through all domains of human experi-ence. We have come to see, through clinical exploration, as well as parent–infant observation and affective neuroscience research, that the levels of psychic organization Berne referred to as second- and third-degree levels of psychological organization are fundamental and vital aspects of being alive. Models based on implicit relational knowing (Lyons-Ruth, 1999; Fosshage, 2010), subsymbolic experience (Bucci, 2001, 2010), script protocol (Berne, 1963; Cornell & Landaiche, 2006; Cornell, 2010), affective neuroscience (Pank-sepp, 2009), and body psychotherapy (Bloom, 2006; Anderson, 2008; Hartley, 2008) are among the emerging paradigms that underscore the necessity of recognizing and working *within* and *through* these pre-cognitive, affective, and somatic levels of organization.

This traditional reliance on strengthening the Adult ego state and its cogni-tive (and allegedly predictive) capacities is mirrored in much of our TA training and preparation for certification, which is heavy on theory, diagnosis, and treatment planning. As I teach in various TA communities and sit on oral examination boards around the world, I see the impact of this emphasis, which fosters a strong bias toward forms of attention and understanding that can be cognitively accessed and named by the professional and the client alike. Yet the second and third degrees of defenses that Berne describes are not organized and maintained at the social/cognitive level, but rather at levels of nonconscious experience (Cornell & Landaiche, 2008; Pierini, 2008; Tosi, 2008), implicit memory, protocol (Guglielmotti, 2008), and bodily experience. Many aspects of evolving TA theory and technique, often now referred to as "relational," are an effort to develop a systematic understanding of how to work at these levels. This broadening of our therapeutic repertoire necessitates a broadening of our training models as well.

In classical TA script analysis, the client and professional step *out of* the transference and analyze it through diagnostic labels (e.g., identifying a "Don't grow up" injunction) and diagrams (the script matrix). In conventional script analysis, as in genetic interpretations typical within a psychoanalytic frame, therapeutic attention is directed to the forces from the past and the psychological impact of historical figures. This is often sufficient for changing script beliefs and behaviors held at the first degree level, but is often not adequate to address script issues maintained at the second and third degrees. In more contemporary approaches to transactional analysis, the client and practitioner are more likely to *stay within* the transference/countertransference dynamics, seeking a more emotional and experiential understanding of what is going on, in the belief that it is only through these nonconscious processes that meaning can be discovered and enacted. The meaning and impact of one's script is now more likely to be explored as it is experienced (and repeated) moment to moment, between client and practitioner and/or among group members. Holding experience in the here-and-now is much more necessary for working at the second- and third-degree levels of defense. I want to emphasize that I don't believe that the work of human relations professionals is only that of resolving script injunctions and other patterns of defense, but also to facilitate the capacity of individuals, groups, and organizations to live with more vitality, aggression, and depth of visceral and creative experience.

I believe that each of us needs to begin our professional work grounded in a theory or two and a set of basic techniques, as much for the security of the practitioner as the efficacy of the work and the learning of our clients. How do we move beyond this initial ground, so that we do not become overly identified with and dependent upon our favored theories and the illusions of predictive knowing that they offer? How do we find the psychological space within ourselves and in relation to our clients to wonder, imagine, and not-know? How do we, as trainers and supervisors, create experiences that facilitate learning through lived experience, in which our theories are secondary containers to a more fundamental process of discovery?

My work as a teacher and consultant has been profoundly influenced by my readings of Ogden (2005, 2009) and my personal supervision and study with Bollas (1999, 2009). Both are elegant, thrilling writers and major contributors to the contemporary psychoanalytic attitudes. Neither affiliates himself with the "relational" Zeitgeist, but neither shies away from fully immersing in the affective and unconscious domains of their patients or supervisees. Both steadfastly refuse to limit their groups to psychoanalysts or to associate with any formal, analytic training programs. Each is committed through their writing and supervision to fostering the capacities for reverie, imaginative thought, and receptivity to unconscious communication, which I see as essential to working at the second- and third-degree levels of somato-psychic organization.

Ogden (2009), for example, sees his primary goals in supervision and teaching as creating atmospheres to maximize the freedom to think and imagine:

> The supervisor is responsible for creating a frame that ensures the supervisee's freedom to think and dream and be alive to what is occurring both in the analytic process and in the supervisory process. The supervisory process is a felt presence that affords the supervisee a sense of security that his efforts at being honest in the presence of the supervisor will be treated humanely, respectfully, and confidentially.
>
> (p. 36)

> Everything about the seminars is voluntary. The groups are not associated with any training program; no certificate of participation is awarded; no one is required to present a case or even to enter into the discussions.
>
> (p. 51)

Ogden's "to think and dream and be alive" captures, in a different language, Berne's own ideal outcome of "autonomy," which he defined as the capacities for "awareness, spontaneity and intimacy" (1964, p. 178). Berne describes awareness as "the capacity to see a coffee pot and hear the birds sing in one's own way, and not the way one was taught" (p. 178). For Berne, spontaneity represented "liberation, liberation from the compulsion to play games and have only the feelings one was taught to have" (p. 180), and "intimacy means the spontaneous, game-free candidness of an aware person, the liberation of the eidetically perceptive, uncorrupted Child in all its naivete living in the here and now" (p. 180).

So much of transactional analysis training and supervision is now so profoundly tied to endless preparation for the examinations and certification that I seldom see this freedom of thought and experience within the TA communities where I work as an independent trainer. Even working with seasoned TA practitioners, years after they have been certified, I see sadly diminished capacities for free thought, imaginative exploration, and discovery, which I see as essential to working at second- and third-degree levels. I have come to further understand training and supervision in human relations work within these non-cognitive realms to be the creation and sustenance of the exploratory, intermediary space that Winnicott (1971, 1989) called "play":

> This gives us our indication for therapeutic procedure—to afford the opportunity for formless experience, and for creative impulses, motor and sensory, which are the stuff of playing. And on the basis of playing is built the whole of man's experiential existence.
>
> (Winnicott, 1971, p. 64)

Play, in Winnicott's conception, is not the exclusive terrain of childhood, nor is it a matter of simply having fun, but rather an essential, exciting, and sometimes anxiety-inducing necessity for self-development:

> ... *It is play that is universal*, and that it belongs to health: playing facilitates growth and therefore health; playing leads into group relationships; playing can be a form of communication in psychotherapy; and, lastly, psychoanalysis has been developed as a highly specialized form of playing in the service of communication with oneself and others.
>
> (1971, p. 41, emphasis in the original)

While Winnicott often cast his discussions of play within the context of his own work with children and parent–child relations, it was an ongoing metaphor for creative adult relations and therapeutic activity. Play in this sense is not necessarily pleasant but represents the freedom and capacity for one to come *up against* other people and the external world in its various manifestations:

> Through play the child deals with external reality creatively. In the end this produces creative living, and leads to the capacity to feel real and to feel life can be used and enriched. Without play the child is unable to see the world creatively, and in consequence is thrown back on compliance and a sense of futility, or on the exploitation of direct instinctual satisfactions.
>
> ... In play an object can be
> destroyed and restored
> hurt and mended
> dirtied and cleaned
> killed and brought to life.
>
> (1989, pp. 60–61)

Here, in his emphasis on literal action into and against the external environment, Winnicott offers an important complement to the states of reverie and internal exploration emphasized by Bollas and Ogden.

I have come to conceive of my teaching and consultative groups as creating a sustained "play" space, providing opportunities to explore and challenge one's self-image, professional ideals, theoretical assumptions and biases, fantasies, imaginative capacities, technical range, and interpersonal relations. In this way, I hope to foster the attitudes and skills needed to work effectively at the second and third degrees of psychic organization. I attempt to attend to experiences at intellectual, affective, and bodily levels as work unfolds. As a teacher, I need also be in a position to have *my* operating assumptions and supervisory understandings explored, discussed frankly, and challenged by a group or supervisee.

What does this look like in actual practice? To use a recent example, I was leading a two-day workshop on transference and countertransference in transactional analysis in a country I'd only visited once before. It was a group of 30, a mixture of psychotherapists, counselors, teachers, child care workers, and organizational consultants. I had prepared a rather thorough set of notes on the topic as presented in the seminar description. As we began, I did a quick tour of the group to ask why people were there, and quickly discovered that their interests had little to do with the workshop description. What emerged in the group was a concern about and fear of their own emotional and bodily experiences, as well as those of their clients. Theory was not what they were seeking. So much for my notes! What followed was a kind of improvisational process between the group and myself—an extended play experience.

I noticed my own bodily reactions as I listened to the initial tour of the group, my fantasies and associations as well. Rather unexpectedly, I started off with a case example of a young man, who came to my mind as I listened to the group talking about their anxieties about their own emotional and bodily reactions to their clients. I felt a strong erotic and affectionate bond toward this guy. He had terminated recently to move to another city. We decided to fully terminate rather than continue working by phone. I referred him on. I missed him a lot, hoped he was doing well, and hoped he was missing me. My body and feelings were certainly present in the room as I worked with this fellow and as we terminated. I didn't have to tell him this in words, as he could sense it in my way of being with him. Unconsciously, and then consciously, I was showing the group, "This is OK, and this is what we're here to talk about. Such feelings don't mean there's something wrong with you, or that they'll all go away when you become more experienced."

I then broke the group into dyads who would become the working partners throughout the workshop. I led them on a guided fantasy of their bodily experiences (which could be framed as countertransference) of a session with their favorite client (or group) and then of their most dreaded client (or group). The rich discussion in the group that emerged from the dyads then oriented my subsequent teaching. The didactic portions of the two days were guided by the thoughts, feelings, interests, and experiences that emerged from the experiential dyads and group discussions. The experiential dyads provided participants with the opportunities for working together, experiencing their anxieties, discoveries, and competencies in the here-and-now. My intention was to open multiple channels of receptivity and learning within the group. The experiential dyads underscore the competencies of the participants while grounding the theory and discussions in a lived encounter with self and other. Case examples from my own work emerged spontaneously in association to the group's interests, and the two clinical consultations with members of the group further elaborated the learning that emerged within the group.

What does it mean to "think"? Healthy thinking and learning goes well beyond our capacities for conscious cognitions. To be fully engaged with our clients in a depth of shared experience, I believe we need to be engaged at the levels of affective, bodily, and frequently unconscious receptivity.

Berne's emphasis on the Adult ego state, his use of diagrams, and many of the techniques he devised to distinguish transactional analysis from psychoanalysis created a highly efficient mode of group and individual treatment to foster cognitive insight. What I have wished to outline here is a perspective that facilitates learning and change through training and supervision within the realms of nonconscious, imaginative, and somatic functioning, which I see as necessary for growth at the second- and third-degree levels of psychological organization.

Chapter 4

The intricate intimacies of psychotherapy and questions of self-disclosure

The cancer scare now seemed to be over, after several weeks of Ben and I anxiously awaiting the results of a series of tests. Many people around Ben waited with him, proclaiming variations of "Oh, it's probably nothing... Everything will be OK...." These were intended as statements of comfort, but Ben experienced them as dismissive and placating. Other than his session with me, there seemed no place where Ben could express his feelings of anxiety, shock, and a bereft anticipation of leaving his young children fatherless.

Ben talked for most of the session about his relief with the positive results, feeling a bit foolish about his level of anxiety while awaiting the results, but eager to stay more and more fully engaged in life. I was deeply relieved. I have a deep regard and affection for Ben, and the thought of losing him to cancer was horrifying to me. As I'd imagined the possibility of his being ill, I had been wondering silently if I would be capable of seeing him through the treatment process.

As he prepared to leave the session, Ben said, "Well, we won't have to talk about cancer any more." I responded, "I think it is something that we will need to come back to for some time, as the possibility of being seriously ill or dying has stirred up many important things that we need to continue talking about." "I think we can let it go," said Ben, "And besides, I don't feel I have the right to keep hurting you." Hurting me? I had no idea what Ben was talking about. I pointed out that he had every right to say things that might hurt me, that it was my responsibility to deal with whatever feelings our work and relationship might stir in me, but I had no idea how he felt he had been hurting me during this period of the cancer scare. Ben explained, "Virtually every time I used the word cancer, it was like a shadow came over your face. Sometimes you looked like you were going to cry. I don't want to cause you pain." I was dumbstruck. His words made instant sense to me. He had seen something in my face that I was not even aware of feeling, let alone showing. I was deeply touched by his noticing and his expression of concern. "I have some idea what you may have been seeing, Ben, and it's important we come back to this next week."

For the next week, I struggled with what, if anything, to say to Ben about the meaning of what he saw on my face. I was stunned and rather embarrassed that something had been evident on my face but not to me. I knew, as soon as Ben spoke, that the sadness he was seeing on my face was there; it was not a projection on Ben's part. My mother died at 40 of cancer, when I was in my late adolescence, my brother and sister in early adolescence. Her young death left deep, unmanaged scars, and my father died ten years later of an intentionally untreated cancer. I could not stand the thought that Ben, who was just discovering the pleasures and satisfactions of his life, could have his young life taken away by this disease, that his kids might lose their father so early in their lives. My admiration and affection for Ben deepened in response to his caring and honesty with me. I knew that if I spoke of my parents' deaths, I could probably not do so without crying. What would that mean to Ben, who had grown up with a determinedly depressive mother and a father who converted all affect into rage, to see his therapist in tears?

In the next session, I told Ben that what he'd seen on my face was undoubtedly a deep sadness that came from my own life. I would talk with him about it if he wished to know and if it would support his therapy. I suggested he take a week to think it over. He replied immediately that he didn't think it was "his place" to know something so personal. I assured Ben it was "his place" to know something of me if he so chose, especially about something that had entered our relationship unbidden and unplanned. The question I wanted him to consider was whether my speaking of myself would support his therapy.

McLaughlin (2005) has stressed that "whether we are analyst or patient, our deepest hopes for what we may find the world to be, as well as our worst fears of what it will be, reflect our transference expectancies as shaped by our developmental past" (p. 187). More than half a century earlier, in his remarkable, though long unpublished, clinical diaries, Ferenczi (1932) noted that it is through the

> unmasking of the so called transference and countertransference as the hiding places of the most significant obstacles to the completion of all analyses, one comes to be almost convinced that no analysis can succeed as long as the false and alleged differences between the "analytical situation" and ordinary life are not overcome.
>
> (p. 212)

For both Ferenczi and McLaughlin, the inevitable humanness and vulnerability of the analyst were simultaneously potential sources of trouble, insight, impasse, and/or mutual influence and understanding.

Ferenczi (1932) also observed a certain merging of psychic realities in the analytic couple that brings affective vitality to the analytic endeavor:

> The emotions of the analyst combine with the ideas of the analysand, and the ideas of the analyst (representational images) with the emotions of the analysand; in this way the otherwise lifeless images become events, and the empty emotional tumult acquires an intellectual content. (?)
>
> (p. 14)

Ferenczi follows this statement with a question mark in parentheses. What does this question mark mean? Does Ferenczi question his own perceptions? Is it a question of what does one do clinically with this observation once it has been made? Is it a question to the reader to take up? Ferenczi's awareness of his own emotional limits and entanglements with his patients led to his experimentation with mutual analysis and his open acknowledgment of his mistakes and mis-understandings with regard to his analysands (Thompson, 1964; Ferenczi, 1932; Aron & Harris, 1993). McLaughlin's response to his own awareness of what he called hard spots and blind spots (2005, pp. 75–76) interfering in the relations with his patients, was to remove himself temporarily from the transference pressures to the privacy of his woodshop, his "transference sanctuary," entering a period of reverie and self-analysis, so that he could return to his patient in a more open state of mind and affect (McLaughlin, 2005, pp. 114–116). He seldom reported the content of his private self-analysis to his analysands; he used it, instead, to bring himself back to the analytic work, the relationship, and the mutual transferences with a clearer sense of self that would enable a more open engagement.

Poland (2005), in a paper delivered in recognition of McLaughlin's contribu-tions to psychoanalysis, mirrors Ferenczi's observations about the psychic impact of the patient upon the therapist's being. He wryly observes, "Positions of subject and object flow subtly and interchangeably. No matter how it seems on the surface, *below* the surface traffic is always two-way" (p. 18).

Stern (2004) argues, "The analyst's role is not defined by invulnerability, in other words, but by a special (though inconsistent) willingness, and a practiced (though imperfect) capacity to accept and deal with her vulnerability" (p. 216).

Poland outlines four areas of danger and vulnerability for the analyst: 1. countertransferential fears provoked by the patient, 2. fears idiosyncratic to the analyst's character that emerge during the course of some analyses, 3. those fears and vulnerabilities intrinsic to the analytic process (object attachment and loss; resistance and relentless negativism on the part of the patient), and 4. "those resulting from the human condition, from the analyst's vulnerability to the demands of reality and fate even when working best" (p. 16). Poland (2005) writes in a deeply personal and self-revealing fashion, and concludes—in contrast to Ferenczi and in accord with McLaughlin:

> A word about self-disclosure. The agonizing personal introspective strife in which I was engaged as part of this woman's analysis was my own task, not to be carried out by my burdening my patient with the details of my private inner work. .... Nonetheless, it was important that I try to resolve my own issues in myself, using them to *facilitate* but not to *complicate* the patient's work. My aim was to *unburden* the patient's analysis, not to burden it with my private labors. The analyst's fear may be triggered or even caused by the patient; the analyst's task is to sort out private issues privately.
>
> (p. 20)

While I admire the clarity and integrity of Poland's position, I would see the choices regarding self-disclosure as variable, dependent on context and the place in time in the evolution of the therapeutic relationship. Would I burden Ben with self-disclosure at this point in his work with me? What kind of disclosure might be most appropriate and therapeutic? These questions are complex, not readily answered by any single theoretical position (Aron, 1991, 1996; Bollas, 1989; Davies, 1994; Leary, 1997; Maroda, 1991; McLaughlin, 2005; Slavin & Kriegman, 1998; Searles, 1959, 1979; Stern, 2003, 2004). Questions of analyst/therapist self-disclosure have been, and continue to be, controversial (Bonovitz, 2006; Eagle, 2003; Gediman, 2006; Greenberg, 1995; Hartman, 2006; Hoffman, 1998; Renik, 1993, 1999; Slochower, 2006). I considered several possibilities as to what, if anything further, to say to Ben should he ask. I might acknowledge to Ben that the shadow he'd seen on my face was a shadow cast by my own history and simply ask for his associations and fantasies. I wondered if I did not disclose anything further about myself, would it hold open the space for Ben's own experience, conflicts, and choices as to whether or not to explore this terrain further? Could further self-disclosure on my part foreclosure Ben's experience of himself? I might say something like, "This is a frightening place I know something about from my own life, so I know something of its importance and am willing to stay there with you in this fear and anxiety." I thought that perhaps my telling something of my own life's losses and feelings toward those I've loved might offer a kind of model and permission for Ben to move into territory that had been forbidden and shameful. I considered telling him more about my feelings for him and his children without telling him anything about my own life. Each seemed like a valid choice.

Over the days between sessions, I found myself thinking particularly about Aron's article "The patient's experience of the analyst's subjectivity" (1991) and re-read the article with Ben in mind. Aron describes the needs of children to reach into the inner worlds of their parents and of patients' desire to know something of the interior lives of their analysts, that this knowing of the other's interiority is an essential developmental achievement in the capacity to think psychologically. I realized that, for Ben, his father's internal world was a black, forbidding, and forbidden box. It was not to be known. In kind, Ben's internal world was of no interest to his father. Any expression of Ben's feelings was subject to ridicule and assault (in adulthood as well as childhood). Early in treatment, Ben had told me that as a child he planted a fruit tree in the yard every year on his birthday. On his fifteenth birthday, he stopped planting trees because "by the time the tree bore fruit, I would be an adult, and I knew that once I was an adult, nothing would taste sweet any more. There would only be bitterness." Ben learned to live a solitary and silent life. It was "not his place" to expect to truly know someone else or to expect to be known.

Much in my own life and development had taught me that those closest to me, in a kind of benign neglect, were most content when I managed myself by myself (Winnicott, 1949; Corrigan & Gordon, 1995; Shabad & Selinger, 1995). Ben, too, had learned to take care of himself and expect little but trouble and judgment from others. From the very beginnings of our work, I had felt an identification with Ben. Our fathers had both fought in World War II and had been deeply scarred. My father came back deeply withdrawn and silent; Ben's father came back self-pitying and violent. As sons, we each grew up with fathers whose internal worlds were deeply disturbed and sealed off. We each lived much of our own internal lives in silence. I decided, should Ben ask me to say more, it was time to tell him something of my own life, to let him learn directly something of my own subjectivity.

The following week, Ben did ask me to speak of the meaning of the sadness he had seen on my face. I told him the story of my parents' deaths and the impact on me, of my fantasies of what might happen to his children should he die so young, and of my admiration for his taking the early warning signs seriously and immediately pursuing help. I did cry. Ben listened to me with tenderness and interest, and something shifted in the shame he had often felt in the face of his own sadness and vulnerability, which he had always seen as "weak." He did not experience me as weak as I spoke frankly with him. Here, at this moment, it was *my* speech rather than that of the client, *my* openness and vulnerability, that served both Ben and myself.

Time passed, and this interchange faded into the background of our sessions. When invited to write a paper for a special issue of a journal, I thought immediately of this experience with Ben and decided to write about it. Early in our work, Ben had given me a couple of his published papers to read. He is very accomplished in his field but had great difficulty with writing about his work. He asked me to read some of his papers, both to understand more about what he does and to help him deal with his writing blocks. I found his work fascinating (though difficult to comprehend), and we were able to address his writing blocks quite productively. In a further step of self-disclosure, I decided to give Ben the first draft of the paper to read for his perspective and also permission to publish something about him. He was deeply moved by the paper, touched that the encounter between us had meant something to me as well as to him. Ben said, "I've always known you were a thoughtful therapist, but reading the paper has shown me something of *how* you think. I learned a lot." He gave me permission to publish what had happened between us.

I could sense that something had shifted in Ben, at least in part as a result of this exchange about the shadow over my face. Ben re-established contact with his father after a couple years of silence following a particularly nasty fight. His father's behavior had not changed, but Ben began to sense that his father was anxious inside, as well as gruff, belligerent, and argumentative. When his father had to be hospitalized for a serious illness, Ben called regularly, and his father was able to express appreciation for Ben's concern. Once he recovered and left the hospital, Ben's father returned to his usual mode, but Ben found himself more accepting of his father's way of being and pleased that he, Ben, had been able to offer his father something different that at least for a little while had been received.

Recently Ben asked if the paper had been accepted for publication. I told him that it had. He said he admired me for writing something so honest and personal, and that he thought it signaled a change in my profession that it had been accepted. Ben had once been in a psychoanalysis which he described as "trying to talk to a stone wall in a dark room," so he thought it was strictly forbidden for a therapist to say anything personal about himself. I asked how the experience I had written about has stayed with him. He said that it has had numerous effects for him, that first of all my sharing myself with him had made me "both more human and more professional" in his mind. My decision to share the draft of the paper with him was "sweet and respectful." Most important for himself, he learned that "to show my vulnerability was OK, healthy, that it makes me feel closer." He said that while I had encouraged his vulnerability on many occasions, he didn't trust it, but that when he saw mine, he could feel what had been only an idea before. "And reading the paper, I had always been ashamed of my withdrawal. But reading the paper I could see that you understood it, and that *you* withdraw sometimes, too, so that really made it OK."

A second vignette illustrates a very different experience of an unexpected self-awareness and unwanted vulnerability. Charlie and I had struggled for years. Unlike the growing closeness and affection I felt for Ben, my years of involvement with Charlie were marked by determination but also bounded by caution and a wary self-protection. Charlie was nearing 50, had never married, had no friends at the start of treatment, and wandered from job to job, working always "beneath his potential" and his academic training.

Over the course of therapy, his job status improved and tentative friendships were in the making. But our relationship seemed forever at the edge of fraying and unraveling. Charlie constantly underscored my failure really to "get him." In my failures I joined a multitude of others who never seemed to "get" Charlie. I would quietly steam, wondering if it ever occurred to Charlie that were *he* to "get" *someone else's* experience, he might have a few friends, maybe even a wife and family.

I was acutely aware of the painful developmental history of Charlie's life, with relentlessly self-involved parents who seemed to see him as a not very attractive piece of furniture that had been delivered, unwanted, to their living room. They just stepped around him. I knew what he felt he needed of me, and I despaired of my capacity (or willingness) to give it to him. I could barely stand how he treated me or others, and there seemed no room to address this with him. I careened between feelings of irritation and urgent anxiety that he would never get a full life for himself and a sense of guilt that I was not more helpful. Regular consultation helped me manage my countertransference and do technically competent work, but in some fundamental way I could not open myself to Charlie in a way that would truly allow me to "get" him with my being as well as my head.

Gerson (2003) describes the transferential relationship as the medium through which unconscious desires can begin to emerge and be articulated, while constantly shadowed and intertwined with memories (and anticipations) of failure, the bedrock of deadly and deadening anxiety and defense. And yet, Gerson argues, "we constantly seek others as transformational objects to make something about ourselves more available to ourselves" (2003, unpaginated talk). The impasse between Charlie and me, the deadlock of our mutual, negative transferences, repeatedly foreclosed our experiences of ourselves rather than made something of ourselves more available to ourselves or each other.

Charlie and I fell constantly into the shadows, the urgency of desire seeming to be a source of irritation and frustration rather than being hopeful and enlivening. I recall some old song about a mutual admiration society; Charlie and I had formed a mutual irritation society. Then one day, quite unexpectedly, a high school acquaintance, a woman in whom Charlie had had considerable adolescent interest, was back in the city for a funeral. She gave Charlie a call, and they met for lunch. In the session, Charlie was uncharacteristically bereft and, also uncharacteristically, upset with himself rather than being upset with the world and everyone in it. "What's wrong with me, Bill? She has a family, a marriage, not the greatest but not so bad. I might have had a life with her. What is it I do wrong? I must do something wrong. You must help me see what I'm doing." I was quiet. I listened. I could feel my wariness yielding, my chest opening. I was afraid to say much of anything, as though I would break this magical spell.

Near tears by the end of the session, Charlie was standing to leave. "She was here for a funeral. If it had been me who'd died, would she have come? Who would have known to tell her I died? If I died tomorrow, who would come from out of state to be at my funeral? No one. Who would there be to call? No one. If I died tomorrow, there would not be enough people who cared to be pallbearers for my casket." He left.

I stood there, barely able to breathe. I felt nauseous and thought I was going to collapse. What Charlie had just described as the fear for his death was the reality of my father's death and funeral. After my mother's death, my father had become so withdrawn, isolated, and increasingly bizarre that by the time he died ten years later, there was no one in his life, there would no pallbearers for his casket, only his mother, brother, two sons, and a daughter to attend his funeral. I had to go to a real estate company where he had worked briefly, and very unsuccessfully, to ask the staff to be his pallbearers. I began to understand my urgency, my irritation, and my inability to open to Charlie, and my self-deadening in the face of his unsocialized behavior and his relentless despair.

The session haunted me the rest of the day. I had to will my attention to my other clients. I went home that night and turned to my personal "sanctuary of transference," music. Bob Dylan, Neil Young, Joan Baez, music that carried me back to my Dad in bitter compassion. I cried, this time in private. I felt the collapse of my Dad's life and the impact of his choices on me. I could feel how deeply, unbearably, and unconsciously I had merged Charlie with my father. I could feel the beginnings of a willingness, an openness, a capacity to undo the knots between us. I did not tell Charlie what had happened to me in that moment when he spoke of his imagined funeral with no pallbearers. Unlike with

Ben, I had no impulse to be personal with Charlie. I recalled a time when I did share a personal experience with Charlie in an effort (rather desperate and un-thought-out) to make a link with him and feel some identification. Charlie responded, "That's really irritating. I don't pay you to hear about your life. I pay you to listen to mine. Please keep your life to yourself. Or pay somebody else to listen to you." Unlike with Ben, for Charlie, given his character and where we were in our developing relationship, such self-disclosure would have been an intrusion, a burden, to use Poland's phrase. At another time in the course of treatment, this might not be the case.

A personal self-disclosure to Charlie would not have facilitated our work or his self-understanding. What *was* possible for me, however, as a result of my self-encounter and realizations, was to return to Charlie with openness, patience, and for the first time, hope. I have no doubt that he felt the difference, though he never spoke of it. He, too, was in a different place after his lunch with his high school girlfriend. He began to question himself, and I was able to engage with those questions without pressure or irritation.

The vulnerabilities and psychic conflicts centered in the tragic deaths of my young parents were within *me*, and deeply affected my work with these two men. The same history inhabited me quite differently with these two very different men. With Ben, probably not coincidentally a father, like me, and self-blaming, like me, my own history of loss facilitated a deep regard and positive identification with him. With Charlie, my history and vulnerability unconsciously evoked in his presence fostered a defensive identification and a relentless wariness. The decisions I made in the context of my work with these men were, therefore, quite different.

Over the past quarter century, various relationally based models of psycho-analysis and psychotherapy have gradually informed one another, though each had been evolving in relative separation from the others from the 1930s until the 1980s. Ferenczi may not have been the first psychoanalyst to notice that the patient was not the only troubled and vulnerable person in the analytic couple, but he was the first to try to work with it clinically and write about it publicly. His experiments with "mutual analysis" may have been brilliant failures, but his emotional honesty inspired many, some of whom emigrated to the United States, offering an alternative to the more classical analytic position dominant in the US before and after World War II (Thompson, 1950; Rudnytsky, Bokay, & Giam-pieri-Deutsch, 1996). Ironically, several of the innovators in relationally oriented models struggled in relative isolation and solitude—Ferenczi in Budapest, Fair-bairn in Edinburgh, Sullivan in Washington, DC, and McLaughlin in Pittsburgh, PA. Others, like Klein and Winnicott in London, and Greenberg and Mitchell in New York, had the advantage of major urban centers of psychoanalytic thinking and a sense of a following of like-minded colleagues, though as one reads their work, one can see that they, too, were not always met with open arms by their more classically oriented colleagues. In the United Kingdom, so often isolated from Europe, a different mode of relational psychoanalysis—object relations—was developing. In the object relational mode, the trouble and vulner-ability within the dyad was seen as centered in the client; disturbances within the analyst were seen as products of the affective and infective impact of the patient, through splitting, projection, and projective identification. In the United States in the 1930s, Harry Stack Sullivan was laboring mostly alone but coming to his own conclusions of the inevitability of mutual influence in the therapeutic dyad. Joined by Clara Thompson, Erich Fromm, Frieda Fromm-Reichman, among other European émigrés, the school of interpersonal psychoanalysis evolved.

It took several decades after the war for these models to reshape psychoanalysis in the US. Jay Greenberg and Stephen Mitchell's *Object Relations in Psycho-analytic Theory* (1983) and Mitchell's *Relational Concepts in Psychoanalysis: An Integration* (1988) were the first major efforts to integrate interpersonal and object relational models into American psychoanalysis, giving birth to what is now known as "relational psychoanalysis." During that same period, McLaughlin was writing a series of important papers exploring the use of the analyst's countertransference and the mutuality of influence within the therapeutic dyad. These emerging models stressed the importance of the analyst's own subjectivity within the psychother-apeutic endeavor.

From the perspective of classical, ego psychological, and object relational models of psychoanalysis, the desires, disturbances, and resistances under study are those within the patient. Within the relational sensibility (although there are many variations of this paradigm), it is understood that *both* therapist and client bring aspects of their unformulated, unconscious experience into the consulting room, that the unconscious pressures of the desired and the prohibited exist in both members of the dyad (Stern, 1997). Hence, at times, there will be the inevitable vulnerability of the analyst that may well affect the work with the patient but does not necessary come from the patient. How to make use of countertransference and the therapist's human vulnerability varies from model to model, practitioner to practitioner. The relational models share a rough consensus that the nature of unconscious experience and the work of analysis are not only the retrieval of rejected and disavowed drives and infantile attachment needs, but a process of unconscious unfolding and discovery of emerging possibilities.

As can be seen from the perspectives of Ferenczi and McLaughlin, two analysts of relentless curiosity and experimentation who wrote with unusual candor, as well as from the clinical vignettes, a therapist's willingness to experience and inhabit his or her own vulnerabilities can deepen the therapeutic endeavor and be of compelling benefit to clients.

Chapter 5

Failing to do the job: When the client pays the price for the therapist's countertransference

> So I experience an ethical obligation to mourn and reflect on my failures yet not look back to engage in the futile violence of self-recrimination. Rather, I strive to learn forward.
>
> (Landaiche, 2014, p. 276)

There are moments, sometimes long periods of time, during which each of us in our professional work lives in the grip of our personal history. There are profound echoes, shadows, voices from the past that remain alive in the present, within the unconscious foundations of each of us, often shaping and distorting how we see, what we want, and how we treat others. These deeply formative experiences, fantasies, and wishes from childhood often remain within our ways of being throughout life and often emerge unconsciously in the therapeutic relationship. This is every bit as true for the professional as for the client.

In this chapter, I will seek to evoke and illustrate the power of our personal histories as they play out in our present therapeutic relationships. The professional literature is filled with papers and books on how the transference dynamics of clients create resistance and trouble within the therapeutic process. Here I will focus on my own (counter)transferential struggles with a client I call "Samantha," struggles that ultimately contributed to an irreparable rupture of the therapeutic process in which we were engaged.

Atlas (2016) used the term "therapeutic tale" (p. 9) instead of "case study," arguing that "What we call a 'case' (assuming an objective observation) is in fact the narrative we are left with, a product of our mind and of the way we process our patients' minds" (pp. 9–10). If the tale told here were presented by Samantha, I am quite sure you would be reading a very different story.

Starting at the end

As I began to formulate this chapter, my thoughts returned immediately to one of the worst failures of my career, my failure with Samantha, now nearly two decades in the past. In what proved to be Samantha's last session with me, I had greeted her in the waiting room and walked past her to go to the kitchen for a cup of coffee before starting the session. When I returned, she was no longer in the waiting area. As we had been locked in a period of intense conflict, I imagined she had decided to leave. I opened my office door to find her already inside, taking photographs. I stood stunned in the doorway as she turned the camera on me to take my picture. When I asked her what she was doing, she continued taking photos, shouting at me, "I'm making a record of this hellhole where you have tortured me all these years." I was horrified and frozen in place. She left. I never saw her again in person. I say "in person" because over the following months I received dozens of angry phone messages that often filled the entire message time. I say "in person" because I made many phone calls to her after this encounter, hoping to get her back into therapy. I say "in person" because, unbeknownst to me, she had purchased pieces of art by various local artists whose work was in my office; these artists found what she had purchased slashed to pieces with a note attached saying that I had forced her to buy "this trash." I say "in person" because there were several times when I looked out of my office window to see her standing in the street in front of the building. But she never re-entered my office or spoke to me directly again.

Before we began working together, Samantha had moved to Pittsburgh after being fired from her previous high-paying position in a major US city. She hated living in Pittsburgh, which she considered decidedly second-class. She would often go into long rants about how the city was full of left-wing idiots. Sessions were frequently filled with contemptuous stories of the idiots and slobs with whom she was now forced to work, and I felt that I was one of them. Her goal was to rebuild her reputation so that she could return to the city that she felt had been taken away from her by the boss who fired her. My job, in her mind, was to give her support and a place to vent.

Samantha had years ago cut off completely from both of her now divorced parents and her brother, so she saw no purpose in talking about them or her childhood. She described her father as a violent alcoholic who treated his children like slaves and her mother as a crass woman who used her and her brother to manipulate her husband. She spoke of them only with contempt. My early efforts to call her contempt into question or to engage her in some sort of personal reflection were met with spiteful fury.

Our work together was marked with frequent conflicts in which Samantha did not feel that I had adequately understood or supported her. Many of my early therapeutic efforts were either script-level interpretations or some form of confrontation of her rigid frames of reference. These were typically dismissed as power plays on my part or narcissistic displays of how smart I thought I was. She wanted my mind and thinking to be the same as hers. She wanted a warm, caring, accepting therapist, which in many ways—consciously and unconsciously—I felt compelled to be, even as I was horrified at her relentless fury and contempt for others.

Whenever I suggested a point of view that differed from hers, she felt like I was trying to take over her mind, and she would fly into rage. Because she had grown up with a violent father and a parasitic mother, her intense, accusatory reactions did not surprise me. I often suggested that what she expected of me was what her mother expected of her. Although there may have been some truth in what I was saying, she heard my words as at best useless, at worst insulting. I moved into an increasingly passive and compliant position.

We had worked together twice a week for more than two years when she lost her position in her firm because of an ongoing conflict with her boss. Because she was very competent in her work, she was given the position of an independent consultant, but this meant a substantial reduction in her income. We decided, reluctantly, to reduce her sessions to once a week. I was concerned about this change in frequency, so I suggested that we have brief phone contact every Monday to maintain a little more continuity between sessions. Samantha readily agreed. I offered to call her because I often traveled and it might be hard for her to reach me consistently. The phone calls never lasted more than ten minutes. They seemed to facilitate our work.

Another year passed in this manner, and Samantha appeared to be doing much better. She found a new job. Her personal relationships were more satisfying. Our therapeutic relationship was considerably less conflictual. I was relieved. I was not sure what was working in the therapy, but something seemed to be, so that was good enough for me. With most clients, I would have been asking what it was about the therapy that was facilitating the changes, but I did not ask Samantha because such questions were so often unwelcome and attacked. This choice not to inquire was to have brutal consequences.

The crisis

As the autumn months were approaching, I knew my schedule was going to change. I had taken on a consultation group on Monday afternoons, so the free time in which I called her would no longer be available. I told Samantha about the impending change in my schedule and that with the start of the group I would no longer be able to call her on Mondays. I suggested, as an alternative, she could call my voice mail and leave an update on what she had been doing and thinking about. She was stunned. She asked me angrily why I had been making those calls for over a year. I explained that I thought we had agreed at the start that this was a way of providing more continuity in our contact, that it was an extension and support for her therapy. She became infuriated. She accused me of humiliating her, asking me if I had a new woman in my life. I had no idea what she was talking about. She went on, shouting, that she had thought I had been calling her every Monday to make myself feel better after a weekend of my being alone and miserable. She told me with absolute certainty that she knew I had been calling her all this time because I was having fantasies of our becoming lovers once therapy was finished. I had never known or imagined that she had such a fantasy; the possibility had never occurred to me. I offered an interpretation that it seemed as though the only way she could understand my calls was as a form of being sexually used (as she had been so many times in past relationships), that she could not imagine that I was calling out of concern for her. I said that somehow our original agreement had changed its meaning in her mind. She felt immediately put down by my comments and mounted an attack on me as a "fucking liberal" trying to make myself feel better at her expense.

Samantha stopped paying for sessions, refusing to pay while demanding that I continue to see her. She missed sessions frequently. She would not attend a scheduled session and then show up in the waiting room demanding to be seen immediately. The sessions were again filled with rants about "the liberal ass-holes" populating our city. Samantha and I, as individuals in a relationship with each other, seemed to disappear from the sessions.

This situation, as unsettling as it was, could have been an impasse or period of enactment that could have served the treatment (Cornell, 2012; Cornell & Landaiche, 2006; Kantrowitz, 1996; Little, 2012; McLaughlin, 2005; Stuthridge, 2012). Contemporary therapeutic tales of impasses and enactments in the transactional analysis literature have often portrayed difficult moments in treatment that led to insight and transformation (Cook, 2012; Maquet, 2012; Murphy, 2012; Novak, 2015; Shadbolt, 2012; Stuthridge, 2012, 2015). But the crisis with Samantha proved to be much more catastrophic than informative or reparative. I could not provide the reflective space needed to find meaning, and new life could not be created. The therapy shattered.

In her writings about enactment, Stuthridge has captured the profound tensions that often inhabit these troubled and troubling periods of treatment. She has observed, on the one hand, that "enactments in therapy provide an opportunity to discover the lost parts of oneself for both client and therapist" (Stuthridge, 2012, p. 249). On the other hand, in a later article, she cautioned this:

> My brief illustrations of this process suggest more ease than the clinical reality presents. Images do not always connect neatly with meanings, new meanings can be profoundly unsettling, visceral experience is always disturbing, and identifying unsymbolized feelings usually involves an inner wrestle with parts of the self we do not want to know.
>
> (p. 114)

Samantha and I were unable to find the means to wrestle with our selves or each other in any productive way. Part of my motivation in writing this is to provide a painful caution about the tendency in the current relational Zeitgesit to valorize, or even glamorize, enactments and countertransference. I failed this woman. Within the transactional analysis literature, Landaiche (2014) has spoken frankly to the lasting emotional impact of failure:

It also appears that the painfulness of failure is often connected to loss, which for me seems linked, in part, to my complicity in the failure, an entangled sense of shock, grief, and mortifications for having somehow violated my sense of rightness and life.

(p. 269)

Seeking consultation

In consultations about Samantha, all too much of the time was focused on my understanding her character defenses and on efforts to manage her projections. The emphasis had been on the importance of my offering a kind of sustained, containing environment. By the time I began asking different questions with my consultant, it was too late.

Throughout the course of treatment, I had been consulting, on occasion, with my supervisor about my work with Samantha. Now we were consulting weekly, and we crafted an effort to bring some semblance of meaning to what was happening. I said to her, "You have been talking for weeks about the liberal assholes of Pittsburgh. It is clear to me that I am the asshole. I think this is what you are trying to tell me. This is what you need me to see and accept. I have been an asshole because I did not see and did not ask what my phone calls represented to you. If I had seen or asked, we could have talked about it. I haven't protected you from the ambiguity of our relationship. How unprotected you have been with me."

Samantha seemed to reject my comments, accusing me of being a narcissist, but I had the impression that my words did mean something to her. However, we still could not move forward. I suggested that we see my consultant together, and perhaps this would help us work through the massive misunderstanding. It had never occurred to her that I might seek professional consultation, which she considered a violation of her confidentiality. Within a few weeks, she would be taking photographs of my office.

When it became clear that the therapy with Samantha had ruptured beyond repair, I continued to work with my consultant. A colleague interviewed me in depth about my work with Samantha as a means of helping me establish the beginnings of some objectivity and reflective capacity about what had happened. With the assistance of the interview and my ongoing work with my consultant, I began to understand how I had come to give up my own mind in the face of hers. My consultant made a powerful observation:

You needed to have clearly, consistently, and at times insistently asked her, "Who am I to you?" You didn't. Over the course of your work together, you must have represented many things to her: asshole, liberal, sadist, narcissist, father, mother, protector, lover, abuser, and savior. You often acted to support and protect her in her life in the world outside your office, and she was able to make use of this. We can see now that you did not protect her from her experience of herself in your office. You did not protect her from the impact of her fantasies. With your phone calls to her she was imagining something that you could not imagine. You didn't ask, and there you failed to protect her.

There are many examples of how I might have more directly and consistently helped her to identify and examine her fantasies about me and her anxieties about our relationship. I became caught up in defending myself against the accusations that were a part of her conscious perceptions of me and did not inquire about her less conscious feelings and fantasies. During the period when things seemed to be going so much better in her life, I accepted it in silent relief. I did not explore the meaning of these periods with her either. If I had, I might have discovered that what seemed to be progress was based on her assumption that when we finished therapy, we would become lovers.

Throughout those years with Samantha, I felt a certain kind of madness within her. Her madness took the form of a profound and rather desperate rigidity in her thinking that could not allow anyone to contribute to her thought process. She could not see that my mind might have something to offer in alliance with hers. She could not call herself into question and rarely allowed me to call her into question. I did not meet her in the moments of this madness. I stepped aside. At one point I suggested medication, which she found to be insulting. Although I did think it might provide her some relief from the anxiety that wracked her, I knew I was also offering a pill as a substitute for my capacity to think. I avoided or submitted to her fury rather than speak to the anxiety that her anger warded off. Without my bringing my own mind to hers in a direct and constructive way, we could not create a space in which we could think together. Her thinking became locked into an ever more elaborate, self-reinforcing web of beliefs that explained my behavior and motivation to her and completely altered her understanding of the meaning of our therapeutic work.

As Samantha became increasingly enraged, I could not see that her fury was, in fact, a plea for my integrity and containment. She was both terrified that my mind would take over hers and at the same time terrified that her mind was too powerful for mine. I was unable to find a way to bring my mind clearly, strongly alongside hers in an accompaniment rather than against hers in an assault. There was nothing in Samantha's history that would have shown her that the mind of another could be both powerful and benevolent. She became lost in the malevolent anxieties generated in her mind. My mind did not show up in a way that offered her something reliably different. Ultimately, in her mind, my mind had become monstrous and malevolent, and from this there was to be no recovery.

Self-examination

In looking back at my failed work with Samantha, I had to start by facing my personal blind spots. With her, my blindness to myself was extreme. Her ways of being evoked in me, unconsciously, a doubling up of my own childhood struggles with each of my parents. Her social isolation and loneliness evoked in me the ghost of my father, who still deeply haunted my psyche. I silently imagined that if the therapy failed, she would live her life, and ultimately her death, bitter and alone, as had my father. I felt an enormous, unspoken responsibility for her wellbeing, as I had with my father. Samantha did not tend to present herself as lonely, but this was my projection. I was simultaneously deeply affected by her isolation, frightened of it, and hesitant to speak to it with any sustained force.

There were few people who knew or spent any personal time with my father. My mother knew many people, but there were few whom she actually liked; she was a relentless critic of the personal flaws of others. With Samantha, the shadow of my mother was evoked in my psyche. My young mother became depressed after her father, my beloved grandfather, died at age 50, and remnants of this depression haunted her the rest of her life. As my father's personal isolation continued and deepened, my mother grew increasingly bitter and volatile. She would rage at my father, and he would sit in numbed, guilty silence. The same could happen with me or my little brother and sister. In these states, she scared me, and I wanted desperately to protect myself and my siblings from her sudden eruptions. I took on the job of keeping Mom happy and calm, and I got very good at it. We were quite poor, so my mother (who never finished school) took in laundry and sewing for extra money. I would sit for hours with her at the ironing board or sewing machine, listening to her acidic tales of woe. Unconsciously, as I sat with Samantha, I was thrown back to my place at my mother's ironing board—a silent sounding board for her hostile and defensive judgments of others.

When the professional can create a reflective space, clients have a better opportunity to see and gradually become free of their scripts. But with Samantha, I was affected in such powerful ways that I could not hold my reactions in consciousness. I could not make sense of my own experience. There were aspects of myself and my personal history that were called into a compelling (though unconscious) being, which I found unbearable. The result was a contradictory and inconsistent combination of my feeling overly responsible, avoidant, and compliant. Without some clarity and distance from my side of the relationship, it became impossible for Samantha to step out of her transferential reactions and demands on me. We became blinded in the dark shadows of our pasts.

Returning to therapy and recovering my capacity to think

I had sought consultation while working with Samantha, which was of some help but not sufficient. It would have been altogether too easy to justify this treatment failure through accounts of the client's psychopathology, resistances, projections, and so on. I needed to engage in serious self-analysis.

It became clear that I needed to return to my own therapy. In my own previous psychotherapy, I had worked through the lingering consequences of my mother's depression and the deaths and other losses that filled and shaped my childhood. But now it seemed that there was something about anger and violence that I needed to face. This seemed strange to me, as I had never thought of my childhood as being one marked with any sort of violence or any real danger.

My previous therapist had been a soft-spoken, gentle man. Now I sought a therapist who was rougher and tougher in his demeanor, though I soon wished that I gone for another gentle soul. My new therapist, whom I will call "Charles," was closer to my own age. He did not mince words. I had found what I was looking for. My first analysis was deeply grounded in the active exploration of the transferential/countertransferential dynamics between me and my therapist, and the work was very useful to me. But Charles had little overt interest in the dynamics of our relationship. His consistent focus was on my activities and relationships outside of his office and (yet another) examination of my childhood. In so doing, he created a triadic space that freed me from my familiar dyadic worlds.

From Charles's perspective, my childhood took on a new shape. My mother's rages were not just viewed as symptomatic of her depression and loneliness but as acts of violence. Charles saw my father's withdrawal as irresponsible and placing me squarely in harm's way—with my mother and with the boys who teased and tormented me because I had no idea how to join in with their aggressive play.

My mother died at 40, when I was in my late teens, and my father ended his life at 50, when I had just turned 30. I was deeply invested in maintaining a positive image of each of them, as troubled but struggling to do the best they could in the face of their own difficult lives. Charles repeatedly challenged my compassionate understanding of my parents' travails as a denial of my anger with them. When I offered my long-dead parents compassion and understanding for their lack of parental guidance, Charles reacted with outrage. I did not like this. When I became angry with Charles, he relished the encounters. But I began to experience what it was to be met by a man in ways I could never have imagined with my father and that were markedly different from how my previous therapist had related to me.

During this period of the work with Charles, I began to see and feel the psychological consequences on my emotional development of my father's withdrawal. Neither my mother nor I could turn to him for much of anything. I was the oldest child, a boy, and my mother turned to me. I was stuck to her and with her. There was little psychological space for me to have a mind and goals of my own. I did not have the freedom to have friends of my own. In primary school, when most kids were finding and enjoying their best friends, I came home to my Mom after school. If I played, I played alone in the woods and creeks that surrounded our country home.

Freud (1924; see also Bollas, 1992; Loewald, 1980) described the crucial developmental phase, which he named the Oedipus period, in which the primary bond between mother and baby is gradually broken by the mother's re-establishment of her primary and sexual relationship with the father. The young child experiences this as a painful loss of a primary and beloved relationship, and this transition is often accompanied by deep pain and anger for the young child. But this transition also grants the developing child freedom from the primary caretaker and a gap—that is, a psychological space—within which it becomes possible to discover one's individuality and sense of agency.

What Freud was attempting to describe is exactly the struggle I lived with my mother. I did not have that space independent of her. My mother was lonely, bitter, and depressed. My father withdrew from his family and stayed to himself. He did not return emotionally to his wife to re-establish the primacy of their relationship. It became my job to make my mother feel better, a job I took very seriously.

In a deeply reflective essay on the developmental period that Freud framed as oedipal, Bollas (1992) suggested that it is a crucial period of psychic evolution through which the child is able to relinquish the primary dyadic bond to the singular, caretaking parent and establish a new object relation—that of the family group (pp. 233–234). He argued that, although the draw toward the comfort of the dyad is never far away, the child who moves through the oedipal dilemma has the freedom and capacity to be a member of a family group and then move on to a civic place of social belonging and group relations. Bollas did not suggest that this process is easy and observed, "Many will cling to an internal loving mother as they refuse intercourse with their peers, while others will reflect the conflict either by assuming the law of the father or hiding in terror" (p. 236). I spent my childhood and adolescence rarely joining my peers but, rather, hiding in quiet terror. Groups frightened and dismayed me. As soon as I graduated university, I moved into a deeply symbiotic marriage, which ultimately ended in a vicious rupture.

I came, unconsciously, to repeat my childhood script over and over again as a psychotherapist, reinforced by the then common models that emphasized empathy and corrective parenting in transactional analysis. It was my experience with Samantha, as well as other clients at that time, that prompted me to join with Francis Bonds-White to write an article exploring the problems of the models of therapeutic relatedness in transactional analysis (Cornell & Bonds-White, 2001). In the idealization of the therapeutic relationship lay both gratification and potential danger within the therapeutic dyad. The therapeutic relationship offers both client and therapist an unusual sense of intimacy and exclusivity. It is a protected relationship that offers a unique and compelling kind of closeness. But it is a closeness that needs to end, that needs to be a temporary foundation that lays the ground for clients to move out into the world. Most of the time, there is an inherent developmental pressure within the therapeutic process that moves the client out toward the world at large. Most of the time, the experience of therapeutic work itself creates a space that challenges the comfort of the therapeutic dyad. But when the therapist and client become locked in an effort to compensate for the pain and losses of childhood, an unhealthy symbiosis forms that can offer comfort and predictability but cuts off the development of emotional maturity, personal agency, and true intimacy.

Years later, because of this period of work with Charles, I was able to deeply grasp the consequences, personally and professionally, of the impact of my lack of differentiation from my mother and the impossibility of establishing an effective relationship with my father. The position I was then able to take in relation to my clients shifted significantly to create much more consistent space for conflict and differentiation.

Charles did not offer much by way of empathy. But neither did he let go. He relentlessly pursued how it was that I felt like I had to avoid crying at all costs. Gradually, painfully, many memories returned, of events I had always recalled—of teasing, beatings, and torments by my peers as a kid and adolescent. At all costs, in the face of those boys, I could not cry. I had always dismissed these experiences as not having been of any real consequence. My parents knew of these situations but minimized them and never intervened. Charles offered a different kind of witness to these memories, which he saw as acts of parental violence.

In my failed efforts with Samantha, I simply had no way at that time of knowing the degree to which I was unconsciously experiencing her volatility, accusations, and rigidity as acts of violence. And so I complied. I tried to minimize the likelihood of conflict. I had disowned my own aggression, which could, at times, have been constructive but at other times retaliatory. I was possessed by my past, unable to reconcile conflicted aspects of myself. My work with Charles brought a sharp and unyielding light to the darker places of my parents' neglect of me and my siblings. It freed me in new and fundamental ways in my work with clients.

Working at the psychotic edge

I began this chapter with an epigraph in which Landaiche argues for the importance of the determination to "learn forward" in the face of professional failures and shame. Bollas' (2013) recent book on working with psychotic breakdowns provides a vivid example of his own learning forward. Written in a deeply personal voice, the book opens with vignettes of working early in his career with two patients who suffered breakdowns. It proved to be failed work that left an indelible and compelling mark on and motivation for Bollas:

> By the early 1980's, however, I was determined to change my practice in working with people on the verge of breakdown. I did not consciously connect this to work with Tim or Lila or other previous patients, but unconsciously I must have been aware that I had failed them, and that something else was needed.
>
> (p. 19)

It was abundantly clear from the many raging voice mails Samantha left that she had fallen into a psychotic state. I had often experienced a kind of madness in our work, but why, I asked myself now, had I never framed it as a psychotic process? Why, I asked both myself and my consultant, had I not been more persistent and insistent on eliciting her fantasies about me and our relationship? I had to face the fact that I had avoided that level of the disturbances between us over and over again and had acquiesced to her ways of focusing and filling the sessions. I gradually came to accept that, although I would never salvage the work with Samantha, there was a great deal for me to learn that would benefit others with whom I would be working.

Since the collapse of the Cathexis School of transactional analysis, remarkably little has been written about the psychotherapy of schizophrenia and psychosis within the TA literature (with the exception of Cornell, de Graaf, Newton, & Thunnissen, 2016, pp. 179–180; Mellacqua, 2014). Mellacqua's 2014 article addressing the functions of dissociation, splitting, fragmentation, and exclusion in the schizophrenic psychoses brought the transactional analysis literature on this complex and troubling subject into the twenty-first century. He concluded as follows:

> Working with psychotic patients reminds us of the considerable importance transactional analysts need to attach to the unconscious-to-unconscious actions ... that are intensely present in encounters with so-called schizophrenics. ... This fact opens up the debate on the nature of regression as well as on the tragic life script classically attributed to schizophrenia (Mellacqua, 2013). It also encourages us to reconsider the role of the transactional analyst who works with psychotic patients while taking into account the protocol aspects (Cornell, 2010; Guglielmotti, 2008; Ligabue, 2007; Stuthridge, 2010) of both the therapist's and patient's life experiences as they emerge in the therapeutic setting.
>
> (pp. 23–24)

In his critique of Schiffian theory and their approach to working with schizophrenia and psychotic processes, Mellacqua (2014, p. 12) argued that the theory fails to recognize crucial aspects of the schizophrenic experience, such as the existential aspects of ego–self dissociation and fragmentation (the uncertainty of being, the subjective sense of feeling lost, the feeling of losing oneself, the emotional withdrawal, etc.); the strongly held subjective sense of the absolute certainty of delusions and hallucinations; the re-enactment of the protocol levels of the disturbed, traumatizing family system; the disruption of personal narrative as manifested by severe thought disorders; and the complex, compelling transferential and countertransferential sensitivities and vulnerabilities of both patient and therapist in the here and now.

Following the collapse of my work with Samantha, now nearly 20 years ago, I had to look elsewhere for an understanding of how I might have worked more successfully with the psychotic aspect of her personality. Through consultation and study with colleagues, as well as reading, I began to recognize some of what had gone wrong in my work with her and others in my failure to adequately grasp the psychotic elements that came to be revealed in the work. Rosenfeld (1987) described the power of delusional projections in psychotic states that "exert a strong hypnotic influence on the analyst" (p. 15), and I began to recognize my experience with Samantha. Rosenfeld observed:

> Psychotic patients seemed typically to show omnipotent attitudes to others and particularly to their therapists. In phantasy they seemed to make insatiable demands on their objects, to confuse self and others, to take others into themselves, and to put themselves into others.
>
> (p. 20)

At this time, I discovered Mitrani's (2001) writing elaborating the concept of adhesive identification as

> an adhesive state of pseudo-relating [in which] objects are *not* experienced as humanly animate, lively entities, existing in a space of their own, but as inanimate "things" which are absorbed, exploited, manipulated or avoided by subjects in a desperate attempt to gain a sensation of existence, safety, and impermeability.
>
> (p. 38)

Finally I was able to gain some insight and compassion for aspects of Samantha's behavior—her assaults on "fucking liberals," her purchase of art works like those in my office, her taking photographs of the "hellhole"—that I had experienced only as hostile and intrusive. I came to appreciate why the ways in which I had attempted to bring my thinking to Samantha were so threatening to her that she experienced me trying to take her mind away from her rather than offering her some kind of alliance. I came to see that, in fact, I had been challenging her mind, rather than seeking an alliance with the nonpsychotic part of her personality as Bion (1957) and Bollas (2013) described. I might, for example, during the periods when the therapy was more productive and she was experiencing more success in her work, have asked her to reflect on what was happening in our work that made this possible. I might have spoken directly to how it could be interesting to see things differently and look together at the world, our minds thinking side by side, seeing things somewhat differently and discovering what we could learn from each other. As Lucas (2009) stressed,

> the psychotic part of the personality attempts to impose a total withdrawal from reality by fragmenting and projecting the sense impressions that are the precursors to the development of thinking, and the attacks on links

between different thoughts. However, contact with reality is never entirely lost, due to the existence of a non-psychotic part of the personality that functions in parallel with the psychotic part, though often obscured by it.

(p. 88)

In conclusion

This chapter is a clinical tale of continuing learning. In the midst of psychotic states, as with Samantha, there is no actual other, only the perceived and dreaded other. In the midst of the dyadic relations that I had constantly created and clung to, there was not sufficient space for differentiation and the recognition of actual others. My therapeutic work with Charles offered a working relationship through which I was able to find a triadic space in which he and I examined (often reluctantly, on my part) my relationships in my daily life and my fantasies about my parents. In this way, I came to think and feel anew about my relationships with my mother and father, my failed work with Samantha, and the recurrent pressures and dynamics I experienced with other clients. In my therapy, I was able to see and confront the psychotic aspects of my own thinking and functioning.

My work and failure with Samantha has no conclusion in the usual sense of how one brings a case discussion to an end. It has been essential to tolerate the lack of closure and seek continuing learning.

Chapter 6

Life script: A critical review from a developmental perspective

Shortly before his death, Eric Berne (1972), using the analogy of a piano player, wondered if he was actually playing the piano or if he was mostly sitting there while a piano roll determined the tune:

> As for myself, I know not whether I am still run by a music roll or not. If I am, I wait with interest and anticipation—and without apprehension—for the next notes to unroll their melody, and for the harmony and discord after that. Where will I go next? In this case my life is meaningful because I am following the long and glorious tradition of my ancestors, passed on to me by my parents, music perhaps sweeter than I could compose myself. Certainly I know that there are large areas where I am free to improvise. It may even be that I am one of the few fortunate people on earth who has cast off the shackles entirely and who calls his own tune. In that case I am a brave improviser facing the world alone.
>
> (pp. 276–277)

This frank and poignant personal observation is filled with fascinating contradictions and implications. Berne's comments seem to reflect his own conflicts about personal autonomy versus the authority of life script, true individual creativity versus psychopathological adaptations of family tradition and societal pressure are apparent throughout Berne's writings. Felsman and Vaillant (1987), in their research and writing about resilient children whose lives seem to defy the expected outcomes of troubled family and social environments, argue:

> Great literature has always provided a balance to the lopsided preoccupation of psychological science with pathology.... In contrast to the reductionism of science, the model of great literature often enlists an interactionist, longitudinal perspective and seeks to illuminate the myriad forces at work within and without an individual. A novelist would never diminish his protagonist with a finite label.
>
> (Felsman & Vaillant, 1987, p. 303)

However, Berne never resolved these conflicts, even though his theory of scripts evolved over time. I think these conflicts remain, undermining the clarity and coherence of script theory and our practice as transactional analysts today. Some eighteen years after Berne's death, the music roll remains the binding image and dilemma in our efforts to conceptualize the nature of life script and to translate those conceptualizations into effective educational and clinical techniques.

What is the nature and function of life script? What are the clinical implications of the script model TA therapists present to themselves and their clients? Although transactional analysts pay careful attention to the "scripty" beliefs and behaviors of clients, do they give equal attention to their own beliefs about script, about the coherence and validity of TA script theory? Does script theory hold up under the scrutiny of developmental theories and research or other theoretical perspectives?

In this chapter, some key developmental perspectives are reviewed and summarized, after which the ideas of major TA script theorists are examined in light of developmental theory and research. Finally, a conceptualization of the evolution and function of the life script process is offered.

An overview of selected developmental theories

Developmental theorists attempt to delineate human development as a definable and predictable sequence of "stages," with earlier stages providing a foundation for later evolution. Whether studying cognitive, affective, social, moral, linguistic, or behavioral development, simpler levels of functioning *develop* into more complex and highly organized forms of psychological organization and function.

Freud

Within the psychodynamic perspective, Freud presented the first developmental theory. Although his work has had a pervasive and lasting impact on the clinical understanding of human development, recently his ideas have begun to yield to current developmental research. Freud (1938) stated unequivocally that

> neuroses are only acquired during early childhood (up to the age of six), even though their symptoms may not make their appearance until much later. . . .. The events of the first years are of paramount importance for . . . [a child's] whole subsequent life.
>
> (p. 83)

Freud's (1917) conceptualization of the oral, anal, oedipal, phallic, and genital stages of psychosexual development was the first formal effort to delineate the evolution of psychological and emotional maturation. Freud's ideas were the product of his psychoanalytic reconstruction of childhood from his clinical practice and theoretical assumptions. His emphasis, and a lasting emphasis in the psychodynamic literature, was on the clinical and pathological implications of "fixation" at any one stage.

Erikson

Erik Erikson (1963), in probably the best known and most widely accepted developmental scheme, significantly altered Freud's model by shifting from a psychosexual focus, with its emphasis on libidinal cathexis, to a psycho-social orientation that attempts to incorporate societal and interpersonal influences in human evolution. Erikson's stages of development reach into adult life. His work opened the developmental perspective to a recognition of social, cultural, and historical forces that influence the developing child's construction of reality. There is a great vitality in his account of human development. For Erikson (1968), periods of developmental crisis are as likely to become opportunities for new growth as occasions of overadaptation and acquiescence.

My first introduction to current developmental research was *Adaptation to Life* by George Vaillant (1977). The book was simultaneously exciting and disturbing. Vaillant presented vivid case studies and substantial data that indicated that the evolution of an individual's psychological construction of reality was anything but linear and certainly not cemented to the dynamics of the nuclear family. This material raised major questions about the validity of TA script theory and was the beginning of a review of the developmental literature that has culminated in this chapter. The brief overview of developmental theories presented here stresses those based on direct, longitudinal studies rather than on clinical theorizing about development derived from adult psychopathology and psychotherapy.

Chess and Thomas

The work of Stella Chess and Alexander Thomas involved long-term studies of normal children, "high-risk" children and families, and children with physical handicaps. Their work presents compelling evidence of the resilience and plasticity of the psyche:

> The deaf child, the blind child, the motorically handicapped child—each can find a developmental pathway consonant with his capacities and limitations, thanks to the plasticity of the brain. By the same token, the environmentally handicapped child is not inevitably doomed to an inferior and abnormal psychological course. Whether the handicap comes from social ideology, poverty, a pathological family environment, or stressful life experiences, the plastic potential of the brain offers the promise for positive and corrective change. This central human potential for plasticity and learning bears directly on a number of issues in developmental

theory—the significance of early life experiences, continuity–discontinuity over time, and sequential patterning of developmental stages.

(Thomas & Chess, 1980, p. 28)

Chess and Thomas (1984, p. 293) conclude without equivocation that simple, linear prediction from early childhood through later childhood, adolescence, and adulthood is not supported by research data. Furthermore, they challenge the reliability of a causal explanation based on clinical reconstruction of childhood from adult problems.

Instead, Chess and Thomas emphasize the importance of the individual child's temperament and capabilities and the "goodness of fit" or the "poorness of fit" with that child's family, social, and school environment. They (1984, 1986) describe psychological development as occurring in a "biosocial matrix," an ongoing, continuous, and *dynamic* interaction of the biological and the social. Their research demonstrates convincingly that significant change can occur at any time in the course of development: "The evolving child–environment interactional process was affected by many emerging unanticipated influences—changes in basic function, new talents, new environmental opportunities or stresses, changes in family structure or attitudes, and possible late emerging genetic factors" (Thomas & Chess, 1980, pp. 103–104).

Chess and Thomas emphasize the importance for future psychological health of the child's development of "task mastery" and "social competence." Using weaning and toilet training as examples, typical Freudian (and script) theory tends to emphasize the experience of loss and frustration. In contrast, Chess and Thomas view these developmental transitions as steps in social competence and task mastery, noting the potential for achievement and satisfaction as well as for loss or frustration.

Vaillant

Adaptation to Life by George Vaillant (1977) was also based on longitudinal study. It summarized the Harvard Grant Study in which 95 Harvard University students were tested and interviewed intensively during college and then followed systematically for 30 years. Vaillant emphasized the evolution and function of ego defense mechanisms in relation to psychological and interpersonal health and psychopathology.

There is striking congruence between Vaillant's view of defense mechanisms as "adaptive styles" or "coping strategies" and the functional, adaptive intent of script decisions as described in TA theory. Unlike Freud, Vaillant (1977) emphasized not the intrapsychic meaning of defense mechanisms, but "discussing defenses as actual behaviors, affects, and ideas which serve defensive purposes" (p. 7).

However, Vaillant's account of defense mechanisms and their development is far richer and more complex than that evident in the writing of most script theorists. Vaillant disputed the Freudian emphasis on fixation and maintained that there are many corrective experiences in the course of an individual's development and many pathways to health throughout childhood and adult life. He observed that dysfunctional thinking and relating in adulthood is

> rarely the fault of any one person or event, for in human development, it is the sustained emotional trauma, not the sudden insult, that does the most lasting damage to the human spirit. No single childhood factor accounted for happiness or unhappiness at fifty.
>
> (Vaillant, 1977, p. 197)

Like Chess and Thomas, Vaillant argued vigorously against linear, causal linkages between childhood experience and adult life. He concluded in his 1977 book that "successful careers and satisfying marriages were relatively independent of unhappy childhoods" (p. 300), and that "the life cycle is more than an invariant sequence of stages with simple predictable outcomes. The men's lives were full of surprises, and the Grant Study provides no prediction tables" (p. 373).

The most relevant of Vaillant's (1977) conclusions for the reconsideration of script theory are: reconstructed, retrospective explanations are fraught with distortions; isolated traumas in childhood rarely have significant impact in adulthood; adaptive (defensive) patterns change both in childhood and adulthood; psychological evolution is often discontinuous; those judged initially to have the "worst" childhoods did not always have the "worst" adult lives; and significant, close adult relationships (spouse, friends, psychotherapist) had major influences on improved quality of life. Thus the Harvard Grant Study offers further evidence of the remarkable resilience, plasticity, and unpredictability of the human psyche.

It is also important to note the work of Robert Jay Lifton (1983a, 1983b) and Robert Coles (1986a, 1986b), both of whom, while not writing specifically from a developmental perspective, based their work on the direct observation of nonclinical populations. The work of both Lifton and Coles is rich with implications that can expand and enliven the concept of script. They have described the yearning of the human mind to *find* and *give* meaning to life, often in the face of severe deprivation or tragedy. In *The Political Life of Children*, Coles (1986b) observed:

> And, very important, a boy demonstrates evidence of moral development, a capacity for ethical reflection, even though both at home and at school he has been given scant encouragement to regard either migrants or Indians with compassion. . ... Children ingeniously use every scrap of emotional life available to them in their "psychosexual development," and they do likewise as they try to figure out how (and for whom) the world works.
>
> (p. 41)

Additional developmental theorists

It is not possible in this chapter to adequately review all developmental theorists. Maslow (1954, 1962) studied primarily healthy, achieving individuals and delineated his developmental hierarchy of needs and a major theory of human motivation. Wilson (1972) provided an excellent summary of Maslow's work in the context of a critique of Freudian psychology. Piaget (1977) addressed the most basic question of "how do people know?" through his direct studies of children's evolving patterns of cognition and other studies of forms of knowledge. His was an interactionist perspective—viewing the child as an active agent engaged with the environment in his or her own learning. More recently, Kagan (1984) extended the study of cognitive development. Kohlberg (1984) researched moral development in children and delineated six sequential stages of morality. Kegan (1982) suggested a developmental theory that is of particular significance in relation to TA script theory. He attempted to integrate a psychodynamic perspective with the work of Piaget and Kohlberg. Central to Kegan's perspective is the ongoing and increasingly complex "meaning-making" in the child's endeavor to comprehend the world and give form to it. Gilligan (1982) challenged the pervasive influence of the masculine perspective in developmental theories stressing individuation and autonomy, and argued persuasively for the recognition of the role of caring and relatedness in human development. Loevinger (1976) addressed ego development, defining the essence of ego function as the striving to master, to integrate, and to make sense of experience. Stern (1985), after years of direct observation of infants, characterized infant development as a creative, highly interactive process. Mahler, Pine, and Bergman (1975) described pre-oedipal development as a creative, highly interactive process. Mahler, Pine, and Bergman (1975) described pre-oedipal development in the infant and toddler's relationship to the mother. In his most recent book, Pine (1985), in contrast to most developmental researchers, writes,

> I find it impossible not to think in terms of the events of the months and years until, say, age three as a primary determinant of psychological functioning …. All have, I believe, not only their origins, but a substantial degree of their final form established in this period.
>
> (p. 4)

While the developmentalists have addressed the nature and problems of human growth from various perspectives, most would agree that it is an interactive, creative, ever-changing process. Most agree that parents are not the exclusive, or even primary, source for a child's construction of reality or coping mechanisms. Most would agree, especially those who have engaged in long-term longitudinal studies, that significant growth and change can occur at any time of life. As Chess and Thomas (1984) conclude:

As the field of developmental studies has matured, we now have to give up the illusion that once we know the young child's psychological history, subsequent personality and functioning are *ipso facto* predictable. On the other hand, we now have a much more optimistic vision of human development.

(p. 293)

Summary and critique of major script theorists

Berne

Beginning with *Transactional Analysis in Psychotherapy*, Berne (1961) offered this description of the nature and function of script:

> Games appear to be segments of larger, more complex sets of transactions called *scripts*. Scripts belong in the realm of transference phenomena, that is, they are derivatives, or more precisely, adaptations, of infantile reactions and experiences. But a script does not deal with a mere transference reaction or transference situation; it is an attempt to repeat in derivative form a whole transference drama, often split up into acts, exactly like the theatrical scripts which are intuitive artistic derivatives of these primal dramas of childhood. Operationally, a script is a complex set of transactions, by nature recurrent, but not necessarily recurring, since a complete performance may require a whole lifetime.
>
> (p. 116)

> Since the dominant influence in social intercourse is the script, and since that is derived and adapted from a protocol based on early experiences of the individual with his or her parents, those experiences are the chief determinants of every engagement and of every choice of associates. This is a more general statement than the familiar transference theory which it brings to mind because it applies to any engagement whatsoever in any social situation whatsoever; that is, to any transaction or series of transactions not completely structured by external reality.

> While every human being faces the world initially as the captive of his script, the great hope and value of the human race is that the Adult can be dissatisfied with such strivings when they are unworthy.
>
> (pp. 125–126)

Thus, from the beginning, script was cast in a highly deterministic mode. Script is a "household drama," with neurotic, psychotic, and psychopathic scripts viewed as "almost always tragic." Script is viewed as the projection and re-enactment of an elaborate transference phenomenon.

Berne was certainly a strong advocate for the intelligence and dignity of the individual in psychotherapy. He seemed at times to be very confident of a person's capacity to change. He wrote in *Principles of Group Treatment*, "Every human being is born a prince or a princess: early experiences convince some that they are frogs, and the rest of the pathological development follows from this" (Berne, 1966, pp. 289–290). For Berne (1966), transactional treatment "aims at getting well, or 'cure,' which means to cast off the frog skin and take up once more the interrupted development of the prince or princess" (p. 290). But how readily can a person cast off the frog skin and recreate a healthy life? Not easily, Berne implied; it was he who introduced the images of witches, ogres, and implanted script electrodes into the language of script theory, a language that suggests the individual is more a product than a producer of script.

Five years after *Principles*, Berne (1970) wrote in *Sex and Human Loving*:

> Man is born free, but one of the first things he learns is to do as he is told, and he spends the rest of his life doing that. Thus his first enslavement is to his parents. He follows their instructions forevermore, retaining only in some cases the right to choose his own methods and consoling himself with the illusion of autonomy. ... In order to break away from such script programs, he must stop and think. But he cannot think about his programming unless he first gives up the illusion of autonomy. He must realize that he has not been up to now the free agent he likes to imagine he is, but rather the puppet of some Destiny from generations ago. Few people have the courage or elasticity to turn around and stare down the monkeys on their backs, and the older they get, the stiffer their backs become.
>
> (p. 168)

Berne's personal optimism seemed to collapse under the weight of a deterministic sense of destiny; he even capitalized on destiny and offered "The Psychology of Human Destiny" as the subtitle of his 1972 book, *What Do You Say After You Say Hello?* For Berne, the process of individuation seemed a courageous exception rather than the natural, common process it is presented to be in the developmental literature.

Much of the literature on development referred to earlier did not exist when Berne was evolving script theory. However, the work of Erikson, Piaget, and Maslow did exist, but does not seem to have influenced Berne's thinking about human development. Like many clinicians, Berne became possessed by the effort to understand psychopathology. He lost track of health. This is a criticism to be made of many clinically oriented theorists. Felsman and Vaillant (1987) emphasize, "Clinical language rarely includes the process of healthy adaptation. What is healthy and going well is often overlooked and obscured in the shadow of illness" (p. 302).

By the time he wrote the material later compiled for *What Do You Say After You Say Hello?*, Berne had given the developing child more choice and authorship in his or her script, but it was still a tale dominated by family drama, parents, grandparents, and intergenerational transmissions. In *Hello*, script was defined as "a life plan based on a decision made in childhood, reinforced by the parents, justified by subsequent events, and culminating in a chosen alternative" (Berne, 1972, p. 446). One wonders about the children Berne described—did they ever change their minds, did their parents ever change, did they have friends, a neighborhood, a culture? There is little sense of excitement and no sense of serendipity in the world as Berne described it.

Berne (1972) wrote that "the first script programming takes place during the nursing period, in the form of short protocols which can later be worked into complicated dramas" (p. 83), for which Berne provided a lengthy, rather nasty list of "breast-fed titles."

Berne's image of the helpless, needy, dependent infant, forever attached to and programmed by mother and family through a literal or symbolic umbilicus, does not hold up in light of current research. Rather, it introduces a severe and inaccurate bias to the foundation for a theory of script formation. For example, according to Chess and Thomas (1984):

> Two striking characteristics of the child's behavior in the first weeks of life are his interest in manipulatory-exploratory behavior and the active social exchange with his caretakers. . . . Along these lines, we have suggested that the primary adaptive goals of the neonate and young infant, for which he is biologically equipped, can be conceptualized as the development of social relations and the mastery of skills and tasks—i.e., social competence and task mastery.
>
> (p. 16)

The observations of Chess and Thomas are verified and extended by the research of Daniel Stern (1985). Stern's conclusions are based on direct observation of infant behavior; he delineated numerous contradictions between psychoanalytic literature on the therapeutically "reconstructed clinical infant" and research on the actual "observed infant." Current developmental research strongly suggests that infants influence and shape their parents as much as their parents shape them. Perhaps even more important is awareness of the child's mastery and evolving competence, an idea central to developmental theory but seriously lacking in Berne's description of script formation. The forces of submission and compromise override the experience of mastery in Berne's writing.

Although Berne did not work specifically within a developmental frame of reference, he offered his most thorough account of psychological evolution in *Hello*. He portrays, in essence, progressive acquiescence. Maturity, for Berne, brings the mortgage, literally and symbolically. He wrote, "During the periods of maturity, the dramatic nature of the script is brought into full flower. . . . In fact, all struggles in life are struggles to move around the [Drama] triangle in accordance with the demands of script" (Berne, 1972, pp. 186–187). What of the struggles between adults that result in individuation and autonomy? What of the struggles that result in the resolution of problems, in deeper understanding and attachment between people, and in sustained love and individual differentiation? If Berne's vision of maturity is accurate for most people, it seems Peter Pan and all perpetual children made logical and compelling choices.

Berne acknowledged the existence of winners, but wrote little about them, and he thought even winners were the product of more affirming and more productive parental programming and permission. Sprietsma (1978), writing from a treatment perspective, took a closer look at the "winner's script" and offered a diagram and language that elaborated on the concept of a winner. Although he did not challenge the concept of a "winner's script" theoretically, Sprietsma offered a useful clinical approach.

Allen and Allen (1972) emphasized factors outside the family sphere that can be crucial variables in a child's evolving script. Based on clinical experience, the Allens delineated a developmental sequence of eight permissions that enhance a person's "readiness" to interact with an ever-widening world. Their article represented a significant widening of the world of script theory. Most current developmental presentations are of a literal hierarchy of development. For example, their "last" permission is that of "finding life meaningful," although it seems clear that children are busy virtually from the start *making* life meaningful. It is the making which the Allens (1987) emphasize in a more recent article.

Groder (cited in Barnes, 1977, p. 20) repeated Berne's observation that there seems to be a self that is "script free," and noted that Berne was not very articulate on the subject. While suggesting that there can be healthy scripts or script-free health, Berne never fully explored the question, and it remains unanswered by subsequent script theorists.

In Berne's view, nearly all the force of the vectors in psychological development is from the parents (sometimes grandparents and other authority figures) *toward* the child. For Berne, the child may have some limited range of choice in the face of the forces that impinge upon him or her, but the child is by and large restricted and formed by these forces. What Berne comes to characterize as the very nature of script is often reflected in the psychological systems of severely dysfunctional families, but it is not the essential nature of script. Both the literature and clinical experience demonstrate that in severely dysfunctional families (especially those that isolate themselves from normal social interaction), a child's range of choice and expression may be drastically restricted. For example, a recent collection of articles on "resilient children" (Anthony & Cohler, 1987) vividly describes the debilitating impact of living with psychotic, neglectful, impoverished, or abusive parents. However, these articles also examine and describe the factors outside of the family and within the child's own style of coping that support resilience and health. These factors are not adequately addressed in Berne's theories of script.

In Berne's thinking, there was an overwhelming sense of self-limiting adaptation and little sense of self-enhancing adaptation. There was even less sense of the child's ability to influence his or her parents and childhood environment. Although it is often striking in clinical work to note the tenacity with which people cling to patterns of "scripty" adaptation, this tenacity is not always motivated by some fearful or defiant resistance, but often by the pride and satisfaction of mastery, of self-expression, of having solved a difficult life dilemma with some degree of success. There is virtually no accounting in Berne's writing for this experience of mastery and individuation in script formation or in the maintenance of styles of adaptation in adulthood.

Steiner

Steiner, too, seems to suggest a preponderance of conflictual compromise in the formation of script; he presents the developing child as victim to negative family and social environments. However, Steiner does give far more importance than Berne did to the social, cultural, and economic forces that influence a child's developing sense of self, autonomy, and possibility. Although a strong and eloquent advocate of individual rights and dignity, his theory of script does little to challenge the deterministic and reductionistic underpinnings of Berne's approach. Steiner (1974, p. 19) even attributed Berne's death to the influence of a life script that called for an early death of a broken heart.

Steiner's (1974) definition of script is as follows:

> The script is based on a decision made by the Adult in the young person who, with all of the information at their disposal at the time, decides that a certain position, expectations, and life course are a reasonable solution to the existential predicament in which she finds herself. Her predicament comes from the conflict between her own autonomous tendencies and the injunction received from her primary family group.
>
> The most important influence or pressure impinging upon the youngster originates from the parental Child.... That is, the Child ego states of the parents of the person are the main determining factors in the formation of scripts.
>
> (p. 55)

Steiner (1971, 1974) developed the script matrix, an elegant clinical tool and a major contribution to TA. The matrix, along with the three stacked ego state circles and the Drama Triangle (Karpman, 1968), provides a central image in transactional analysis. As a therapeutic tool, it is clear and impactful. As a central element in theory, however, it is restrictive and deterministic, placing much too much power within the nuclear family, with the ego states of the parents drawn above the child, script messages literally descending on the child. Since its introduction, numerous variations on the script matrix have been presented in the TA literature, although there has been little challenge to its theoretical limitations.

For example, in the script matrix, the central emphasis on the nuclear family does a disservice to our understanding of the range of factors that significantly influence human development. Even limiting the image of the script matrix to the nuclear family, it would be more accurately drawn as shown in Figure 6.1.

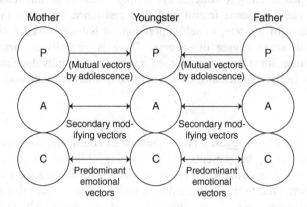

Figure 6.1 The script matrix

The concept of script and the images used to represent it need to include the active influence of the developing child upon the environment. Both Berne's and Steiner's conceptualizations of script are embedded in oedipal theory and Freudian assumption, with little acknowledgment of the curiosity, spontaneity, and expressiveness of childhood. Neither children nor adults create psychological organization primarily around negative messages and experiences in childhood, as suggested by Berne and Steiner.

Levin

Within the TA literature, Levin has made a strong effort to present a developmental perspective. Ironically, however, of all the script theorists, Levin's account is the most deterministic. According to her:

> We record our entire personal history in our ego states. The way we were as children doesn't go away when we get older. It remains a dynamic part of us, motivating our current experiences. If we didn't get what we needed as children, we continue to seek it symbolically through dramatic scenes enacted in the here-and-now. The scenes are taken from our "script," our personal story or collections of early decisions and unmet needs, now long forgotten. We continue to use them to program our current experiences, even without being aware of them. Scripts represent our attempts to get needs met which were not met originally. When we play out our script as grown-ups, we act in ways which are symbolic of the original unsatisfactory childhood experience. Thus, script behavior is

predetermined. We are controlled by yesterday, as if we were haunted by demons or hunted by witches.

(Levin, 1985, pp. 29–30)

Levin (1985) describes infancy (birth to six months) as "Stage One: Being the Natural Child," and characterizes it as follows:

> The events of the first six months of our lives are crucial to all the rest of our development. The way we experience our existence for the rest of our lives is largely determined by the foundation we create while we are still helpless. Our first basic "set" or program is the building block upon which we support all our later developmental experiences and decisions. This is our basic position in life, our OKness, our right to be taking up space in the physical plane. It is our basic existential position. All the experiences from which we derive our first program are recorded in ego states which we call the Natural Child. They are on film and on file in each of us, a personal documentary of how we each arrive at our basic life position.
>
> (pp. 60–61)

This description of infancy and the establishment of a basic existential life position is not only in contradiction to the research on infant and child development, it is inconsistent with Berne's own conceptualization of the basic life position, which he saw as a phenomenon of later psychological development. Levin's emphasis on script as an effort to get "un-met" needs "met" and on needs as the primary focus of therapy distorts and severely limits our understanding of both pathological and healthy human development. A comprehensive theory of the evolution of self and script must attend to the influence of wants, desire, excitement, hopes, dreams, chance, and culture.

In *Cycles of Power*, Levin (1980) acknowledges that

> Repeating the stages of development implies that we naturally change, advance and mature even though we use the same pattern as before, building on the early skills in the same way that we build walking skills on the ability to crawl.
>
> (p. 7)

At the same time, she presents "normal symptoms," which she suggests are indicative of unresolved issues at various developmental stages. Such clinical literalism is simply not supported by developmental research. In *Cycles of Power*, Levin's references are drawn almost exclusively from TA literature, virtually disregarding the vast clinical and research literature on development. This parochial approach, seen all too often in TA literature, does transactional analysis and TA clients a grave disservice.

Chess and Thomas concluded from their research that similar causes can lead to different symptoms, and similar symptoms can evolve or "be chosen" in response to different causes. Likewise, Daniel Stern (1985), in *The Interpersonal World of the Infant*, also addressed some of the clinical implications of data drawn from direct observation of infants rather than from interpretive reconstruction of infantile experience from psychotherapy with adults. Stern's (1985) central conclusion was that:

> The traditional clinical-developmental issues such as orality, dependence, autonomy, and trust, have been disengaged from any one specific point or phase of origin in developmental time. These issues are seen here as developmental lines—that is, issues for life, not phases of life. They do not undergo a sensitive period, a presumed phase of ascendency and predominance when relatively irreversible "fixations" could occur. It therefore cannot be known in advance, on theoretical grounds, at what point in life a particular traditional clinical-developmental issue will receive its pathogenic origin.
>
> (p. 256)

The "theoretical infant," Stern concluded, does not exist. However, he did point out that the "clinical-developmental" literature may, in fact, offer useful therapeutic constructs or metaphors, even if these are not empirically valid. He also suggested that the "clinical-developmental" perspective (which would include much of TA script theory) may be more accurate for later phases of childhood, when symbolic functions play a more crucial role in psychosocial evolution.

The developmental literature indicates that the binding nature of psychological and emotional difficulty is the pervasiveness and the *chronicity* of the family dynamics, not a stage-specific problem. It also seems clear that even when the family difficulties are chronic, the impact of the family can be significantly altered by the child's own attitudes toward the difficulties and by extra-familial experiences. For the clinician, the developmental literature suggests that the careful, continued attention to the effectiveness of a client's present-day functioning is more apt to facilitate self-enhancement than the therapeutic "re-doing" of a specific developmental period.

Babcock and Keepers

Within the TA literature that incorporates a developmental perspective, *Raising Kids OK* by Dorothy Babcock and Terry Keepers (1976) is consistent with current developmental theory and research, and effective in its presentation of an active, evolutionary model of script formation. The process and importance of mastery, attachment, change, and individuation are well presented in Babcock and Keeper's book. Written primarily as a child-rearing manual for parents, it makes an important contribution to the TA literature. Babcock and Keepers present life script as an ongoing formative process usually not set until adolescence, describing it as the consolidation of family patterns, the child's "favorite" and "preferred" modes of managing, and cultural and historical influences. They emphasize the psychosocial perspective on human development and a stage-specific hierarchy. They also emphasize continued learning, re-learning, and change, presuming a drive toward health and satisfaction. The child's experience of mastery in social relations and task competence, central for many developmental theories, is evident throughout Babcock and Keeper's presentation, and they acknowledge the impact of the baby and growing child on the parents.

Gouldings

Robert and Mary Goulding made a major shift in script theory by demonstrating that script is the result of active decisions made in childhood rather than from injunctions imposed on (or implanted in) a developing child. The Gouldings (1978) observed:

> Although patients remembered remarkably similar early scenes and injunctions, each individual reacted uniquely. Our clients were not "scripted." Injunctions are not placed in people's heads like electrodes. Each child makes decisions in response to real or imagined injunctions, and thereby "scripts" her/himself.

(p. 213)

The Gouldings' conceptualization of script emphasizes the "injunction–decision complex," an interactive process between the growing child and his or her parents in which the meaning the child attaches to parental injunctions and attributions is the binding force of the script.

For the Gouldings, script is flexible and changeable during its formation in childhood. The home environment is central in script formation, but the Gouldings acknowledge the influence of school, neighborhood, television, and the world environments on the life decisions made during childhood. Their observations about the importance of the child's efforts to comprehend, adjust to, and influence his or her family and social environments are much more in keeping with the findings of developmental researchers. The Gouldings' approach to script in theory and technique challenges the determinism inherent in so much of script theory. Their treatment approach also brings humor, vitality, and action to script analysis and change. They seat the client in front of the piano, place his or her fingers on the keyboard, and encourage the audience to applaud. They train therapists to work within the client's construction of reality (past and present) and to allow for important script influences within and outside of the family.

The Gouldings' approach does, however, take on a reductionistic cast in their efforts to identify ten basic injunctions. This author has heard countless TA clients and TA therapists speak of "having" a "Don't Be" injunction or a "Don't Grow Up" script, thereby missing both the subtleties and variations of an individual's childhood experience and meaning. It seems both more theoretically accurate and therapeutically useful to encourage clients to find their own words to express script conclusions, to articulate their own "meaning-making." It is also crucial *not* to restrict the analysis of script to negative, restrictive decisions.

Erskine

In his article on "Script Cure," Richard Erskine (1980) offers a significantly different definition of script as: "a life plan based on decisions made at any developmental stage which inhibit spontaneity and limit flexibility in problem-solving and in relating to people" (p. 102). Erskine does not reduce script to childhood and the family. Here script is presented clearly as a mechanism of psychological defense, of coping, rather than as a debilitating, unconscious strategy for life. It directly mirrors the concerns of task mastery and social competence so central in much of the developmental literature. It is clear in the developmental literature, and in clinical practice, that a person relies on defense mechanisms, however limiting, to cope with trauma or life problems that cannot be adequately managed by current skills, knowledge, and environmental sup-ports. For example, Thomas and Chess (1980) offered the following:

> Operationally, defense mechanisms can be defined as behavioral strategies with which individuals attempt to cope with stress or conflict which they cannot or will not master directly. This definition does not assume, as Freud did, that defense mechanisms are necessarily unconscious.
>
> (pp. 169–170)

These difficulties are not exclusive to childhood, nor are childhood coping mechanisms necessarily more compelling or permanent than those of later life.

Consistent with most script theorists, Erskine's definition stresses the pathologi-cal nature of script. Although he makes an important addition to the concept of script by clearly indicating that restrictive life script decisions can be made during any phase of life, Erskine does not address the individual's capacity to re-open and change those decisions in subsequent phases of life (in response to new and different life experience as well as therapeutic interventions). This is a theory of pathology, not one that adequately addresses the nature of human development and spirit.

Kegan (1982) is critical of the psychotherapeutic/psychopathological attitude toward life. He calls psychotherapy "unnatural therapy" and urges therapists to remember the "natural therapy"—stressing that "theories are needed which are as powerful in their understanding of normal processes of development as they are in their understanding of disturbance" (p. 262).

Groder

Perhaps the most pointed and existential definition of script in the TA literature is provided by Martin Groder (cited in Barnes, 1977, p. 19): "Each of us has the task each morning to recreate the universe from our central focus and this responsibility is unavoidable. Unfortunately, we tend to be habit-ridden and do the same lousy job every morning. This is what scripts are all about." For Groder, the essence of script is the daily, unavoidable psychological construction and reconstruction of reality. Groder appears to agree with those authors already quoted: The script is habit-ridden, restrictive, self-limiting, and hence pathological. Interestingly, Alfred Adler (1956, p. 191), in his discussion of "the style of life," elegantly described the daily "pathology" of "being in script." He observed that once individuals settle into a "style of life," they remove aspects of thinking, feeling, and relating from the "criticism of experience." The process of script formation and "meaning-making" in life is not inherently pathological; "being in script" becomes dysfunctional when it involves hanging tenaciously on to certain beliefs about self and the world rather than allowing for the surprises and opportunities presented in actually living.

English

Fanita English is virtually alone among the major TA theorists in considering scripts to be valuable assets, another advantage humans have over other animals. English (1977) states without equivocation, "Our scripts enable us to blossom, rather than preventing us from doing so, even though they may contain certain 'conclusions' out of early childhood that can be dysfunctional or downright dangerous" (p. 288). English's conceptualization is strongly influenced by Piaget, and particularly congruent with the ideas suggested by Kegan and Vaillant. As she says in "What Shall I Do Tomorrow? Reconceptualizing Transaction Analysis":

> We all need a script. The child's need for a script reflects an inborn human need for structuring the time, space and relationships that are ahead of him, so that he can conceptualize boundaries against which to test his ongoing experience of reality.... By constructing the outline of a script, he can hold together his hopes, his fantasies, and his experiences. This becomes a basic structure out of which he can develop a perspective about his life.... During the script-structuring age period, the child experiences the intense excitement of being a living human being with ideas.
>
> (English, 1977, p. 290)

More than any other TA theorist, English captures the essence of "meaning-making" which is fundamental in much of the current developmental literature. However, consistent with many script theorists, English still places too much emphasis on childhood as the primary time for script formation and uses too literal an adaptation of developmental stages.

English (1977) does not ignore the dysfunctional, even pathological, aspects of script; she contextualizes them:

However many irrational elements there may be in script—including horrible devouring monsters, pitfalls, dangers, and even, in many cases, terrible endings for the unwary hero or heroine—there are also fairy elements of excitement, adventure, love, beautiful fantasy, and all kinds of magical tricks and prescriptions as to how calamity can be circumvented and how misfortune can be turned into good fortune. It is these latter aspects that offer clues as to how a person can fulfill himself through his script rather than in opposition to it and in fear.

Even a script generated under the worst environmental circumstances contains within itself the Child's own genetic intuitions as to how he might fulfill his inner goals creatively, if certain malevolent fairies and cobwebs can be neutralized. Without a script, the Child ego state would be operating only out of a vacuum of time and space within which there would be no content from which to connect the past to the future, so he would be rootless, like a leaf in the wind. I suspect that certain cases of psychosis represent lack of script formation, as a result of which the individual has no background from which to experience the foreground and, therefore, he operates out of a condition of total disorganization.

(p. 290)

There is tremendous power and vitality in English's conceptualizations. Her ideas are enlivening in the clinical context and more theoretically valid than most script theory. For her, script formation is *determining* rather than *determined*, formative rather than acquiescent, unpredictable and creative rather than reductionistic, focused on the future rather than embedded (mired in the past). "Survival conclusions" for English are an aspect of script, not its primary purpose.

Summary

TA as an approach to therapy stresses the dignity of people and their ability to change. This perspective is supported by developmental research which has repeatedly demonstrated the enormous flexibility and resilience of the human psyche. Unfortunately, much of the script theory as it has evolved is inconsistent with this perspective on human nature.

Although TA began as social psychiatry, it seems increasingly to have collapsed into a psychodynamic framework. The interpersonal is too often lost to an over-emphasis on the intrapsychic.

It is not the intent here to remove the intrapsychic focus from script theory. The psychodynamic perspective brings a richness and depth to clinical understanding. It is one intention of this chapter to return the intrapsychic emphasis that permeates much of script theory to a place within a context of the interpersonal and cognitive/behavioral fields.

Script theory has become more restrictive than enlivening. Script analysis as it has evolved over the years is overly psychoanalytic in attitude and overly reductionist in what it communicates to people about human development. In addition, the incorporation of developmental theory into script theory has too often been simplistic and inaccurate, placing primary emphasis on psychopathology rather than on psychological formation.

[2018 note: This paper was published in 1988, and the "psychoanalytic" attitude to which I refer here was based on my knowledge at the time of classical psychoanalysis and ego psychology. It was somewhat ironic that it was in this same year that I discovered the work of Christopher Bollas and, through him, Donald Winnicott. A new world of psychoanalysis opened to me after I wrote this paper.]

The richness, depth, and complexity of current developmental research and theory is not well represented in the TA literature, although it has a great deal to teach TA practitioners about the contexts in which people learn and change. Developmental studies of healthy individuals and longitudinal studies of human growth and psychological formation challenge some of the basic assumptions and attitudes underlying transactional analysis. Called particularly into question is the TA emphasis on the pervasive role of childhood and family—central experiences in determining adult behavior.

Although life script is not inherently pathological, it may be hopelessly imbued with pathological meaning in TA theory and practice. Transactional analysts need to either significantly challenge and broaden the current conceptualization of script or introduce a second, parallel term—such as psychological life plan—to describe healthy, functional aspects of "meaning-making" in the ongoing psychological construction of reality. Perhaps it would be more inclusive to use a term such as psychological life plan to describe the ongoing evolution of healthy psychological development, with "life script" used to describe dysfunctional, pathological constructions.

By integrating the evidence from current developmental theory, life script could be more comprehensively defined as follows: Life script is the ongoing process of a self-defining and sometimes self-limiting psychological construction of reality. Script formation is the process by which the individual attempts to make sense of family and social environments, to establish meaning in life, and to predict and manage life's problems in the hope of realizing his or her dreams and desires. Major script decisions can be made at any point in life. Times of crisis, during which a person experiences severe "self failure" or "environmental failure," or chronic "environmental failure," will likely foster more rigid, and therefore more dysfunctional, elements in an individual's script.

Chapter 7

Babies, brains, and bodies: Somatic foundations of the Child ego state

Babies and brains have been getting a good deal of attention in the laboratory over the past couple of decades. Contemporary neurophysiological research and studies of infant–parent interaction are leading to radical revisions of theories of psychic development, with equally radical implications regarding the nature of the psychotherapeutic process with adults.

In this chapter, I hope to convey some of the clinical and theoretical implications of such research for Eric Berne's model of the Child ego states, which is at the heart of the clinical practice of transactional analysis. Although Berne developed his theory of ego states as an extension of the work of Federn (1952) and of the brain research carried out by Penfield (1952), the clinical corollaries Berne based on Penfield's speculations no longer hold up. Taking this into account and drawing on my understanding of current research and my experience, in addition to transactional analysis, as a body-centered psychotherapist, I will suggest a significant revisioning of what TA therapists have come to think of as the Child ego state.

Most clinical writing in the transactional analysis literature emphasizes the historical, fixated, and regressive nature of Child ego state functions. Parallel to this emphasis on the nature of the Child ego state are the models (or metaphors) of the therapeutic relationship, common among transactional analysts, as some sort of parenting, corrective, or compensatory relationship, intended to be responsive to the traumas and environmental failures of childhood. In this chapter, I hope to demonstrate the limits and errors in conceiving of the Child ego state as a fixated repository of childhood experiences, and as the infrastructure for characterological games and defensive scripts. I will also challenge the corrective/compensatory models of therapeutic relationships that seem to be an outgrowth of an out-of-date conceptualization of the Child ego state.

I do not deny regressive aspects of some Child ego state patterns, but in my view there are also powerful *progressive* and *exploratory* functions to those aspects of the human psyche that we transactional analysts have come to label as the Child ego state. I have come to think that it is a fundamental error to conceptualize the Child ego state as a repository of historical experience. I have come to understand that the level of mental organization transactional analysts call the Child ego state forms *subconsciously* and *unconsciously* within a matrix of emotionally and somatically based motivational forces, which are organized and reorganized throughout the course of one's life. I suggest that what we have come to call the Child ego state involves subsymbolic (Bucci, 1997a, 1997b, 2001) neural, emotional, and sensorimotor processes that are crucial forms of psychic development and organization. These processes are perhaps not best conceptualized as states of the ego, or even as functions of the ego, but are better understood within some of the more recently emergent language in the transactional analysis literature, such as activation states (Hine, 1997, 2001) or states of mind (Allen, 2000).

I want to emphasize at the start of this chapter that baby and brain research is unfolding at an extraordinarily rapid rate (Tronick, 1998, 2001; Fonagy, 1999, 2001; Lyons-Ruth, 1998, 1999; Panksepp, 1993, 2001; Emde, 1999; Lachmann, 2001). While I am not an expert in either field, I have been reading in both for many years as a fascinated clinician, drawing upon a now rather distant academic background. The clinical implications are exciting, but since clinicians are in the earliest stages of digesting this work, its generalizability to psychotherapy with adults is not at all clear. Green (2000), among others, offers an especially compelling critique of the too-literal applications of mother–infant research. Similarly, Panksepp (2001), a psychobiological researcher with decades of experience, cautions, "Despite remarkable advances in neuroscience and psychology during the past few decades, our attempts to relate core psychological processes to neural processes remains rudimentary" (p. 139). Therefore, this chapter is speculative in intent, falling far short of a definitive statement. With these caveats in mind, I offer the following musings about babies, brains, and bodies in order to raise important questions and thus contribute to the evolution of ego state theory in transactional analysis.

The roots of transactional analysis in ego psychology

Berne's own training in the late 1940s and early 1950s was in psychoanalysis, which was then dominated in the United States by models of ego psychology, a departure from the drive theories of classical Freudian analysis. In fact, Paul Federn and Erik Erikson, Berne's two training analysts, were among the leading theoreticians of the ego psychology movement at that time.

In the glossary of terms in Berne's (1947) first book, *The Mind in Action*, which he wrote when he still identified with psychoanalysis, Berne defined ego this way:

> [It is] that part of the mind which is in contact with the outside world on the one hand and with the Id and the Superego on the other. It attempts to keep thoughts, judgments, interpretations, and behavior practical and efficient in accordance with the Reality Principle. Here we have used the word somewhat inexactly as almost synonymous with the conscious part of the mind.
>
> (p. 303)

In the body of the text itself, writing in his typically more informal fashion, Berne characterizes the ego as "a system which in some mysterious way can look at itself" (p. 66). When *The Mind in Action* was revised in 1968, with Berne now famous for creating transactional analysis, sections on TA were included, and Berne added a definition of ego states to the glossary. However, his definitions and descriptions of the ego in both glossary and text remained unchanged. Freud's own understanding of the ego and its functions was complex and changed over the course of his writings (Laplanche & Pontalis, 1973, pp. 130–143). The understanding of the ego as "an agency of adaptation which differentiates itself from the id on contact with external reality" (Laplanche & Pontalis, 1973) was brought to the United States before and after World War II by emigrant analysts. The ego psychology school of psychoanalysis became dominant in the US through the middle of the 20th century. Berne's understanding of the ego seemed to change little over the course of his writings.

In leaving psychoanalysis to create transactional analysis, Berne sought to create a metapsychology and a therapeutic process that were more interpersonal and phenomenological than the dominant analytic models of his day. Nevertheless, his new model was based squarely within the tenets of ego psychology. Reviewing Berne's theory of the ego and ego states, Rath (1993) concluded that "ego psychology represents the basis of the theory of personality structure and dynamics in transactional analysis" (p. 209). Today, this grounding in ego psychology seems taken for granted by transactional analysts, even as they graft on subsequent (and often contradictory) psychoanalytic models, such as self psychology, object relations, and attachment theories.

The problematic Child ego state

The tenets of ego psychology served much of Berne's efforts quite well, but he ran into trouble with the limits of this model as he attempted to delineate what he first called the "archeopsyche," and subsequently described as the Child ego state. The Child ego state, as conceptualized by Berne, has been the problem child of TA theory from the beginning. Berne himself never resolved his understanding of the Child ego state, and his writings about the Child are full of contradictions.

Berne's varying descriptions of the archeopsyche and the Child ego state created a theoretical hash that has profoundly affected clinical assumptions and techniques ever since Berne's original writings. The concept of a psychic organ suggests a *capacity of* the mind with a sense of the potential for action, whereas the concept of an ego state suggests a *structure within* the mind with a sense of fixation. Although Berne tended to use the terms of archeopsyche and Child almost interchangeably, I think that the archeopsyche conceived as a "psychic organ" is a more inclusive concept that can incorporate some of the aspects of mental development that I will discuss in this chapter. In fact, with his idea of the

Child, Berne hypothesized a supposed state of the ego that was founded in realms of experience that I suggest are far more accurately described as both pre-ego and sub-ego, that is, preceding the developmental capacities for ego organization and underlying the functions of the ego throughout the course of life.

Berne's conceptualization of ego states evolved during the writing of a series of early papers in the late 1950s, which were collected together after his death and published as *Intuition and Ego States* (1977). However, even then, before he had articulated the TA model, his efforts to distinguish between the archeopsyche as a mental capacity and the Child ego state as a more clearly bounded mental/emotional structure were already in trouble. The Child ego state was presented as a sort of homunculus of the past, seated in the brain: "The Child in the individual is potentially capable of contributing to his personality exactly what a happy actual child is capable of contributing to family life" (1977, p. 149). Later, in *Transactional Analysis in Psychotherapy*, Berne put it this way:

> When a previously buried archaic ego state is revived in its full vividness in the waking state, it is then permanently at the disposal of the patient and the therapist for detailed examination. Not only do "abreaction" and "working through" take place, but the ego state can be treated like an actual child. It can be nurtured carefully, even tenderly, until it unfolds like a flower, revealing all the complexities of its internal structure.
>
> (1961, p. 226)

This version of the Child ego state seems to suggest a sort of resident child in the adult client's psyche and a visiting child in the psychotherapist's office. The clinical consequences of Berne's creation of direct parallels between the Child ego state and child*hood* and his reification of the Child ego state as a virtual little being in the brain have been theoretically rather troublesome, to put it mildly.

Confusion about the nature of the Child ego state is intensified in Berne's more colloquial style of writing within the texts themselves. For example, Berne writes:

> Each person carries within a little boy or little girl, who feels, thinks, acts, talks, and responds just the way he or she did when he or she was a child of a certain age. This ego state is called the Child. The Child is not regarded as "childish" or "immature," which are Parental words, but as childlike, meaning like a child at a certain age, and the important factor here is the age, which may be anywhere between two and five years in ordinary circumstances. It is important for the individual to understand his Child, not only because it is going to be with him all his life, but also because it is the most valuable part of his personality.
>
> (1972, p. 12)

Here we have conceptual confusion and a reification of the Child ego state as an actual childlike presence and as childhood remnants within the adult psyche, remnants that can be both fixated (on a bad day?) and precious (on a good day?). Also, we have in this formulation the crucial, formative years of the Child ego state identified as two to five, when the developing youngster is becoming motorically and linguistically autonomous and does, indeed, have the beginnings of true ego functions. Significantly, however, much of Berne's writings seemed to ignore the significance of the years from birth to two, which are emerging in current brain and infant research as crucial to psychological development, as well as to the psychotherapeutic process.

In contrast to some of his more informal, colloquial writings, the formal definitions of the Child ego state Berne presented in his books were more consistent. "Child ego state is a set of feelings, attitudes and behavior patterns which are relics of the individual's own childhood," stood as the original definition provided in *Transactional Analysis in Psychotherapy* (1961, p. 77). In *Principles of Group Treatment* (1966), he defined the Child ego state as "An ego state which is an archaic relic from an early significant period of life" (p. 362). And in *What Do You Say After You Say Hello?* (1972), he wrote that the Child is "an archaic ego state. The Adapted Child follows Parental directives. The Natural Child is autonomous" (p. 442). (One wonders how an ego state can be simultaneously archaic and autonomous?)

Many transactional analysis clinicians have emphasized the archaic, fixated, defensive functions of the Child. Rath (1993) extended this perspective as follows:

> The archeopsyche or Child ego state (colloquially known as the Child) is defined by a set of inadequate (pathological) states of the ego displayed in thoughts, feelings, and behaviors, which manifest themselves in the here-and-now during the development of the elements stored in the archeop-syche and which are, from the phenomenological point of view, regressive elements and psychic reactions to earlier stages (of development).
>
> (p. 210)

Erskine (1998), in a similar fashion, has argued:

> The archaic state of the ego is the result of developmental arrest which occurred when critical early childhood needs for contact were not met. The child's defenses against the discomfort of unmet needs became egotized—fixated; the experience cannot be fully integrated into the Adult ego state until these defense mechanisms are dissolved.
>
> (p. 17)

According to this view, the archeopsyche/Child is viewed as a kind of storage container for archaic psychopathology, seemingly more of a container for weeds than the tenderly unfolding flowers sometimes suggested by Berne.

Clarkson and her colleagues at the Metanoia Institute (Clarkson & Gilbert, 1988; Clarkson & Fish, 1988) struggled perhaps the most mightily among TA practitioners with the theoretical dilemmas created by Berne's writings about the Child. Clarkson (1992) wrote:

> Ego states were initially conceived of as vividly available temporal record-ings of past events with the concomitant meaning and feelings which are maintained in potential existence within the personality (Berne, 1980/1961: 19). However, he distinguishes from this multitude of Child ego states: (1) Child as archaic ego states and (2) Child as fixated ego states. . . . Child ego states might be better referred to as *"historical ego states"* since a person's vivid experiences of today will be stored in natural psychological epochs, archaic by tomorrow.
>
> (pp. 44–45)

Although in this conceptualization the Child is still understood as a phenomen-ological repository of the experiences of history consistent with Berne's basic definitions and his emphasis on childhood, we also see some effort to resolve the question of how the Child can be viewed as fixated, adapted, *and* as autonomous in function and expression.

Transactional analysis theoreticians and clinicians have been aware of this quandary for a long time now, but it has yet to be resolved satisfactorily. Some have challenged the conceptualization of the Child as an archaic, fixated ego state. Schiff and her colleagues (Schiff et al., 1975), for example, viewed the Child this way:

> The Child ego state is the source of all energy and is in control of cathexis. . . . Psychopathology can be thought of as the development of adaptations which control the Child as opposed to the Child controlling the adaptations.
>
> (p. 26)

The Gouldings (1979) argued:

> Some TA therapists believe that the Child ego state stops developing at an early age. We see the Child as ever growing and ever developing, as the sum total of the experiences he has had and is having in the present.
> . . . The Child develops. We have stressed that the *Child* does the work. The Child both experiences and copies, and then incorporates.
>
> (p. 20, italics in original)

Blackstone (1993) extended the argument for the activity and changeability of the Child ego state, and presented a model of the intrapsychic dynamics of the Child ego state, drawing upon object relations theories.

I am not arguing that it is mistaken to include historical and fixated elements within the definition of the Child ego state. Rather, I am suggesting that an emphasis on these elements does not sufficiently account for the nature of the Child ego state, and that continued reliance on Berne's definitions maintains a serious limitation in theory and significant bias in clinical work.

Implicit and explicit knowing

Our earliest means of learning and mental organization occur at the level of subsymbolic, sensorimotor, and affective experiences that cannot be accurately described as states or functions of the ego. These realms of organization developmentally precede the capacities of the ego and underlie/accompany/inform/shape/color the nature of the Child, Adult, and Parent ego states throughout the course of life. Seen from the perspective of current neurophysiological and memory research, the psychological states of organization that transactional analysis calls the Child ego state does not develop until the middle of the second year of life. An immense amount of enduring learning is occurring in those first eighteen months of life, and throughout the life span, through avenues other than the functions of the ego.

Brain and memory researchers (McClelland, 1998; Milner, Squire, & Kandel, 1998), while often using different terminologies, are converging on a quite consistent differentiation of implicit (procedural) and explicit (declarative) memory processes. Implicit memory precedes the evolution of explicit memory, which requires cortical functions that develop later. Implicit memory is not replaced by explicit memory but continues to operate in parallel with explicit memory, providing the unthought realms of knowing. Siegel (2001) summarizes contemporary research this way:

> The process of memory and those of development are closely aligned. For the first year of life, the infant has available an "implicit" form of memory that includes emotional, behavioral, perceptual, and perhaps bodily (somatosensory) forms of memory. ... When implicit memories are activated, they do not have an internal sensation that something is being recalled. They merely influence our emotions, behaviors, or perceptions directly, in the here and now, without our awareness of their connection to some experience from the past.
>
> By the middle of the second year, children begin to develop a second form of memory, "explicit" memory (Bauer, 1996). Explicit memory includes two major forms: factual (semantic) and autobiographical ("episodic") (Tulving, Kapur, Craik, Moscovitch, & Houle, 1994). For both types of explicit memory, recollection is associated with an internal sensation of "I am recalling something now."

(p. 74)

The felt sense of implicit memory is captured in Bollas' (1987) now famous phrase of the "unthought known." Implicit knowledge is formed and sustained through somatic activity and emotional experience. As summarized by Pally (2000), implicit memory is understood as memory for aspects of experience, historical *and current*, that are not processed consciously, that is, patterns of learning and experience that influence functioning but are not experienced as conscious remembering. Kihlstrom (1990) and Izard (1993) define a broader range of forms of implicit *cognitions*, which includes perception, memory, and learning. These realms of implicit experience and learning are also taken up and extended within models of both research and clinical practice by Bucci (1997a, b) as subsymbolic processes, Ogden (1989) as the autistic-contiguous mode, Mitrani (1996) as unmentalized experience, Tronick (1998) and Lyons-Ruth (1998, 1999) as implicit relational knowing, Shahar-Levy (2001) as emotive motor memory clusters, and La Barre (2000) as nonverbal behavior.

Berne's writings about the Child ego state and script theory were primarily rooted in explicit memory, though what he defined as the script protocol is more reflective of implicit memory. Current transactional analysis perspectives based in attachment and empathic attunement models reach back into realms of implicit memory, although these have little to say about the infant's sensory, affective, and motor organization (i.e., the baby in relation to its own body, outside of relational experiences). In articles on the implications of neurodevelopmental research for transactional analysis, Allen (1999, 2000) also discussed the relevance of implicit and explicit memory for transactional analysis theory and observed:

> Implicit memory develops earlier than explicit memory. It is nonverbal and nonsymbolic, but it is not less rich or more primitive. It is not replaced by explicit knowledge. It involves how we feel and is a major element in relationships. Complicated music is understood implicitly.
>
> (2000, p. 262)

It is important to note that implicit, nonverbal, subsymbolic experiences are not limited to the first year of life. They are constant elements in the psychic organization of experience, co-existing side by side with explicit and declarative realms of experience in the here and now. Life that can be languaged is not necessarily healthier, richer, or more mature; it simply has a different kind of psychic organization. Healthy functioning requires both implicit and explicit knowing, subsymbolic/nonverbal and symbolic levels of organization. A complete psychotherapy must work within both levels of mental organization. While it is certainly a primary therapeutic task to foster the development of the capacity for symbolic and verbal representation, it is not necessarily true that sensate and subsymbolic experience is in some way regressed and pathological or will be improved by the achievement of symbolic or languaged knowing. Just consider how societies build museums and concert halls for the work of those who are able to carry us through sensation, sight, and sound into unthought and unlanguaged realms of experience.

In actual life and in psychotherapy, the realms of implicit knowing and subsymbolic experience can simultaneously contain elements of past, present, and future. I offer a case example to illustrate. Ben, an accomplished physicist, began individual therapy as an adjunct to marital therapy. Both he and his wife had engaged in extra-marital relationships at the time of their youngest child entering college. While the marital crisis had precipitated therapy, Ben's attention quickly turned to the pervasive deadness in all aspects of his life. The brief but intense sexual liaison with a new partner had startled him with an experience of his own vitality and passion. "Most of the time," Ben said, "I'm so dead to the world, lost in my head, that I could fall off the edge of the world and not notice."

Therapy proved extremely difficult. Sessions were filled with bitter and deadening complaints about himself, his marriage, his work, his colleagues, me, the therapy. "Just what was it that I am paying you for?" was the disdainful question that ended most of sessions. My efforts at observation, confrontation, or empathic elaboration were typically met with some version of, "I think we already know that one. Perhaps you could come up with something new the next time we meet." His impatience and disdain colored everything. He saw no purpose in talking about his parents or his history, as he "knew all of that already." I found it increasingly difficult to speak. I didn't know what to speak about; our talking seemed useless. I wondered to myself how it was that I found myself so often speechless in the presence of a man I both liked and admired, whom I was also quite certain felt considerable regard and affection toward me.

Then one evening I ran into Ben and his wife at a baroque concert. He opened the next session with, "I feel a bit silly saying this, but I was watching you during the concert. You never sat still. It was like you were dancing in your seat. What was going on in you?" Rather hesitantly, I replied, "I can't listen to that music and sit still. I don't think that music was written to settle people down. I think it was written to inspire people, to move them. It moves me, and I move when I'm moved." Then Ben asked, "What goes on inside of you when you listen to music?" "I think I'm supposed to ask you that sort of question," I parried. "I asked you first," Ben persisted. I told him, describing body sensations, dancing in my seat, humming aloud, feeling a range of emotions, imagining what the original rooms and audiences looked like, wishing at moments I had a sort of belief in a god that seemed to inspire that sort of music, anger at my parents for never letting me learn to play an instrument, wondering if the performers traveled with their lovers or if some of them slept with each other. "What," I then asked Ben, "goes on inside of you?" "I analyze the structure of the music and try to see the notes on the page. Quite a contrast, huh? It's what I do with every aspect of my life. I analyze it and kill it."

"Kill it:" suddenly the session was filled with memories, sensations, and images of Ben's childhood: the deadness of his parents; his inability to somehow move his parents; his desperate and ultimately bitter wish to somehow touch and inspire his parents (and then his wife); the atmosphere created by his mother's depression and bitterness, which was ever present and always unspoken; his father's constant withdrawal and solitude, including images of father sitting alone at the breakfast table to start his day and finishing alone in the garden reading the newspaper. Ben felt how he himself was killing off so much of his life, his own vitality, that the deadness of which he so often complained was of his own making. Like his parents, Ben was a "killer." He now knew why he was in therapy.

This example illustrates both the regressive and progressive aspects of the Child ego state. Rarely in psychotherapy do we create new patterns of emotional and relational processes for the future without first circuiting back, if even briefly, into memories of the past (perhaps a powerful factor in why it has been so easy to equate the Child ego state with actual childhood and psychopathology). As we wrestle in psychotherapy with wishes for a future different from the past, the possibilities of the future seem inextricably bound up and blinded by the strictures of the past. Dropping into the realm of sensory experience that our discussion of the baroque concert opened up for him threw Ben back in time, into a wealth of visceral/sensate/visual memories, *and* threw him *forward* into a realm of unthought desires that had long seemed unthinkable, foolish, and impossible. Would I suggest that this conversation and the subsequent therapy brought him out of a Child ego state into an Adult ego state (an integrated or integrating Adult, as is often suggested in current transactional analysis theory)? I would not. Rather, I think these experiences strengthened his Adult ego state, deepening his self-reflective capacities. I would also suggest that these experiences strengthened his Child ego state functions in the here and now, providing an intensification and enrichment of his sensate and emotional capacities. I see these somatic experiences as inherent to the nature of the Child ego state, not simply as remnants of childhood but as current and constant accompaniments of other aspects of psychic and interpersonal functioning.

Emotion and the brain

I have come to understand the Child ego state in procedural rather than structural and historical terms, which is to say, as a coherent and enduring system of organization and motivation. This system has deep, often compelling, historical roots, but it is a system that lives and changes in the present. The complexities and apparent contradictions of the simultaneously old and current elements in our emotional reactions are examined by Levenson. Levenson asked, "Is the human emotion system a masterpiece of design or the ultimate kludge?" (1999, p. 482). He answered in this way:

> This conundrum results from the fact that of all of the building blocks that make up human beings, some of the evolutionarily oldest as well as some of the newest, are found in the emotion system. This confluence of old and new makes an extremely complex system, one that often serves us extremely well

as we navigate the stresses, challenges and opportunities of life, but at other times bedevils and plagues us, even undermining our health.

(p. 482)

The implications of this two-system design of the brain, as discussed in such pivotal books as Lichtenberg (1989), Schore (1994), LeDoux (1996), Bucci (1997), DeMasio (1999), and Pally (2000), as well as in countless articles in professional journals, have profoundly deepened and altered my understanding of the nature of the psychotherapeutic project in general and, as I attempt to address in this chapter, of the Child ego state in particular.

Berne developed a theory and therapy of primarily the conscious mind, with ego states as manifestations of different levels and kinds of consciousness. Like most ego psychologists of his era, he viewed emotions and affect with ambivalence, suspicious of their disruptive, regressive, irrational qualities. But things have changed since then! Levenson (1999), for example, offered a contrasting perspective that is rich in its clinical implications:

> Emotion appears to function as a master choreographer, the ultimate organizer of disparate response systems. Emotion orchestrates the action of multiple response systems so that they act in a unified way in the service of solving problems. This view of emotion as an *organizer* stands in stark contrast to the oft-expressed view of emotion as a *disorganizer* or *disrupter*. In this latter view, emotion is the enemy of purposeful behavior and rational thought
>
> (p. 495, italics in the original)

Likewise, Emde (1999) challenged the long-held biases of classical psychoanalysts and ego psychologists about affect and emotion to emphasize, "Affective processes enhance developmental change in an everyday sense, not just at times of transition, and they are linked to cognitive processes" (p. 323).

Panksepp (2001) pushed this perspective on the organizing and motivating functions of emotions even further, concluding in language that is uncannily familiar to transactional analysts:

> Because emotionality is remarkably ancient in brain evolution, there is every reason to believe that the underlying brain systems served as a foundation for the emergence of basic social and cognitive abilities. The basic emotion systems of the brain imbue environmental events with values (i.e., "valence tagging"), and deficiencies in emotions may lead to psychiatric problems characterized by distinct cognitive and social idiosyncrasies. In developing infants such processes may be psychologically decisive. Infants may fundamentally project their emotions into the world, and initially assimilate cognitive structures only in highly affective ways. . . . The rich interpretation of emotions and cognitions establish the major psychic scripts for each child's life.
>
> (p. 141)

How do we reconcile these views of the role of emotion and affect in the organization of the brain and in the motivation of behavior with the ego state model of transactional analysis? This is not an easy task as the ego state model now stands. Clearly, the researchers just cited see emotion as *rooted* in the very earliest stages of life, but this is quite different from seeing it as *fixated* or *archaic*. They suggest that emotions and affective states shape and inform cognition throughout the life span. Does Berne's (1961) definition of the Adult ego state as "characterized by an autonomous set of feelings, attitudes and behavior patterns which are adapted to current reality" (p. 76), or the subsequent theoretical elaborations of an integrat*ed* or integrat*ing* Adult ego state, adequately embrace the models of emotion and cognition that these researchers describe? I think not. I see the Child ego states as *a matrix of emotionally, somatically based organizing and motivating systems*. Grounded in sensorimotor and implicit, procedural forms of knowledge, the Child provides systems of organization and motivation quite distinct from Adult and Parent states of the ego.

Movement and sensorimotor organization

One thing that babies and brains have in common is that they are firmly and permanently attached to a body, although the actions and organization of this body receive remarkably little attention in clinical theorizing. As one of the consistent voices on behalf of considering the body in theory (not to mention the consulting room), Boadella (1997) reminded psychotherapists:

> Every patient brings to the session not only his problems but also his body: he can never leave it behind, even if he forgets it's his (as in depersonalization); or treats it as a mechanical object (as in the schizoid process); or as a source of threat (as in hypochondria).
>
> (p. 33)

Significantly, the psychological and relational significance of sensorimotor organization and activity is now receiving attention in the body-centered literature (Marcher, 1996; Boadella, 1997; Downing, 1996; Rothschild, 2000; Frank, 2001). Within the transactional analysis literature, there have been a few writers touching upon the sensorimotor realms (Steere, 1981, 1985; Ligabue, 1991; Waldekranz-Piselli, 1999). Downing speaks to the rather obvious but often overlooked fact that, for the infant, the body is the means, the vehicle, to all that is outside. Seen from a developmental perspective, the inattention in clinical theory to sensorimotor processes is a curious oversight, one reflecting a long history of bias and blindness against the body within psychology and psychoanalysis, many philosophical traditions, and countless religions of associating the brain and the mind while setting the body and mind in opposition.

Researchers Thelan and Fogel (1989) threw down a conceptual gauntlet:

Developmentalists, like other psychologists, have been concerned primarily with the formation of the complex symbolic and affective processes of the "life of the mind" and have paid less attention to the translation of ideas into movement—a "life of the limbs." Infants, however, are born with much movement and few ideas and, for the first year or so, lack symbolic and verbal mediating mechanisms between their mental state and the expressions of their bodies and limbs. At this stage of the life cycle, then, the link between the developing mind and the developing limbs may be especially direct. We see this formulation in no way competing with theories that focus more directly on mental structures but rather as a complement and supplement to understanding the development of cognition.

(p. 23)

A substantial body of research has been developed within the general rubric of "dynamic motor theory" which suggests that many psychological phenomena presumed to arise from brain processes may actually develop more fundamentally from the activities of the muscles and limbs (Fischer & Hogan, 1989); that the movements of the body organize and reorganize the brain.

Fischer and Hogan (1989) described the unfolding of levels of cognitive development linked the sequencing of sensorimotor competencies. In the first weeks of life, the infant has a limited repertoire of reflex movements, such as turning the head to orient toward the mother's face, which come quickly under voluntary control. By 10 to 11 weeks, babies have the capacity to carry out a limited but flexible sensorimotor sequence of action, such as following a ball with their gaze while opening a hand and extending an arm in the direction of the moving ball, in contrast to a singular movement of one part of the body. Sensorimotor activities quickly reach more complex layers, or "mappings," and by the end of the first year, have become flexible systems of sensorimotor competencies, such as "complex systems of sensorimotor actions: infant moves a rattle in different ways to see different parts of it" (p. 280). Not until some time between 18 to 24 months are young children able to translate complex sensorimotor systems into representational systems (i.e., a child can pretend a doll is walking, walk the doll, and say, "Doll walk"). As Boadella (1997) observed, "The movement vocabulary of the child, during the first year and a half, is the foundation of his communicative rapport with the world: he interacts by means of motoric and vocal signs long before there is the capacity for semantic use of language" (p. 33). Call (1984) referred to this process as the "grammar of experience," by which he suggested that the development of language is grounded in the sensorimotor organization of the infant and toddler in relation to caregivers and the physical world.

Downing (1996), drawing on the work of Winnicott, Stern, Mahler, and others in particularly creative ways, writes with clarity and specificity about the importance of sensorimotor organization in the patterns of infant–parent interactions and its significance for adult psychotherapy. He stresses the importance of the infant's development of "affect-motor schemas" and affect-motor beliefs" that are an elaboration and integration of the infant's sensorimotor development within the relational and affective patterns with the caregivers. These patterns are not encoded in language but in literal affective and motoric experiences, that is, the somatic infrastructure. Downing conceptualizes these affect-motor schemas as forming pre-linguistic, sensorimotor belief systems for connectedness, differentiation, and bodily effectiveness. He hypothesizes

> that certain physical parent-infant bodily interactions... leave a trace... that this trace can be understood as a shaping, an influencing, of the infant's motor representational world.... that the vestige of these early motor beliefs will later affect adult behavior and awareness.
>
> (p. 150)

He stresses the importance of the parent–infant relationship fostering for the infant a sense of embodied agency, that "the infant's ability to impinge upon the other must equally be unfolded" and that the infant "must build up a motoric representation of the other as engagable, and of himself as able to engage" (1997, p. 169).

Attention to the sensorimotor regions of the brain and realms of mental organization remind us in an essential way that the infant is developing a relationship not only to an other(s) but also, equally importantly, to his or her own body and is developing a sense of selfhood. Infants spend many waking hours alone with themselves, discovering the pleasures of their bodies (Lichtenberg, 1989, p. 234), in relation to the body itself and the inanimate world as well as the interpersonal world. This becomes even more pronounced when the child begins walking, and the world opens up dramatically. As Call (1984) describes it, "for the first time the child experiences what must be something like a kinesthetic art gallery. The world changes as the child moves in the world" (p. 19). Thus, as the research of Thelan and her colleagues also demonstrates, while the brain and its neural activities can direct the movements of the body, the movements of the body and the acquisition of new sensorimotor patterns change the brain and its neural paths as well.

All of this is to underscore the tremendous amount of learning and organization occurring during infancy *and throughout childhood and adult life* that is outside of the purview of the traditional definitions of the ego and most definitions of the Child ego state. The body brings the world to life not only for the developing baby and the growing child, but also for adults and their psychotherapists. Shapiro (1996), as an example, has attempted to bring awareness of the body—both of the client and the therapist—into the consulting room and the therapeutic process. She has criticized other psychoanalytic theorists who have attempted to include a sense of somatic experience within the therapeutic process as having tended "to view these experiences as more primitive and pathological than verbally symbolized experience" (p. 299). She described the range of bodily experiences that are present in the therapist's office (whether they are attended to or not) as "a complex experience which includes the whole range of somatosensory phenomena: our breath, pulse, posture, muscle strength, fatigue, clarity and speed of thought, sense of boundedness, our skin, mucous membranes, bodily tension, facial expression, taste, smell, pulse, vitality" (p. 298) that have the potential to enliven the therapeutic process and its participants, to have an "interanimating and interpenetrating" experience of somatic and verbal interplay. In this regard, Waldekranz-Piselli (1999) has made a major contribution to TA clinical technique, elaborating— within transactional analysis theory—an account of sensate and affect-motor explorations and the client's being "active in the process of discovering his or her being and living his or her own body as well as how this affects relating to others" (p. 46).

Sensorimotor processes clearly provide a means of knowing and relating to "reality" from the there and then *as well as* in the here and now. These are not patterns that are simply "remnants" from childhood, though they begin in childhood. These are means of exploring, knowing, and shaping the world throughout one's life. As Thelan wryly observes, "the motor system is capable of generating novel form, as even an ageing psychologist can learn to tap dance or to ski or to play a musical instrument" (Thelan & Fogel, 1989, p. 28). I recall the first time I stood, at the age of 45, at the top of a black diamond ski slope, which a friend of mine (an expert skier) had decided I was ready to manoeuver. I was terrified, and as I tried to follow his instructions, I fell repeatedly. Finally, my friend told me to simply follow him and "Do whatever I do." No words, no thinking, just doing, physically imitating his movements, developing a *sense* of how to use my body, my sensorimotor systems, in Thelan's language, generating novel forms and new possibilities. I made it to the bottom of the slope without falling, acquiring in the process substantial new skills in the life of my limbs. Skiing, like so many aspects of life involving the body, improves by doing it, rather than talking about it.

Subsymbolic experience

We are just beginning to develop terms and concepts that adequately convey the nature of pre-linguistic, subcognitive experience. As transactional analysts have extended and deepened the reach of their clinical work, they have come to increasingly work within these realms of subsymbolic experience. Many transactional analysis theorists have desperately stretched the conceptualization of the Child ego state to address these arenas of developmental and clinical experience, as we see in the common notations of P-0, A-0, C-0. Taken from Berne's effort to establish a standard nomenclature for the TA literature, these zero-based ego states were meant by Berne to signify "at birth" (1969, p. 111). The notations were taken up by Schiff and her colleagues (1975), to try to reflect the very earliest stages of motivation and organization within the ego state model. This notation was extended and formalized within Mellor's account of third-degree impasses, which "relate to primal protocols (Berne, 1972); that is, they originate during very young experiences, perhaps even pre-natal" (1980, p. 214). As TA theorists have attempted to describe these earliest, pre-cognitive realms of experience, the concept of the third-degree impasse has taken an important place in the literature (Levin-Landheer, 1982; Giuli, 1985; Clarkson, 1992; Cox, 1999; Waldekranz-Piselli, 1999). Waldekranz-Piselli accounts for the P-0, A-0, C-0 levels of organization purely in terms of sensate levels of experience, reflective of the development of affectmotor schema in a way that is more consistent with direct body experience than with ego function. I find this extension of an ego state model more obfuscating than clarifying, and think we find far more accurate and clinically viable models outside of conceptualizations of the ego. Here I have found the work of Bucci most useful.

Bucci (1997a, 1997b, 2001), through her explication of subsymbolic pro-cesses, has made an especially important contribution from cognitive psychol-ogy to clinical theorizing and research within the realms of sensorimotor learning, implicit knowledge, and psychotherapy with adults. Subsymbolic processes refer to those means of mental organization and learning that are not dependent on language. This perspective has much to offer transactional analysis. According to Bucci (2001):

> Subsymbolic processing accounts for highly developed skills in athletics and the arts and sciences and is central to knowledge of one's body and to emotional experience.... Balanchine communicated to his dancers primar-ily through these modalities. His communication was intentional, conscious, systematic and complex—within the motoric mode... he did not resort to motoric or sensory modalities because verbal representations were repressed, but because the information existed only in a form that could not be captured in words.... We should emphasize that the prefix "sub" here denotes the subsymbolic as *underlying* symbolic representation, not as an inferior or primitive processing mode.
>
> (pp. 48–49, italics in the original)

Bucci (1997b) effectively evokes a sense of the body that is deeply familiar within the experience of doing body-centered psychotherapy:

> These sensory experiences occur in consonance with somatic and visceral experience of pleasure and pain, as well as organized motoric actions involving the mouth, hands, and the whole body—kicking, crying, sucking, rooting and shaping one's body to another's... these direct and integrate emotional life long before language is acquired.
>
> (p. 161)

We kick, cry, suck, experience pain and pleasure, shape our body to another's (with any luck at all!) throughout the course of life. These are not simply manifestations of infancy or archaic remnants of childhood, but also of intimacy, play, eroticism, fighting, sexuality, and nurturing throughout the full span of one's life. In these subsymbolic realms, the therapeutic process becomes a kind of exploratory, psychosomatic partnership (quite different and distinct from a corrective, pseudo-parent–child relationship) that can be often wordless, but rich in meaning nonetheless.

A clinical example further illustrates the organizing and reorganizing potential of sensorimotor and subsymbolic activity. Abby was one of four siblings, two sons and two daughters, born to ambitious, upper-middle-class parents. The family prided itself on its social and political accomplishments, the children pressured to be outgoing, independent, socially competent, and academically accomplished. Abby, both as a child and as an adult, felt she often fell short of the mark. Her therapy tended to focus on professional concerns and self-doubts and the stresses of being a professional woman while raising very active children. In discussing struggles with colleagues or family members, Abby was intensely self-critical, rarely feeling or expressing anger or disappointment toward those around her. She was able to express anger and disappointment toward me, though with considerable apprehension and difficulty. The issues she raised with me were substantial and brought up in a way that enhanced the work rather than disrupted it or distanced from it. Sessions were productive, and yet no underlying theme seemed to emerge. Abby remained uncertain as to why she was "really" in therapy, whether she could justify the time and expense.

During one session, she mentioned in passing that she had become preoccupied with a photograph she'd seen in a magazine, one that both fascinated and disturbed her. She thought several times of bringing it up with me but hesitated, feeling embarrassed and uncertain of what to say about it. She finally decided to draw it, hoping she could then discover its meaning. After drawing, redrawing, and reworking the image several times, she asked to bring the drawing to a session.

The image was of three football players walking off the field, hunched over, soaked in rain and covered with mud. The figures were somewhat obscured in the rain and mist, their faces hidden by their helmets. The figures communicated both a menace and a fatigue. The men were physically close, touching each other, clearly part of a team. The drawing was very finely rendered and quite moving as a drawing in and of itself.

As Abby began to associate to the picture, she thought of her father, his pride in his body and his athleticism, his preference for his sons over his daughters, his bullying and narcissistic authority and self-righteousness. All of this was familiar material from her previous therapy, Abby reported, and she expressed bewilderment at not being able to get through to whatever it was that made the image so compelling for her. I suggested that rather than drawing the image or talking about it, she *become* it physically, literally taking it on with her body.

A series of sessions ensued in which she worked standing up, mimicking each of the figures, gradually entering the posture of each, walking and moving in the way she imagined they would move. Each session would begin with her discussing whatever events of the week she wanted me to know about or that she needed to think through, and then she would stand up, put the picture on the floor, and begin to *do* some part of the picture. We spoke very little. I stood near her, offering no interpretations, simply asking her to relate what she experienced if she was so inclined. She did a lot and said very little, occasionally commenting on sensations in her body, on what she was feeling, on what she sensed the men in the picture might be feeling. No new memories or insights emerged, but she did begin having a new sense of her body. She began to notice a different sense of herself between sessions, feeling more substantial in herself with her thoughts and feelings. She realized she felt angry more often. She was moving into a way of being that had captivated her in the photograph, one that had been denied to her as a daughter in the family. Language and insight followed and were informed and enriched by her bodily activity and exploration.

As diverse strands of research about babies and brains come together with clinical theory, we are beginning to recognize the force of subsymbolic and sensorimotor processes that create formative and enduring states of mind, to use Allen's (2000) phrase. In the first of these strands, contemporary neurophysiological and brain scan research is demonstrating with increasing clarity the mutually influencing interactions of the subcortical, limbic functions with cortical (symbolic/verbal) functions (Hadley, 1989; LeDoux, 1996; Bucci, 1997a; Siegel, 2001; Schore, 2001). We now know that two distinct, concurrent, and lifelong modes of experience, the symbolic and the subsymbolic, the cognitive and the somatic, constantly shape psychic life. Both symbolic and subsymbolic realms of psychic experience are open to influence and alteration at any stage of life.

In a second crucial strand of research, more than two decades of direct observation of infants has dramatically altered our understanding of the nature of infancy, the infant–parent dyad, and the social construction of the human brain. From birth, human beings begin to form non-linguistic schema of an affective and sensorimotor world that function as subcortical, pre-cognitive templates which influence and are influenced by all subsequent cognitive and relational development. We are seeing the beginnings of a coherent theory of the somatic, affective, and nonverbal foundation of human functioning, as exemplified by Lichtenberg's (1989) description of the perceptual-affective-action mode, which operates without verbal representation or symbolic formation, and by Bucci's accounting of subsymbolic processing.

Evolving concepts in transactional analysis

It is clear that current infant and neurophysiological research reflects a range of neural developments that cannot be adequately captured in Berne's model of ego states. We shall never see an ego state light up in a PET scan in a particular area of the brain. Clarkson (1992) addressed the limits of theories of ego states in transactional analysis by introducing the language of states of self. Hargaden and Sills (2001, 2002) have extended the conceptualization of self states within the Child ego state to address the more unconscious aspects of human functioning while retaining the basic model of the Child ego state. Rath (1993) attempted to broaden the conceptualization of ego states by utilizing the idea of self-organizing systems. In a related fashion, Gilbert (1996) developed the idea of ego state networks, drawing on research models of schemas and generalized representations.

Hine (1997) carried the model of neural networks further, synthesizing neurophysiological and infant research to offer hypotheses as to the development and differentiation of ego states, describing the bridging between implicit and explicit knowing. Hine (1997), drawing on the work of Churchland (1995), Edelman (1992), Nelson and Gruendel (1981), and Stern (1985) among others, offered a theory of ego state development and organization based largely on implicit memory and learning. She emphasized the concept of generalized representations of experience, concluding that "this fundamental neural process builds up into coherent networks of representations functioning as wholes, interlinking each other with increasing mental complexity. Ego states appear to be an evolved example of this impressively powerful process of structuralization" (p. 278). She observed:

> Ego states exhibit several characteristics of GR [generalized representation] systems... Ego states become comparatively stable and coherent systems, as do GRs. ... In ego states the mental activity can be broad and can include thinking, feeling, and behaving. This is similar to the make up of a "generalized experience" as described by Moscovitch (1994). ... In ego state systems the ego states have their own characteristic styles and give their own meaning to internal sensations and external perceptions.
>
> (p. 283)

Hine went on to suggest that the differing forms of mental activity characterized for each ego state reflects "the way each ego state system forms and how the perceptions that give rise to each system are processed and organized" (p. 284). From this perspective, she has sustained a model of discrete and differentiated systems of mental activity and organization.

Allen (2000), while not directly proposing a change of terminology, suggested a change of language that points a way out of the theoretical dilemma we have inherited from Berne. Drawing on contemporary brain research, Allen writes:

> *States of mind as precursors of full ego states*: How is the activation of widely distributed neural circuits regulated? This function seems to be performed by what has been termed a "state of mind," the total pattern of activation in the brain at a given time. It brings together several different

neural networks, any one of which can become the dominant energy and information-processing unit of the moment....Over time, these cohesive states become more and more easily activated and coalesce into self-states. As Post and Weiss (1997) concluded, "Neurons which fire together and survive together and wire together" (p. 930).... In transactional analysis, we label the manifestations of such neural network activations "ego states."

(p. 261)

Hine's and Allen's descriptions of systems of neural network activation speak more accurately, at a theoretical level, to the understanding of dynamic mental processes that is emerging in contemporary research than does our more familiar theory of ego states as psychic structures within the mind. Allen's reference to states of *mind* rather than states of *ego* opens up the frame of reference in accounting for the growth and change of somatic, emotional, cognitive, and behavioral organization. Allen seems to suggest that when schemas of neural organization reach the point at which "they also include socially shared and communicable language," they may then be conceptualized as ego states rather than states of mind.

Allen's perspective also mirrors one common to body-centered therapists, many of whom are trained to differentiate evidence of differing states of mental organization, usually defined as visceral/affective, sensorimotor, and cognitive. From a developmental perspective, the visceral/affective systems of the limbic regions dominate the earliest stages of neurophysiological and interpersonal organization, facilitated and extended by sensorimotor development, and capped by the cognitive processes of the cerebral cortex. Each system is necessary for healthy functioning. While the visceral/affective and sensorimotor systems dominate early infant development, they do not then become remnants and repositories of the past but remain vital systems of mental organization co-existing with cognitive systems throughout one's life. These same subsymbolic systems are active (and hopefully utilized) in the ongoing psychotherapeutic process of linking thinking and feeling, past and present, in the midst of trying to create meaning and effectiveness in one's life.

It may well be that the most direct (and theoretically sound) means of change within the subsymbolic and affect-motor realms of experience involve systematic attention to various forms of nonverbal experience and communication, including such means of intervention as: direct work with the body, increased focus on sensory awareness, attention to the interplay of the transferential/countertransferential relationship, and exploration of unconscious fantasy. It seems increasingly clear that when we are working within these foundational realms of mental organization, we are dealing with *process not structure*. While these processes (implicit, procedural, unconscious means of knowing) have definite coherence, they do not have the fixity of those states of mind we could call self or ego. We are dealing with *how things happen*, in addition to the more familiar questions of what happened and who did what.

In these realms of the therapeutic process, it is the activity and experience of seeking, moving, and exploring that create the therapeutic edge and the means of change.

Clinical implications

Transactional analysis psychotherapy is alive, well, and growing. When we look at psychotherapy from the perspective of somatic processes and brain development, the field of the therapeutic *process* opens widely, far beyond the scope of the models of the therapeutic relationship most common in transactional analysis today. The models and metaphors of parental, patriarchal, or maternal presences have powerful draws for therapist and client alike. After all, if a client is unable to soothe himself, who better to provide the service than the therapist; if unable to understand herself, who better to provide the understanding than the therapist? Winer (1994) has challenged this parental model and its many variations in psychotherapy:

> It is too comfortable for therapist and patient to view themselves as parent and child, even seductive we might say. We all long for a wise and protective authority. The patient invests her therapist with that power and the therapist finds security in identifying with his patient's idealization of him.
>
> (p. 64)

Tronick (2001) has sought to deepen the understanding of the process of psychotherapy through the insights gained from infant studies. He has suggested the model of "dyadically expanded states of consciousness" through which "the collaboration of two individuals (two brains) is successful, each fulfills the fundamental system principle of increasing their coherence and complexity" (p. 193). He is cautious about simple applications of the infant–parent research that tends to turn psychotherapy into some form of parent–child relationship. I quote Tronick at length here, as his perspective raises crucial questions about our understanding of the Child ego state and our approaches as transactional analysts to the therapeutic process:

> The adult was a "being" who once had infant capacities but who no longer has (or no longer only has) infant, toddler, or child capacities. ... It is with these fundamentally and qualitatively different capacities that adults experience, even re-experience (interpret), their experiences. ... We must not apply models of mother-infant/child interaction to the therapeutic situation in a simple-minded, noncritical fashion. Infants are not patients. Mothers are not therapists. ... It seems to me we can learn a great deal about both by comparing and contrasting them to each other. Nonetheless, we should not confuse and confabulate mothers and infants, patients and therapists.
>
> (pp. 189–190)

Bonds-White and I (Cornell & Bonds-White, 2001) examined the clinical implications of the subtle and not-so-subtle models of mother–infant and parent–child relationships that are so common in TA psychotherapy. We have suggested thinking more in terms of relatedness rather than relationship to provide a conceptualization that shifts away from the parent–child metaphors. We emphasize the establishment of a therapeutic *space* (in contrast to relationship) which allows the means to reflect, wonder, explore, and move. Seen from a body-centered perspective, psychotherapy is a means through which the client discovers personal agency. In working systematically with implicit knowing, bodily activity, and sensate/motoric organization, therapy can help bring the body into the mind of the client. It is my hope as a therapist to promote a kind of bodily learning and agency which will remain in the body of the client, an implicit somatic knowing that will remain with a client outside of the office and our relationship.

What happens to our images of ourselves as psychotherapists if we cast psychotherapy into the broad fields of activity and desire, beyond those of parenting, nurturing, and understanding? Psychotherapy becomes a field of uncertainty and potentiality, of play and exploration, of action and aggression, of desire and imagination. Knoblauch (1996), a psychoanalyst and jazz musician, captures the flavor of somatic and interpersonal enlivening in his title "The play and interplay of passionate experience: Multiple organizations of desire." I think that the conceptualization of the roles of play and desire within the therapeutic process point a way out of the long-standing binds and blind spots of transactional analysis theory, which has become imbued with variations of parenting and corrective models of therapeutic activity. "Play and interplay" conveys the sense of mutual exploration, motoric activation, and the unconscious matrix of transference and countertransference within the therapeutic process. Play and interplay offer a therapeutic model more consistent with the emerging discoveries of research with babies and brains, rooting those babies and brains in active, moving bodies, as well as within minds and ego structures.

There is a rich, emerging literature on the place of desire and passion in psychotherapy (Davies, 1994, 1998; Winer, 1994; Benjamin, 1995; Knoblauch, 1996; Eigen, 1996, 1998; Mann, 1997; Dimen, 1999, 2001; Billow, 2000; Cornell, 2001, 2018) that has many implications for the issues raised in this chapter. These articles go beyond the scope of this chapter but warrant the attention of those seeking to extend their thinking about the nature and purpose of psychotherapy.

Play and the creation of potential space were certainly crucial to Winnicott's (1971) understanding of both child development and the therapeutic process. Play is a complex and multifaceted phenomenon. Among the contemporary brain researchers, Panksepp has worked extensively with studies of brain development in older children and has undertaken numerous studies of the role of play. Panksepp (2001) has stressed that "young children tend to be very active a good deal of the time," and that "all children need daily doses of rough and tumble (R&T) activities, for this may help to optimize brain development" (p. 146). Panksepp (1993) outlined the importance of play:

> Human play has been divided into a large number of categories, including exploratory/sensorimotor play, relational/functional play, constructive play, dramatic/symbolic play, games-with-rules play, and rough and tumble play. Probably this last form, roughhousing play, is presently easiest to study in animal models, but... it has received the least attention in human research. This is understandable, for roughhousing is boisterous and often viewed as disruptive and potentially dangerous by adults. Of course kids love it (it brings them "joy"), and animals readily learn instrumental responses to indulge in it.
>
> (Normansell & Panksepp, 1990, p. 151)

In subsequent writing on the long-term psychobiological consequences of infant emotions, Panksepp (2001) described four primary and enduring emotional systems of seeking, play, lust, and care. Most psychotherapeutic models (certainly transactional analysis) have the care component nailed down thoroughly. My readings of the baby and brain research strongly suggest that we, as psychotherapists, are long overdue in adding much more systematic attention to seeking, play, and lust. I think we need a more rough-and-tough approach to the psychotherapy of adults, bringing the full range of possibilities of two adult bodies and minds to bear upon the psychotherapeutic project.

Conclusion

Am I suggesting that we throw out the concept of the Child ego state? No, certainly not. There are certainly aspects of ego function—archaic, fixated, and defensively organized—that are very much as Berne described them in his accounts of the Child ego state, and as we often see reflected in the TA literature. I would agree that these states are indeed aspects of ego function. I am, however, arguing that as transactional analysis has significantly extended its clinical reach, we have run into serious theoretical trouble as a result of the limits of ego state theory, especially in our conceptualization of the Child. I am suggesting that the Child ego state emerges from a matrix of implicit, affective, and motoric systems of subsymbolic (pre-ego) organization and motivation. These are states of mind or neural organization that precede ego development and are the unconscious and preconscious realms of mental organization. The Child ego states reflect means of functioning in reality that may sometimes contain historically rooted distortions and defenses but at the same time involve a wealth of affective and procedural forms of knowing that enrich daily life and relatedness. We must articulate a theory of process as well as structure. I think that we are now (and this will be evident in many of the chapters of this book) seeking to evolve a clinical theory of the unconscious, procedural, somatic states of motivation and organization that come alive in the *process* of in-depth psychotherapy.

Consistent with the implications of contemporary research with babies and brains, we must begin to reconceptualize the level of bodily and emotional organization from that of Child ego states to that of fundamental and ongoing processes of neural activation, organization, and change. We can then conceptualize transactional analysis psychotherapy as a means and place for the activation of desires, the exploration of possibilities, and an enlivened, rough-and-tumble relatedness.

Chapter 8

"My body is unhappy": Somatic foundations of script and script protocol

> Protocol is a kernel of nonverbal, somatic experience that may be touched or triggered in intimate relationships. Such moments are often impregnated with both hope and dread. When the experience of a therapeutic relationship evokes protocol, the Child ego state is deeply opened, and the transference dynamics that may be played out become more anxiety provoking and more difficult to tolerate, understand, and resolve for both client and practitioner.
>
> (Cornell & Landaiche, 2006, p. 204)

It had been a year since I last consulted with Lara and Emily. The previous year Lara had asked that I consult with her regarding her client, Emily, with whom she'd been working quite productively for three years addressing Emily's eating disorder, body shame, and sexual anxieties. Emily was a successful young attorney, then involved in her first serious relationship. She was "fed up" (so to speak) with her constant preoccupation with her eating and her weight, and fearful that her bodily shame and preoccupations would ruin this loving relationship. The therapeutic work to this point had enabled Emily to value herself and be able to stand outside her "issues" enough to pursue this relationship. But as this man became more important to her, her body anxieties came flooding back. Lara, deeply saddened by Emily's struggle, became trapped in a cycle of reassurance, while Emily's sense of self-worth seemed to utterly collapse into series of images of a fat, undesirable body. They were at a point of impasse and decided to seek consultation. Emily felt it important to have the point of view of a male therapist; Lara agreed and was particularly interested in a body-centered perspective.

We agreed upon a rather unusual structure for the consultation: Lara and Emily would discuss their experience of their work together and of the current point of impasse with me listening; I would then do a therapeutic session with Emily with Lara watching and probably participating; then the three of us would discuss the work together. Listening to the opening conversation between Lara and Emily, two things were immediately apparent: the first was that there was a deep affection and intimacy between the two; the second was that Emily's experience/account of her body was almost exclusively in visual terms, that is, how she saw herself and imagined others saw her. This visual frame of reference unconsciously directed both Emily's and Lara's attention to the surfaces of her being. Emily's use of a visual frame of reference was so dominant and familiar that it had become "invisible," unnoticeable to Lara and Emily, which I thought was contributing to the impasse in the therapy. Emily experienced herself only as a visual object, constantly subject to scrutiny. This experience was so familiar and compelling that it was recreated within the therapeutic couple, even though the intentions of their lookings were benign. As I have so often experienced myself in seeking consultation at points of impasse, the consultant (or peer group) is an outside force, not so intimately subjected to the states of being and relatedness induced within the therapeutic relationship, thus more able to see, feel, and imagine things anew. What seemed so familiar to Emily and Lara seemed sad and limiting to me. In keeping with our contract for body-centered exploration, I wondered what it would be like for Emily to use her eyes actively, aggressively in response to those around her.

Eyes became the focus of this first consultation. I worked with Emily to use her own eyes, rather than lose herself in the actual or imagined gaze of others. We experimented with her using her eyes to repel unwanted expressions from others, to make demands upon others, and most importantly to hold Lara's eyes with her eyes. These experiments were a relief and source of excitement for Emily. As the body-centered work came to an end, the three of us then spoke of the meaning of these somatic experiments, both in the literal use of her eyes in relation to those around her and as a kind of metaphor for shifting from passive/receptive reactions to emotionally significant people to active/aggressive engagements.

A year later, Emily's relationship was deepening, the work with her eyes continued to foster a sense of independence and mastery, and eating was not at the center of her concerns. But gradually, as her years-long vigilance about food waned, Emily had put on a few pounds. While virtually invisible to anyone else (except, not coincidentally, her mother and her maternal grandfather), Emily's perceptions of herself became graphically distorted, and she once again saw herself held and judged disgusting in the eyes of others. She abruptly canceled a beach vacation with her boyfriend. She knew this time that her reactions were entirely irrational but was unable to contain them. Lara, for her part, was bewildered and feeling ferociously protective in ways she knew might not be productive. They decided on having another in-person consultation.

As we began the new session, Emily told me that in her mind everyone could see the extra weight, that people stared, joked about her behind her back, found her disgusting. "I know it's not true, but that is how it feels, and it feels entirely real." She was deeply upset with herself for this setback. She felt it started when she went to lunch with her maternal grandfather, and he commented constantly on how FAT everyone around them was. She was certain (and very likely correct) that he had noticed her weight gain and was indirectly commenting on it. Her mother (now in her 60s and bulimic for at least 40 years) had immediately noticed the weight gain and told Emily that her boyfriend would soon leave her. As I listened, I wondered (but did not say) if the deepening intimacy with her lover might also have triggered a step back into the safety and familiarity of a script-based focus on weight and undesirability. Her mother was convinced that Emily's father had abandoned them because he found his wife too fat, and that her weight was the fatal cause in the ending of every relationship she'd ever had. Emily described the experience of her sense of her body changing and being invaded again by the gaze of others. She felt helpless, unable to hold her gains from her therapy. She became convinced that Lara was just saying nice things to make her feel better.

And then she said to me, "My body is unhappy when it is fat." I responded with, "You mean that you feel happier with your body when it is thinner. You are unhappy with your body when you put on weight, and you imagine every-one else is, too." "No," she insisted, "my *body* is happier when it is thin, not me. My body is unhappy when it weighs too much. My body knows when it puts on weight." "My god," I thought to myself, "what an extraordinary statement." I suddenly found myself imagining this body of Emily's literally absorbing the anxiety and disgust of her mother's body toward itself and toward Emily's body when one/the other/or both were "*too fat.*" I imagined her young body literally an unhappy body in the grip of another's/mother's unhappy body in a symbiotic fusion, the sensations merged, the sensation of literally making her mother's body unhappy, the sensations of disgust. Only thinness brought some possibility of relief, acceptance, fleeting happiness. I imagined the literal, unspoken, flesh-to-flesh transactions that must have impinged upon Emily's body from birth. A phrase kept flashing through my mind, "the *weight* of the gaze of others." I felt that weight in my own body, as well as a sadness and fierce protectiveness toward Emily. I could identify with Lara's wish to ward off the mother, reassure Emily of her worth and attractiveness, argue with her Parent ego state, and protect her.

I asked Emily to close her eyes and bring our conversation into her body. How was she sensing/feeling our discussion in her body? Could she put words to the experience of her body? "I feel heavy... heavy like fat and heavy like sad, ... weighted down," were Emily's first words, continuing, "the eyes of the others are always so heavy." I repeated her words, slightly amplifying their intensity. I suggested she begin to *feel* the eyes of others surrounding her, intruding, judging, shaming, weighing her down. I asked that she feel how it is to be noticed for her exterior, the surface and size of her body. "What is it that people see and know (or think they know) about you when they see your size and surface?" I asked her quietly, several times over. "What is it about you that is not seen?" "What is it that is of no interest to these eyes at the surface?" I did not want Emily to speak in response to my questions but to be with these questions in her body. I asked Emily to feel the *weight* of these eyes upon her body. As time passed, I asked her to both *describe* and *show* what was happening in her body. "I'm being crushed. It crushes me." "*Show* me the crushing," I urged Emily. Her body began to collapse, I moved behind her, and Lara moved in front to take my place. As her body began to collapse against me, Emily suddenly said, "*I* want to crush *them!*" She opened her eyes, looked at Lara, took Lara's hands, and began to press her back forcefully into my chest. She pushed long and hard until I finally gave way. Then she pulled herself forward into Lara's arms, crying. Gradually, Emily opened her eyes, locking them on Lara's, challenging her mother in a torrent of words, and speaking of Lara's importance to her with the force of both gaze and voice growing.

In time, she shifted her gaze from Lara to include me and began to reflect on the experience of her body. We spoke of the literalness of her body being happy rather than she herself being happy, of her sense of herself being so concretely tied to her bodily perceptions and sensations. Emily asked how this was possible and what to do about it. I described to her my fantasy that the "happy/unhappy body" was originally that of her mother, not her, but as her mother could literally not tell herself apart from her daughter, it all felt one and the same. How could her body as a baby, a growing girl, be happy when enveloped, nearly possessed, by her mother's profound anxiety and unhappiness with her own body? I wondered aloud about the confusion she may have felt in the midst of these crazy, destructive projections on her mother's part that were also ferociously loving and protective in their intent. Her mother seemed (and seems) to have had no sense of self separate from the external appearance of her own body, so how could she have helped Emily develop that separation? Emily needed to develop a new relationship to her "unhappy" body and to explore the conflict between these two felt, sensate aspects of her self-experience (Stern, 2004; Wood & Petriglieri, 2005). She needed to find ways to bring her "unhappy" body to her boyfriend, to Lara, and eventually to others who enjoy and value her, so as to experience others' bodies that were happy to be with her, whatever the state and shape of her body. She knew this in her mind, but her body quite literally did not "know" this and needed very much to learn.

Twenty years ago

Before taking up a detailed discussion of this session as an exploration of the nature of script and possibilities of script intervention, I want to take a theoretical interlude that can help inform the case discussion.

It has been twenty years since I wrote, "Life script theory: A critical review from a developmental perspective" (1988), which I can look back on with real satisfaction. It turned out that that article was to be the first in a series that I have written to challenge some of the basic tenets of transactional analysis theory and practice. At the time, I was troubled by several aspects of script theory and its clinical applications: Were the developmental stages so clear cut as we were taught and practicing? Was developmental arrest as permanent and causal in script formation as our theories suggested? Were script-related childhood events so readily available to recall? Was most script decisional? Was script inherently defensive or pathological? Were there just ten or twelve script injunctions or exactly five miniscript drivers? Did what we were teaching hold up to contemporary developmental research? In that article, I strongly argued that creativity, meaning-making, and mutuality of influence were inherent in the process of script formation and enactment. I concluded:

> Script theory has become more restrictive than enlivening. Script analysis as it has evolved over the years is overly psychoanalytic in attitude and overly reductionistic in what it communicates to people about human development. In addition, the incorporation of developmental theory into script theory has been too often simplistic and inaccurate, placing primary emphasis on psychopathology rather than psychological formation.
>
> (p. 281)

I smile now as I read the bit about script theory being "overly psychoanalytic in attitude," as I was then not at all a fan of psychoanalysis and am now often accused by some of my TA colleagues of trying to turn transactional analysis back into psychoanalysis. The aspects of psychoanalysis I was quarreling with in the late 1980s were essentially the same as those Berne was arguing against in the 1950s and 1960s. Ironically, right at the time I was writing my script critique article, I was discovering the work of Winnicott, Bollas, and McLaughlin, psychoanalysts who were not the least bit reductionist in their thinking. Their work opened new vistas to me, and my interest in contemporary analytic work has grown ever since. During this same period of time, I discovered the work of Stephen Mitchell, and in 1991 *Psychoanalytic Dialogues* started publication, introducing me to the emerging relational theories of contemporary psychoanalysis.

At the time of writing the critique, I was quite nervous as to whether I was accurately representing the developmental researchers and theorists whose work I only knew through their writing. I sent each of them the first draft of the article to check on the accuracy of my understanding. To my surprise, almost all wrote back thoughtfully and with significant interest. I was particularly touched by a letter from Stella Chess, handwritten from her hospital bed after hip surgery. She wrote that she was delighted to know that "TA was still around," that she and Alexander Thomas (Chess & Thomas, 1984) had been quite enthusiastic about TA but thought it had died out. She went on to say how much it meant to her as a researcher to see their work understood and applied clinically, that they often felt their work had little impact in the actual practice of psychotherapy, that practitioners didn't read research. That experience set the basis for my circulating early drafts of papers to authors outside of my personally known circle of colleagues whose work I reference in major ways. That process has constantly informed and pushed my learning, found new colleagues among diverse disciplines, and let people outside the TA community know that TA is still very much alive.

Since writing that article, my understanding of script and how to work therapeutically with script-based processes has continued to evolve. My attention has been particularly drawn to third-degree script (what Berne called "tissue level") and to script protocol. This interest is drawn in part out of my enduring interest in the somatic component of psychological and emotional experience. But the driving motivation for my exploration of the body (in theory and practice) is the fact that most of my clients have had very difficult lives, so the issues brought into treatment were anchored at a somatic, "tissue" level and simply were not affected in any enduring way by the traditional TA means of cognitive/interpretive interventions.

At the point when I was writing the critique of script theory, my clinical work was carried out in two parallel modes—one based in the cognitive/behavioral/ interpersonal model of transactional analysis, and the other grounded in a neo-Reichian, body-centered cathartic model. I was not happy with either the process or the results. Windows of new understanding began to open as I read people like Bollas and Winnicott, the relationalists, and the mother–infant research. Through supervision with Bollas and a Jungian analyst, I began to learn how to work more effectively with affective and unconscious states through the transference–countertransference matrix. I became more effective in working with states of both intrapsychic and interpersonal conflict, and the therapy became more intimate. My work with script emphasized the conscious and unconscious efforts at meaning-making and psychological structure more than fixation and defense.

But my body-centered work, stuck in the Reichian model of muscular armor and emotional discharge, evolved more slowly. Reading Winnicott gave me new insights into the gestural/communicative meanings of nonverbal behavior (Cornell, 1997). Body-centered theorists were beginning to speak of a model of three realms of mental/somatic organization—the cognitive, sensorimotor, and visceral (affective/limbic)—which needed to be increasingly integrated in somatically based psychotherapy. This was the first real break from the cathartic model, and my work began to change. However, the door of my thinking about the body and somatic processes blew wide open when I read a series of articles and a book by Wilma Bucci (1997a, 1997b, 2001, 2002) elaborating her research into the interface of cognitive science and psychoanalytic theory, utilizing what she calls a multiple code theory of symbolic and subsymbolic processing. It is her work that I wish to elaborate here and then use in my discussion of the case consultations with Lara and Emily, and in application to my current understanding of script theory and the therapeutic process.

Applying Bucci's multiple code theory to script and script protocol

The "multiple codes" of Bucci's model are three major interacting and interdependent systems of mental and emotional representation and processing: Symbolic verbal, symbolic nonverbal, and subsymbolic. These three systems are fundamental and lifelong, although the verbal symbolic, the mode that tends to be valorized in psychoanaysis and most forms of psychotherapy, is the last to come "online" in psychological development. As Bucci (2007) argues:

> We are not accustomed to thinking of nonsymbolic processes, including somatic and sensory processes, that cannot be verbalized or even symbolized and that may operate outside of intentional control, as systemic and organized thought. It changes our understanding of pathology and treatment when we are able to make this shift.
>
> (p. 58)

The symbolic verbal is the dominant realm of most human relations work, be it psychotherapy, counseling, psychoanalysis, organizational consultation. It is the mode of experience and communication most readily available in language and relatively open to reflection. This is the mode in which script decisions and type I impasses are organized, recognized, and can be communicated. Memories in this mode are available for conscious, narrative recall.

The symbolic nonverbal is the realm of psychological organization that is both known and shown through nonverbal behavior and nonverbalized processing, likely experienced and/or expressed in visual, auditory, motoric, or tactile modalities. Though lacking words, the nonverbal symbolic generates reflective meaning that can be brought into words. Bucci suggests that this is the mode currently theorized in psychoanalysis as transference–countertransference enactments, that is, experience that is *shown* first as a way of becoming *known* and may then be available for languaged reflection. I would suggest that this is the mode that Berne characterized as ulterior communication, that level of script which is more accurately characterized as the introjects of the unspoken parental patterns and expectations, and the core of type II impasses.

The subsymbolic mode includes affective, sensory, somatic, and motoric modes of mental processing, which are not experienced in language, though may be brought into language to some degree. As described by Bucci, subsymbolic processing is:

> experientially immediate and familiar to us in the actions and decisions of everyday life—from aiming a piece of paper at a wastebasket or entering a line of moving traffic, to feeling that the rain is coming, knowing when the pasta is *almost* done and must be drained to be "al dente," and responding to facial expressions or gestures. Subsymbolic processing accounts for highly developed skills in athletics and the arts and sciences and is central to knowledge of one's body and to emotional experience.
>
> While subsymbolic functions maybe highly developed and organized and may occur within attentional focus, the special nature of the computation is such that it cannot be expressed fully in words.
>
> We should emphasize that the prefix "sub" here denotes the subsymbolic as *underlying* symbolic representation, not as an inferior or primitive mode.
>
> (2001, p. 48)

Bucci draws upon the writing of Bollas to illustrate the emergence of subsymbolic processing in the therapist's process of discovery and understanding within the therapeutic work. She quotes Bollas' self-description, "I know I am in the process of experiencing something, but I do not as yet know what it is, and I may have to sustain this not knowing for quite some time" (1987, p. 203), and uses his now-famous phrase, the "unthought known," to illustrate subsymbolic processing. She goes on to distinguish subsymbolic knowing from the standard conceptualizations of the unconscious:

> This experience occurs on a level that has been characterized as unconscious; the analyst knows, however, that he is "in the process of experiencing something"; the state that Bollas describes is not unconscious but involves consciousness—knowing *and* thinking—of a specific sort.
>
> (2007, p. 58)

From the perspective of script theory, I see the subsymbolic modes being the dominant form of organization and processing for type III impasses and what Berne considered the underlying somatic/relational protocol out of which script evolves.

While thinking about the therapeutic process from a psychoanalytic perspective, Bucci challenges certain aspects of psychoanalytic (and, without knowing it, transactional analysis as well) biases:

> Whereas Freud's deep and generative insight concerning the multiplicity of the human psychical apparatus remains valid, the psychoanalytic premise of lower or more primitive systems—unconscious, nonverbal, irrational—being replaced by more advanced ones needs to be revised in the light of current scientific knowledge. We now recognize that diverse and complex systems exist, function, and develop side by side, within and outside of awareness, in mature, well-functioning adults throughout life. ... The goal of treatment is better formulated as the integration, or reintegration, of systems where this has been impaired, rather than as replacement of one system by another.
>
> (2007, p. 53)

The access to, and interaction of, all three modes (which Bucci calls the referential process) is essential to psychological health and functioning. From Bucci's perspective, it is the interference or dissociations within the referential process that underlie psychopathology, and the goal of psychotherapy and psychoanalysis is to re-establish and strengthen the referential capacities among these three modes of experience and expression. When our childhood and developmental environments (and I would include here our adult life environments as well) are reasonably predictable, relevant, and responsive, these three domains of experience are more likely to remain accessible to one another, open to new stimuli, and fluid in response to the environment and within the intrapsychic referential process.

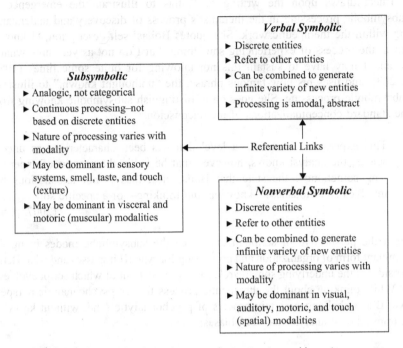

Figure 8.1 Bucci's model of the three domains of experiencing and knowing

There is an uncanny mirroring of fundamental aspects of transactional analysis theory in Bucci's model. I see here the three levels of games and script described by Berne: social/verbal symbolic; psychological/nonverbal symbolic; and "tissue" or somatic/subsymbolic. I see the three types or levels of impasse. It is important to recognize that no one mode of experience/organization is seen as "healthier" than the others; one is not privileged over the others—though they often are in theoretical models and clinical practice. All three modes are valid, essential, and lifelong means of experiencing, learning, and organizing. Health has to do with the capacity to utilize all three modes, to shift among them consciously and unconsciously, so that each can inform the other; this is what Bucci calls the referential process. Therapy can be understood as a process to facilitate and reinforce an openness and awareness of all three modes. Bucci further elaborates a model of emotion schemas (2007, pp. 57–61) quite consistent with those described in the recent transactional analysis literature (Hine, 1997; Allen, 2000, 2001; Gildebrand, 2003).

The beauty of Bucci's work for me is that it is independent of any particular theoretical frame of reference, as she sees this process being carried out (though not always intentionally) in a variety of therapeutic modalities. I have found it enormously clarifying in my thinking about both transactional analysis and body-centered psychotherapy, as well as the blind spots and limits of psychoanalytic thinking and technique.

While there is an obvious kinship between subsymbolic realms and those levels of experience now described in terms of implicit/procedural memory and knowledge, there is an important corrective balance in Bucci's conceptualization of the subsymbolic and its centrality in human experience. In the clinical field, the model of implicit memory is best known and most often applied within the context of mother–infant research and the notion of implicit *relational* knowing (Lyons-Ruth, 1998). Bucci's model offers a vital correction in noting that not all subsymbolic or implicit knowing is relational and relationally based. The subsymbolic also includes vast arenas of somatic and self-learning, organization, and expression that are not interpersonal but fundamentally intrapsychic and sensorimotoric (Cornell, 2007). The subsymbolic shapes, experientially and often unconsciously, explicit memory and the verbal symbolic. It is the sensori-somatic container within which much of our symbolic and verbal capacities develop. Alan Fogel (2004), a developmental researcher and theorist, offers a succinct synthesis of perspectives on implicit memory:

> Implicit memory is primarily *regulatory*, automatized, and unconscious (Bargh & Chartrand, 1999). Implicit memories do most of the work of mediating between perception and action, as when stimuli are unconsciously evaluated, approached or avoided. Implicit memories are operating all the time and account for the organization and regulation of most of our adaptive behavior.
>
> (p. 207, italics in original)

> Regulatory implicit memories, then, seem to be composites of repeated early experiences rather than accurate records of single incidents (Epstein, 1991; Stern, 1985). These generalizations create an unconscious predisposition to act or feel in particular ways in particular situations. ... They are unconscious and, under ordinary conditions, unable to be explicitly accessed.
>
> (p. 209)

Psychotherapy and psychoanalysis are, of course, interpersonal processes designed to enhance both self-cohesion and interpersonal capacities. Fogel has expanded the concepts of implicit and explicit memory to include that which he calls "participatory memory," a concept I see as very relevant to our thinking about script, script protocol, and the case material I present in this chapter. Fogel suggests, "there is a third type of memory, participatory memory, that forms a bridge between implicit (unconscious) and explicit (conscious) experience and may be one of the primary pathways for integrating infancy experiences into the autobiographical self" (p. 207). He argues further:

Participatory memories are lived reenactments of personally significant experiences that have not yet become organized into a verbal or conceptual narrative.... When experiencing a participatory memory, one is not thinking about the past. One is directly involved in a past as if it were occurring in the present.

(pp. 209–210, italics in original)

When I wrote earlier in this book of Jim McLaughlin's confronting me by saying "the closer something is to your heart, the quieter you become," he was describing this level of memory, known at some level and at the same time unknown and not understood—an essential element in my script protocol. When I took Jim's comment to my analyst, it gradually became clear that I had, as a very young child, kept much of my love and enthusiasm quiet, profoundly so, as I was living with parents and grandparents who were endlessly sad and depressed. I loved them, needed them, and to be too happy, too exuberant, too visible, seemed like a sin. What Jim observed and commented on so succinctly was my script protocol, participatory memory, in action. My theoretical wonderings are not separate from my personal questions, one often compelling and informing the other:

Protocol is not a set of adaptive or defensive decisions like a script. It is not remembered in a narrative fashion but felt/lived in the immediacy of one's body. Protocol is the literal embodiment of the repetitive, often affectively intense, patterns of relatedness preceding the infant's capacity of ego function.

(Cornell & Landaiche, 2006, p. 204)

And now we can return to the case.

Case discussion: Script protocol in action

Thirty years later, verbally and nonverbally, Emily's mother is still communicating the same, affect-laden messages to her daughter and her daughter's body. As I reviewed my notes in preparation for writing this chapter, I asked myself what it was about this single consultation that came to mind as I imagined the issues I wished to address in this chapter. Why did this particular session stay in my mind in such a compelling fashion? I realized that there was something very moving in the stark contrast between the closeness of Lara and Emily and their dedication to her wellbeing and the malignant, incessant intrusion of Emily's mother, both unconsciously in Emily's being and in her actual, present-day interactions with her mother. I thought of the passage that I've used as the epigraph from Bollas to this section. Whose body is Emily actually experiencing? Who is in treatment, Emily, her mother, her maternal grandfather, the dyad of Emily and Lara, perhaps all of them? As I thought about my own therapy, pressing against the silences around my heart, whose hearts were being experienced? I think now of a young man, about to be married and hoping soon to become a father, who recently came to me for therapy. The son (product, he might say) of a brutal, certainly narcissistic, if not psychotic, father, he said to me with breathtaking clarity in the first session, "I spent my life defying the father's will. Now I'm about to be married, I want to be a father myself, and all I can find is my father's mind in my mind. I feel like I am in his body. I have to have my own mind before I get married. I'm scared, and I don't understand this." At the tissue level of script, script protocol, unconscious enactment, participatory memory—framing it as you will—there is no clear distinction of self and other, mind and body.

In working with Emily and Lara, in keeping with work at the level of script protocol, I did not base my interventions on behavior change, behavioral permissions, support, cognitive interpretation, or empathic interventions. My interventions were fundamentally somatic and experiential, sensing and feeling our conversation and the eyes of others in her body, the subsymbolic. Her experience was first expressed in sensation and movement, within the subsymbolic. In my mind were notions of hysterical Rolfings, enigmatic signifiers, maternal narcissistic possession. These notions helped open my body to Emily's bodily struggles and to find a way to bring that struggle alive in the room within her body and among the three of us, in what Fogel would call a participatory memory.

The focus in my first consultation with Lara and Emily was at a somatic level, working directly with her eyes. The work was quite useful and self-sustaining until strained and ultimately overwhelmed by the deepening erotic intimacy with her boyfriend (my interpretation) and the encounters with her mother and grandfather. Emily could not sustain her ownership of her body. As we all do so often, Lara sought to relieve Emily's suffering, and I think we have all experienced the limits of those interventions. When the impasse is rooted at the "tissue" level, client and therapist must typically enter the suffering, live it together, to experience an understanding in the mode in which the problem is being held and enacted. Emily captured this level of reality when she said, "I know it isn't true, but that is how it feels, and it feels entirely real."

When Emily said, "My body is unhappy," initially hearing this statement as a script belief, I redefined what she meant by saying "*You* are unhappy with your body." But Emily meant what she said in the way she said it—this was a description of experience at the level of protocol (the subsymbolic). I realized then that a different level of intervention and involvement would be needed. I slowed myself down, shifting my attention into myself, noticing the ideas, fantasies, images, body sensations that came up for me as I stayed with this statement, "My body is unhappy." Bits and pieces of things I've read came to mind, as did a few of my own clients. The phrase "the weight of the gaze" kept floating through my mind. I began to feel a continuity of the previous year's session with what was happening now, that is, a shift from Emily's experience of her own eyes, to the impact of the eyes of others, real and imagined. As I often do, I was trying to experience in my own body what Emily was describing in hers, and I began to sense a place to start, the sense of being *weighted down*.

We shifted to the subsymbolic level of experience as I asked Emily to bring our conversation into, to *feel* our conversation in, her body, I was, in essence, inviting her to think *with and through* her body, rather than think *about* it. This was a grounding in the subsymbolic, a grounding for an evolving referential process of connecting to other modes of experience. "*Show me the crushing*" is a very different intervention to "tell me about...," anchoring the work in her body and body movement. We reached an understanding in her body, through her somatic experience, rather than through her (or my) cognition.

Emily's spontaneous rush of words against her mother and her physical move toward Lara, unleashed by the expression of aggression in her body, began the shift from the sensate/somatic subsymbolic experience to that of the nonverbal symbolic and then to the verbal symbolic. She was then able to spontaneously include me in the dialogue with Lara, and the three of us could begin to reflect on the meaning of what had happened and to look to the future. It is a testimony to the quality of the work and the level of trust between Emily and Lara that we were able to cover so much ground in a single session. It is probably no coincidence that the presence of a third, especially a male, helped to open the physical, sexual space between Emily and Lara for action and exploration (but that is probably the topic of another paper). Emily will need, repeatedly, to bring her body physically (subsymbolically) to her boyfriend and Lara; so, too, she will need to bring her body experience verbally (symbolically) to those who can support *and delight* in her separation from her mother and reclamation of her body and sexuality.

At the level of protocol, it is extremely hard to tell who is having what experience, to whom this feeling or fantasy belongs. In this terrain, I have learned the most from the writings of André Green (1986), Bollas (1999, 2000), Jean Laplanche (1995, 1997, 1999), McLaughlin (2005), and Ruth Stein (1998a, 1998b, 2007). It was the work of these authors that came to my mind when Emily insisted that it was her *body*, not her, that was unhappy with *its* weight. It was the work of these authors that helped me comprehend the impregnation of Emily's body by that of her mother. Stein (2007) summarizes a central point of Laplanche's perspective, that of the enigmatic signifier:

> The enigmatic signifier... is a perplexing and impenetrable communication that is overloaded with significance, not only for the child who is its receiver, but for the adult who is transmitting it as well. .... These messages introduce themselves into the infant's world through the most innocent and mundane gestures.... Such messages implant themselves as foreign bodies, haunting questions, in the child's psyche.
>
> (pp. 179–180)

Obvously, the Laplanchian notion of a mother who normatively and regularly mystifies her child is quite different from the view on which the mother co-constructs a mutual choreography with it. Mother's "idiom" (Bollas, 1997), her unique style and personal approach to herself and her infant, is assumed by Laplanche to be experienced as that of a beckoning, meaning-dispatching, yet profoundly alien and dispossessed caretaker. Such a picture is far from a "harmonious mix-up" (Balint) or attunement-disruption-attunement moments (Stern).

(p. 182)

We might think of Emily's therapy and her relationship with Lara as being a fundamental reclamation project, extracting her body and sexuality from that of her mother.

In conclusion

In preparing for this chapter, I thought about Emily, my own therapy, the young man who came for treatment, and others. How does it happen that, sometimes, one's heart, one's mind, one's body, one's sexuality is not one's own? There are, to be sure, important things to be learned from the infant–parent research, attachment theorists, models of implicit/procedural memory. These are avenues of study that have fundamentally altered our understanding of our work. And yet, in my experience at least, there is something more irrational, more compelling, more anguished at the foundation of the human psyche, at what we in transactional analysis would most likely call the level of script protocol. There is something essential within the realms of the sexual, erotic, unconscious experience that is absent in theoretical models based in systems of memory and patterns of attachment. These models, while informative, are a bit too far removed clinically from the disturbances that we often live within our intimate relations and self-conflicts. It is no accident that the level of protocol, participatory memory, and enactment emerge often during periods of the most intense personal growth, the most intimate stages of psychotherapy, or the deepening of our intimate relations.

I have often remarked that it was an aspect of Berne's genius that he conceived a therapeutic system that could be applied in many realms of therapy, counseling, education, and living, sufficiently flexible to utilize cognitive, behavioral, and interpersonal interventions. His is a system that continues to test itself, to evolve, and extend its reach of efficacy. Work at the somatic level has been an enduring interest of mine. Work at the somatic level significantly extends our efficacy in working with these nonverbal, foundational levels of psychic organization. It is my hope that the presentation and discussion of this single session will illustrate the meaning of subsymbolic organization and ways of thinking about and working with the somatic realms of script protocol.

Chapter 9

Aspiration or adaptation?: An unresolved tension in Eric Berne's basic beliefs

Eric Berne was at his most creative during the last decade of his life, as he sought to break free of his psychoanalytic roots and write in his own singular and provocative voice. Any close reading of his writings reveals a creativity marked by brilliance, bravado, defiance, and internal conflict. Berne's major writings all took place during the ascendance of the humanistic tradition in American psychology and psychotherapy (Anderson, 1983; Bugental, 1967; Rogers & Stevens, 1967), an emerging tradition that infused Berne's thinking and challenged the dominant psychoanalytic ethic of the time. This chapter will focus on a particular aspect of an ongoing and, I would suggest, unresolved conflict in his life's work, which I will summarize here as unresolved tension between the psychological power of aspiration versus adaptation, or growth versus survival. While Berne's untimely death cut short his work and prevented its continued unfolding, my reading of portions of *What Do You Say after You Say Hello?: The Psychology of Human Destiny* (1972) suggests that he had begun a reassessment of his work, with his concept of "aspiration" central to his evolving thinking. This chapter will focus on Berne's notion of aspiration and related pro-growth concepts in his theories and the implications of these ideas for our work as transactional analysts.

Pro-growth concepts in Berne's writings

Berne's conceptualizations of *physis*, the human hungers, and aspiration form the core of what I see as his recognition of essential factors in human nature that propel one toward growth and vitality, inherently containing the capacity to challenge the forces of acquiescence, life script, and social adaptation.

Even before his development of transactional analysis as an independent theory, Berne had introduced the concept of *physis*, attributed to the Semite philosopher Zeno, which was defined as "the force of Nature, which eternally strives to make things grow and to make growing things more perfect" (1947, p. 68). He introduces this idea in his first book, written while still identified as a psychoanalyst. He mentions it in the context of the debate between the Freudian concepts of libido [or life instinct] and the Kleinian theory of the death instinct (pp. 69–70). Even here, he is ambivalent:

Perhaps Physis does not exist at all, but in spite of our inability to be definite about this subject, there are so many things which happen *as if* there were such a force, that it is easier to understand human beings if we suppose that it does exist.

(p. 68, italics in original)

In spite of his ambivalence, this is a term he returns to repeatedly in the pages of his 1947 *Mind in Action* and retains in his later edition, *A Laymen's Guide to Psychiatry and Psychoanalysis* (1968), published then with several chapters on transactional analysis. Even in the 1968 edition, while there is evidence of his sexual naivety and stereotyping when he writes that "*physis* directs him toward vaginal sexual intercourse as his preferred aim" (p. 226) and that "homosexuality nearly always means a thwarted *physis* and a troubled superego" (p. 228), Berne is applying the concept of *physis* as a kind of positive life force. Although most would now firmly disagree with these particular applications of the term, Berne does seek to describe a sense of this force of nature, defining *physis* in the 1968 glossary as:

The growth force of nature, which makes organisms evolve into higher forms, embryos develop into adults, sick people get better, and healthy people strive to attain their ideals. Possibly it is only one aspect of inwardly directed libido, but it may be more a basic force than libido itself.

(1968, pp. 369–370)

He returns to the concept of *physis* in *The Structure and Dynamics of Organizations and Groups* (1963) and in *Hello* (1972).

In *Games People Play* (1964), Berne does not refer directly to *physis*, but in the midst of his discussion of defensive motivations, he does say, "But there is something beyond all this—some force which drives people to grow, progress, and do better" (p. 88). In *Principles of Group Treatment* (1966), he does not use the term *physis*, but there is again a very similar attitude conveyed in his description of the therapeutic attitude:

The therapist does not cure anyone, he only treats him to the best of his ability, being careful not to injure and waiting for nature to take its healing course. ... When the patient recovers, the therapist should be able to say, "My treatment helped nature," and not "My love overcame it"—a statement which should be reserved for the patient's intimates.

(p. 63)

Principles of Group Treatment contains what is probably Berne's most thorough exposition of his beliefs and values about the therapeutic attitude. Berne's attitude here echoes his definition of *physis*, which is seen as a force of nature seeking greater health.

Berne did little to develop this idea or hold it center stage in such a way that it became incorporated as part of the transactional analysis canon of theory. Little has been said about *physis* by subsequent authors, although Clarkson (1992a, b) and Cornell and Landaiche (2008) have highlighted it, with Clarkson commenting that "the importance of *Physis* as a generalized creative drive towards health is only equaled by its neglect in the theoretical literature since Berne" (1992a, p. 12). Building on Cornell's 1988 critique of script theory and his emphasis on the meaning-making functions of script, Clarkson argues that in Berne's conceptualization of *physis*, "It is precisely this emphatic insistence on cure, progress, and evolution that differentiates transactional analysis from its psychoanalytic cousins" (1992b, p. 204). In Berne's thinking, *physis* does not seem to be so much an unconscious force as an impersonal, biological force of nature that takes a great deal of inhibition and obstruction to thwart.

Turning our attention to Berne's conceptualizations of the human hungers and aspiration, we witness his efforts to describe more personal, individual forces that propel people toward the world and richer and, perhaps, more intimate lives.

Berne's ideas about human "hungers" (1972, p. 21), which may be understood as his effort to humanize Freudian drive theory, recur in most of his books (Berne, 1961, 1963, 1966, 1972). The hungers are seen as elements in people's need to structure their time: stimulation, recognition, and structure hunger. To summarize in his words:

> The first is *stimulus* or *sensation hunger*. Far from trying to avoid stimulating situations, as some people have claimed, most organisms, including human beings, seek them out. ... The second drive is *recognition hunger*, the quest for special kinds of sensations which can only be supplied by another human being, or in some cases, by other animals. The third hunger is *structure hunger*, which is why groups tend to group into organizations, and why time-structures are among the most sought after and the most highly rewarded members of any society.
>
> (1972, p. 21, emphasis in the original)

In *Principles of Group Treatment*, Berne links recognition hunger to the theory of strokes and structure hunger to the derivative "leadership hunger" (1966, p. 239). Berne's ambivalence about the fundamentals of human nature is again apparent in his writings on the hungers. On the one hand, he suggests that "only a relatively small proportion of people are able to structure their time independently" (1963, p. 216) and argues, "People are willing to pay almost any price to have their time structured for them, since few people are capable of structuring their own time autonomously for very long" (1966, p. 230). He links the structuring and satisfaction of the hungers to central, psychological functions of game and script formation.

On the other hand, there is the sense of possibility in Berne's descriptions of human hunger of a compelling longing for novel experience and intimacy. There is the possibility of growth beyond oneself toward others and the world at large. Attention to the human hungers in human relations work carries with it the potential of recognizing and seeking more fulfillment of one's fantasies and desires.

Berne's third concept, that of "aspiration" (1972, pp. 128–132), emerges only in his last book and is rich in implication and possibility. In this book, which proved tragically to be his last, he begins to wrestle with questions of destiny, the nature of script, the possibilities of change and its limits, and his own theories. It conveys some of the qualities of Freud's classic paper, "Analysis terminable and interminable" (1937), in which Freud, nearing the end of his life, reflects on the efficacy of psychoanalysis and the limits of psychological change. I cannot read *Hello* without wondering how its content was affected by Berne's declining health. In the chapter on how script is possible, much of which is pessimistic to nearly cynical in tone, Berne writes in a startlingly poignant voice about the possibility of a "real person," drawing on the image of the piano being played by the music roll rather than the person, who is merely pantomiming a musician:

> As for myself, I know not whether I am still run by a music roll or not.... Certainly I know there are large areas where I am free to improvise. It may even be that I am one of the few fortunate people on earth who has cast off the shackles entirely and calls his own tune. In that case I am a brave improviser facing the world alone. But whether I am faking on the player piano, or striking the chords with the power of my own mind and hands, the song of my life is equally suspenseful and full of surprises as it rolls off the pulsating sound board of destiny—a barcarole that either way will leave, I hope, happy echoes behind.
> (1972, pp. 276–277)

Berne does not elaborate why it is that he imagines that if someone has thrown off the shackles of script to become a brave improviser, he then faces the world alone. Captured in that statement seems to be his persistent belief and perception that the vast majority of people must compromise and adapt in order to ensure survival and belonging, seeming to suggest that there is something fundamentally dangerous about autonomy. In his discussions of group theory, he repeatedly maintains that the primary function of a group is to maintain its own survival (e. g., 1963, p. 90), thereby ensuring the survival of its individual members. But I also wonder if in that passage Berne might be reflecting an observation from his therapeutic practice, that is, that those who stay relatively free of script-creating forces and who significantly break out of script are by nature or choice more willing to be loners, to choose a certain degree of solitude as the price of autonomy.

Earlier in *Hello*, in the chapter on the script apparatus, there is a startling contrast to the piano roll imagery in the brief section on aspiration (pp. 128–131). Here, Berne writes in nearly poetic language:

> Caught in the mesh of his script apparatus, Jeder meanwhile has his own autonomous aspirations. These usually appear to him in daydreams in his

leisure hours, or in hypnagogic hallucinations before he falls asleep.... All men and all women have their secret gardens, whose gates they guard against the profane invasion of the vulgar crowd. These are visual pictures of what they would do if they could do as they pleased. The lucky ones find the right time, place, and person, and get to do it, while the rest must wander wistfully outside their own walls. And that is what this book is about: what happens outside those walls, the external transactions that parch or water the flowers within.

(1972, p. 130)

The *Hello* volume is, rather sadly, much more about the forces that parch than those that water, and I cannot help but imagine that his next book might have been one about watering those secret gardens, so they need not be so secret and might flourish in the light of day and the eyes of others. Berne describes a range of possible mechanisms that can provide some release or relief from the coercive forces of one's script: The demon, permission, an internal release, an external release, the anti-script, stressing "even winners are programmed, too" (p. 131). These mechanisms, while freeing to some extent, Berne defined as within the script apparatus. Intimacy and autonomy seem more of a passing fancy or fleeting possibility than a normal or reasonably common condition of life and love.

With aspiration, however, Berne suggests something different—more robust and resilient. In a modification of the script matrix, he diagrams aspiration as an arrow rooted in the Child ego state, forcing its way upward, piercing through Adult and Parent with the statement, "I want it my own way" (p. 128). He says, "The object of script analysis is to free Jeder and Zoe so that they can open the garden of aspirations to the world" (p. 131). In these four short pages, Berne suggests a great deal about the nature of aspirations and how we might recognize and support them in our work with clients and groups. Aspirations are experienced within the realms of fantasies, images, and dreams. I have quoted Berne here at some length because I see something rather unusual for Berne is these segments, an urgency and sense of personal passion quite different from his more typical tone of wit edged with cynicism.

What does this mean for how we look, listen, and relate to our clients to recognize and enhance the capacity for aspiration? Before taking up this question in terms of attitude and technique, I want first to turn to the clinical, educational, and organizational implications of studies of resilient children.

Lessons in resilience

A rich literature has been evolving over the past forty years based in studies of children and adults who have defied the odds of deeply disturbed childhood circumstances or other challenging life experiences (Coles, 1964, 1986a, 1986b;

Vaillant, 1977; Chess & Thomas, 1984; Anthony & Cohler, 1987; Dugan & Coles, 1989). Anthony (1974a, 1974b, 1978, 1983, 1987), an early researcher in studies of children who defy the odds of stressful and traumatic life circumstances, contrasts the vulnerable and resilient individuals in this way:

> Following a traumatic exposure, hypervulnerable individuals move not toward spontaneous recovery, but toward the development of lasting defects of the personality, such as an impoverishment of ego functions, a diminished interest in the external world, and a readiness to withdraw from contact with reality, all summarized in the picture of a general restriction of the personality.
>
> (1987, p. 9)

Here, Anthony is describing what Berne would most certainly have characterized as a "hamartic script" (1972, p. 447). Anthony's description of the resilient individual echoes more of what is evoked in Berne's notion of aspiration or a self-liberated pianist:

> In contrast, there may be others who respond to stress by maintaining a confident control over the environment, remaining hopeful and helpful in distressing situations, and by taking responsibility for what occurs to them. In some studies, the internal locus of control expectancy has been equated with competence, coping ability, and *relative invulnerability* to debilitating effects of stressful events (Campbell, Converse, & Rodgers, 1976).
>
> (1987, p. 7, emphasis in original)

Anthony describes the evolution of ideas about the nature of psychological "invulnerability," later to be more accurately characterized as resilience, and the coming together of research in medical and child development fields.

The medical strand came from studies of individuals with coronary heart disease, comparing those who were more debilitated by the disease to those who remained comparatively healthy and lively (Hinkle, 1972, 1974). The researchers described patterns that they named psychoimmunity with individuals who were self-determined to a point of an "almost sociopathic flavor" (p. 5). Anthony goes on to characterize "this detachment, this defensive distancing, [which] insulates him from all disturbing psychosocial impingements from the environment" (p. 8).

Anthony then draws upon the research in child development based on ego resilience and the mechanisms of defense (Hartman, 1950; Kroeber, 1963; Redl, 1969; Murphy & Moriarty, 1976), which elaborates Anna Freud's model of the ego and the mechanisms of defense (1936). Freud, of course, emphasized the function of ego defenses in the context of managing intrapsychic conflict. In the 1950s and 1960s in the United Kingdom, Bowlby and Winnicott were stressing the development of the child within the context of actual interactions with the parents. In the United States during that period of time, Murphy (1956, 1962), among others, was also reframing the child's development of defenses and coping strategies with relation to external circumstances and actual parents. This, of course, was one of the main arenas of Berne's departure from and challenge to the ego psychology brand of the psychoanalysis of his day. Script theory is fundamentally based on the child's reactions with and decisions in the face of real-world interactions. I can find no evidence in Berne's references of his familiarity with Murphy, Redl, Anthony, Chess and Thomas, or other developmentalists of his time, but his conclusions coming from his clinical observations mirror the questions and theories that were emerging from a developmental perspective. One would think that Berne would have been influenced by Erikson (1959, 1975), who was certainly deeply interested in the child's relationship to the external world, but perhaps the souring of their personal analytic relationship resulted in Berne's giving little acknowledgment to Erikson.

The resilience research certainly indicates that healthy, responsive parent–child relationships provide a resilient (secure) base for the meeting and management of life's later stresses and assaults. However, many of us are not so fortunate. Even among the fortunate, Anthony suggests that resilience is not an inevitable outcome:

> The "mother's undisputed darling" can succumb to chronic setbacks in a world that is indifferent to mothering him.... On the other hand, the "ugly duckling" ... may become "immunized" by the early challenges and be gradually changed not only into an attractive swan, but a highly robust one.
>
> (1987, p. 36)

There is always an interaction of internal (intrapsychic) traits and external factors that support resilience. Mazzetti (2008), in his clinical work with immigrant refugees and traumatized populations, describes the duality of individual and social factors influencing the vulnerability or resilience of immigrants. Given the intense needs and limited resources of refugees, Mazzetti stresses the establishment of active intervention strategies (pp. 297–300) that stabilize life and increase the opportunities for a more resilient second chance. What is of particular interest here, however, in this exploration of Berne's concept of aspiration, are those individuals who have what would be seen from the outside as a profoundly and chronically disturbed base of early parental relations and environmental factors, but still create a thriving life.

Several personality characteristics and social patterns emerge repeatedly in the studies of resilient children. One factor often evident in these studies is that these are children who find a way to stand, at least in part, outside of the family dynamics and beliefs. We could say that they do not introject the family beliefs but construct a Parent ego state largely out of their own perceptions and experiences from other sources. Another key factor in resilience, very much related to the capacity to stand outside the family's frame of reference, is the determination to *move* outside the nuclear family so as to find and maintain an attachment figure—most often a teacher, minister, an aunt, an uncle, a neighbor, a grandparent. This person is able to take the child out into the world, to indicate a different world, to offer a different kind of relationship. Dugan (1989), writing about variables in the establishment of resilience during adolescence, describes an aggressive determination to seek a substitute care-taker, so as "rather than being someone 'who has been neglected,' he is 'someone who has been found'" (p. 165). Dugan stresses the "appeal of an extrafamilial social role" that provides "a sense of himself amongst peers, and a look to the outside for affiliation, involvement, and affective connection" (p. 161).

Another aspect of the research in resilient children is that these are children who get attached to some form of work, a project, an interest outside of the family, which provides a crucial sense of identity and mastery. Significantly, this interest does not necessarily involve other people, but it is an investment in something in the world that is engaging and important to the child. It provides meaning, a sense of personal agency and competence. The importance of work is that it also provides a kind of protection from the trauma, the chaos, of the family system (Vaillant & Vaillant, 1981; Good, 1992). Chess writes that her many years of work with marginalized but resilient children has led her to "a stronger belief in the power of reinforcement of work dedication," such that there is "a high virtue in distancing from noxious familial onslaughts and underminings, in leaving behind irreconcilable conflicts, and in substituting alternative constructive, social involvements which have the power to protect and to provide a second—or even a third—chance" (1989, p. 198).

Reading this research and case studies, I would say that these are children who have maintained the right and capacity to *dream*. They have the sense that life, their lives, *mean* something—or *should* mean something. Often, this sense of life has been communicated or modeled by an adult outside the nuclear family. Sometimes this is discovered through reading, in movies or television, or religious teachings.

There is another factor common to resilient children, which is that, as adults, they often have problems with intimacy. Dependency and attachment are less desired and often threatening, as resilient characters tend to be better at autonomy than at intimacy or dependency. This autonomy can be quite brittle. Here, we see a particular task in our work with people to be able to support an individual's intelligence, initiative, interests, work, while providing an environment in which it gradually becomes safe to invest in another person. We can provide the experience of being a reliable other in their lives.

Cornell (2009), drawing on his earlier work (1988), provides a compelling portrait of one man who defied the odds of his chaotic upbringing in Soweto, South Africa. This portrait is consistent with many of the elements that emerge in the literature on resilience. English (2008) tells her personal story of her recovery from life-threatening burns and dependency on pain-killing drugs, linking it to her ideas of the "vital impetus" of human nature, compelling people unconsciously toward more life. Although she does not reference Berne, her ideas certainly echo his of *physis* and aspiration. Similarly, Landaiche (2009), in his examination of social pain and shame dynamics in human relations, stresses the need for courage:

> Courage is not a function of professional direction, challenge, or pressure. Nor is it a process of toughing things out. The choice must be made from the individual's determination to reverse a pattern of withdrawing or rejecting. Courage is strength that comes from personal conviction—an innate resource, albeit rarely one as instinctive as our capacities for rejecting and social pain. Our courage must often be willed into life.
>
> (p. 237)

These words capture the dynamic tension within Berne's writings of the forces of script and aspiration. We cannot say that resilient individuals are "script free," but I think we see in these patterns something fundamentally akin to the process Berne is trying to convey in his concepts of *physis*, the human hungers, and aspiration, which is the capacity in some to defy the predictable (hamartic scripts) and maintain a robust sense of self and life's purpose.

Aspiration and resilience: Berne's aspiration in action

What are the implications for these ideas in our work as transactional analysts? In our work as educators, consultants, trainers, counselors, and educators, how might we actualize these concepts in practice so as to identify and support one's aspirational forces? I see several key areas of attention: 1) value autonomy as well as relatedness; 2) actively attend to the dialectic tensions within the script; 3) listen for conscious and unconscious fantasies; and 4) work with the enlivening transference and countertransference dynamics. These are not distinct categories or sets of techniques, but more intertwined and intertwining attitudes and processes.

The place of autonomy

We are in period of a relational Zeitgeist: attachment, mother–infant, empathic, relational, and co-creational models seem to dominate the contemporary theoretical landscape. These models can create the impression that we always learn, or learn and change best, in the presence of another. With the iconic image of the secure base, some seem to suggest that we have the responsibility to provide an atmosphere of safety and understanding to ensure growth. This was not exactly Berne's cup of tea, nor is it a reality supported by the developmental literature. In this era of the "*we-go*" (Emde, 2009) and mirror neurons (Gallese, 2009), there is still an ego, and there is an aspect of the solitary implicit in Berne's description of aspiration. Children learn and grow under threatening life circumstances, as well as comforting ones, reflected in Berne's idea of aspiration. Infants, children, and adults spend enormous amounts of time *alone* and still learning. There is a particular kind of learning and satisfaction that comes from being alone and being in the world on one's own, a particular sense of mastery, which is captured in Berne's valuing of autonomy.

I recall the many times one or another of my children told me to leave them alone so that they could do something on their own. Children thrive in the privacy of their own rooms and minds as much as at a parent's knee or the family dinner table.

Pink (2009) offers a compelling argument, presented in the context of motivational theories for businesses, for the fundamental need for aloneness and autonomous exploration. Drawing on long ignored research by Harlow (1950, 1953) and Deci (1972, 2008), among others, Pink argues, "According to a cluster of recent behavioral science studies, autonomous motivation promotes greater conceptual understanding, better grades, enhanced persistence at school and in sporting activities, higher productivity, less burnout, and greater levels of psychological well-being" (pp. 90–91). Pink's stories and examples illustrate what I think Berne sought to convey in his ideas of aspiration and autonomy. Aspirational forces often have the effect of taking one *away* from others and *toward* one's self—one's own capacities and desires, regardless of how they may or may not be welcomed by others. This is the quality of attachment seen in resilient children to activities, projects, and work.

Pink describes primarily conscious experiences of autonomous motivation and exploration. Another layer, one that I think Berne hints at without using the word "unconscious," is fundamentally unconscious in nature. It is in this terrain that Bollas (1992), in his descriptions of the development and experience of self, emphasizes that "certain objects, like psychic 'keys,' open the doors to unconsciously intense—and rich—experience in which we articulate the self" (p. 17), forming the basis for what he terms "psychic genera" (pp. 66–100). The objects to which Bollas refers are not only people, but an entire range of life experiences that a person seeks to nourish self-discovery and psychological aliveness.

What I am suggesting here is that if we are to support aspiration and resilience in our clients and working groups, we need to create zones of aloneness, of being on one's own, of getting out of our clients' way at times—to be willing to step aside or away, in addition to toward and in; as one of my young sons grew so fond of saying, "Dad, would you please let me do it myself?!" Respect and support for work and private effort are essential.

The dialectic tensions inherent in script

Script theory in transactional analysis, especially as conveyed in such ideas as the script matrix and injunctions, can be profoundly reductionist and predictive. How many times have I heard trainees or clients say, "I have a 'don't be' script"; "I'm in my 'Be Perfect' driver"; "I'm in a 'Hurry Up'"; "I have a 'don't feel' injunction"; and so on. Such language and styles of intervention reinforce (consciously or unconsciously) the power of adaptation with a singular focus.

Awareness of the desires of what Berne referred to as *physis*, the hungers, or aspiration may emerge through attention to the dynamic tensions within the script, so as to enter the "secret gardens" that Berne suggests contains our aspirations. We do not discover a sense of aspiration through diagnostic slogans or diagrams but through imagination, dreams, and daydreams, in as Berne put it, the "almost infinite amount of dialogue he has stored in the dim-lit caverns of his mind" (1972, p. 130). Berne continues, "There are complete answers to questions he never even dreamed of. But if the right button is pushed, sometimes they pour out in sheer poetry" (p. 130).

We often stress the importance of permissions, confrontations, and other external interventions offered by the therapist, consultant, or counselor. These are important. But here Berne seems to be pointing to something else, giving attention to the dissonant voices and desires submerged within the Child ego state, often held out of awareness, silenced by the dominant voices of script. Here, Berne speaks to the liberating forces waiting within the individual's psyche, available to challenge the demands of script and adaptation. In a similar fashion, Bollas (1989), with his concept of one's "personal idiom" (pp. 33–34), argues passionately that people are driven to fulfill their "inner idiom through familial, social, cultural, and intellectual objects" (p. 34); I think it is important to note here the range of fields of experience that Bollas recognizes as essential fields of self-expression—the interpersonal being but one. For Bollas, the therapeutic process, "becomes a procedure for the establishment and elaboration of one's idiom rather than simply the deconstruction of material or the analytic mapping of mental processes and the fate of internal objects" (p. 35). Very much in keeping with Berne's spirit of aspiration and *physis*, Bollas notes, "If we can say of most people that they have memories, so too they have futures" (p. 41). Here we have the dialectic tension between the forces of past and future. We need to demonstrate as much interest in our clients' futures as in their histories.

The centrality of fantasy

I find that no matter how strong the script, there are always internal images, urges, fantasies, memories, or furies that stake a different claim on the individual's psyche and life potential. These are present from childhood and sustain into adult life. Berne suggests that aspiration is not experienced so much in language as in imagery, fantasy, and wishes for the future. Here is an arena of transactional analysis that Berne left under-developed. He hints at it in his last book. These are not realms of experience we access through diagrams, slogans, or cognitive-behavioral interventions. Ogden (2005) fully captures what Berne hints at:

Not knowing is a precondition for being able to imagine. The imaginative capacity in the analytic setting is nothing less than sacred. Imagination holds open multiple possibilities experimenting with them all in the form of thinking, playing, dreaming and in every other sort of creative activity.

(p. 26)

Here, we live with our clients not only in the realms of what had been, but also what was lost and what might still be. This is not necessarily pleasant or welcomed territory, as it is often one filled with anguished loss as well as determined hope.

Enlivening transference and countertransference

To this point, I have emphasized some aspects of the non-relational qualities I see in Berne's pro-growth forces. There is, of course, also a relational component—the transferential/countertransferential matrix. Here the consultant or therapist represents a figure (to self as well as the client), consciously and unconsciously, who stands not for some particular outcome or accomplishment but for the right to life itself, to vitality. This is similar in some ways to the meanings of erotic transferences and countertransferences as described by Mann (1997, 1999) and others, but there is a distinctly different quality and meaning I wish to convey in this discussion of aspiration and resilience. While transferential dynamics are typically linked to the past, Bollas describes those that are linked to the *future*, as does Gerson (2003) in his description of the "enlivening transference," in which "the relationship to the analyst and analysis is infused with a sense of passionate interest" (unpaged manuscript). Transference is not simply a recreation of the past or an effort to undo it:

> Transference, when conceived of as a means of creatively synthesizing experience, can then be thought of as a form of language that includes not only communicative speech practices but performative ones as well, practices whose aim it is to make real that which was imagined. ... In the enlivening transference the motive is the evocation of desire itself rather than the object.
>
> (unpaged)

The object is not the other but the experience and articlulation of self through, or perhaps in the presence of, another.

This is not a singular, unilateral transaction. The enlivening matrix must be profoundly mutual in order to create life and movement at this level. Bollas and Gerson emphasize that the therapist must enter and engage with the enlivening, generative desires of those with whom we work. Director (2009) writes of being "an enlivening object," elaborating Alvarez's descriptions of the therapist's proactive "reclaiming" of clients' right to life (Alvarez, 1992; Edwards, 2001). None of these therapists describe this enlivening process as a pleasant path. Bollas, for example, writes that this is "work of great personal struggle, as any change of one's [fundamental] status quo involves emotional struggle" (p. 70). Gerson,

Director, and Alvarez (all writers whose work has helped me see how to work in this terrain) describe the intense interweaving, the inevitable dialectic, between growth and exploration, on the one hand, with the anxious and deadening retreats, on the other. The secret gardens to which Berne so longingly and passionately referred are filled with delicate, precious, but precarious hopes, seeking a life structure that can finally bring them to fruition and realization. It is not an easy path. In Gerson's words, "we can only hope that our solitude and desire are enabled by others who, in the embrace of their presence, permit us to both suffer our aloneness and to revel in our excitements" (2003, unpaged).

Conclusion

Much of *What Do You Say after You Say Hello?* was written while Berne was not in good health. While we'll never know if he was anticipating his premature death, he was working on the manuscript right until his death. In this reader's eye, Berne was beginning a major reassessment of his life's work. Transactional analysis was born within the emerging humanistic tradition of the 1950s and 1960s—informing and infusing Berne's perspective. Transactional analysis also represented Berne's defiant and rebellious departure from the ego psychology of the classical psychoanalytic techniques in which he had lost confidence, further fueled perhaps by a sense of personal betrayal. He sought to create a new paradigm, but he never quite finished the project. The ego psychologies in which he was trained stress adaptation and defense. Berne sought to create a different vision of people and of the psychotherapeutic process that was present in the background of virtually all of his writing. He never quite got there. In the dynamic tension within his own work between his emphasis on script as the apparatus of adaptation and acquiescence, on the one hand (which I attribute to his psycho-analytic training), and to aspiration and autonomy, on the other hand (which I see as expressions of his own aspirations), theories of adaptation dominated his work. In *Hello*, I see Berne as beginning to adjust the balance of attention between these two fundamental forces of human nature. But his aspirations were cut short by his early death. I hope this chapter will extend Berne's thinking and encourage transactional analysts of all disciplines to periodically return to a close reading of his work—there is always something new to discover. I wish only that Berne had had a longer life, as his was a life of discovery.

Chapter 10

What do you say if you don't say "unconscious"?: Dilemmas created for transactional analysis by Berne's shift away from the language of unconscious experience

For reasons never directly articulated, between the publication of *Principles of Group Treatment* (1966) and his writing of *What Do You Say after You Say Hello?* in the years immediately following, Eric Berne dropped the word "unconscious" from his personal lexicon. In the glossary of *Principles*, the book in which Berne most fully articulates his values and philosophy of treatment, he defines script as "An unconscious life plan. In some cases it may be preconscious or conscious" (1966, p. 368). In *What Do You Say after You Say Hello?*, published posthumously, script is defined as "A life plan based on a decision made in early childhood, reinforced by the parents, justified by subsequent events, and culminating in a chosen alternative" (1972, p. 446). The phrase "life plan" remains, but "unconscious" is gone, with the new definition now referring to early childhood "decisions."

How did the word "unconscious" come to be taken out of Berne's writing in his final years? Why did Berne seem overtly to shift to a decisional model of script and interpersonal dynamics? He did not speak to this change of terminology overtly, in a clearly articulated theoretical fashion, but this change of language certainly suggested a significant change in his thinking. I say "overtly" because there is much in *Hello* that still suggests that many aspects of psychological motivation and organization are not conscious. For example, Berne opens the chapter, "How is the script possible?," with the metaphor of Jeder at the piano, but the piano is a player piano, Jeder's fingers only appearing to be responsible for the music. The tune that is emerging from the piano is actually controlled by the piano roll. Berne writes that Jeder

> is under the illusion that the music is his own, and has for his witness his body, slowly wearing out from hour after hour and day after day of pumping. Sometimes, during the pauses, he rises to take a bow or a boo from his friends and relatives, who also believe that he is playing his own tune.
>
> (1972, p. 244)

If this is not a metaphor for unconscious motivation, I don't know what is! It may also have been a parable for Berne's feelings about his own life, slowly wearing out as he sat with his endless role of paper writing away in the study behind his house.

Perspectives from members of the original San Francisco TA Seminar

In his preface to *What Do You Say after You Say Hello?*, Berne thanks the teaching members of the International Transactional Analysis Association (ITAA) and the members of the San Francisco TA Seminar for their contributions to the development of transactional analysis and to his thinking. To better understand the context for the changes in Berne's thinking, I decided to write to all those still alive who were members of the San Francisco TA Seminar between the period of 1966 till Berne's death. I asked them why they thought Berne removed "unconscious" from his definition of script, and why Berne had described *Hello*, in the midst of writing it, as his most difficult book to write. The responses I received were fascinating and quite consistent. I will present a summary of their comments. I will then discuss the relevance of unconscious experience in contemporary transactional analysis and offer a perspective that seeks to address the pitfalls that Berne was attempting to avoid in the Freudian concept of the unconscious.

Fanita English, Marty Groder, Len Campos, Steve Karpman, Claude Steiner, and Pat Crossman each responded to my inquiry about the erasure of "unconscious" in Berne's later writing. First and foremost, each emphasized Berne's growing rejection of psychoanalysis and disavowal of his analytic background in his efforts to create a new theory of TA.

Fanita English (personal communication, October 19, 2006) wrote most bluntly:

> Berne was very conflicted about psychoanalysis and psychoanalysts. Several times I heard him say: "I am a better Freudian than the analysts" (and he was extremely well read). He got to hate the psychoanalysts. ... A big blow to his (narcissistic) ego was the lack of recognition by psychoanalysts of *The Mind in Action. Instead of stroking and admiring his major contribution to clarifying psychoanalysis for unsophisticated readers, he was criticized for making it too simplistic!!!!!* ... *TA was a definite nose-thumbing to THEM.* ... The central question is about Berne and the use of the concept of Unconscious should be seen in the context of the almost pathological anger/dislike/hatred/suspicion he (especially his Child) progressively developed about psychoanalysts and psychoanalysis (and I must say some deservedly—they all looked down their noses at him and TA). Berne's Adult knew darn well that there is an Unconscious—he tried to get around it... Berne never denied that archaic processes and memories affect us in the Now!!!!

Pat Crossman (personal communication, October 31, 2006) similarly observed:

I met Eric Berne in the fall of 1964 and I left the seminar in 1969. In 1964 Eric was "small time." In 1969 he was "big time" and famous. And this is what killed him. He was like Sisyphus, always rolling the stone up the mountain but never quite making it. But what happens if he makes it! *Games People Play* was a runaway best seller and Eric was on top. That spoils the game. Eric became depressed and very unhappy and some of his disciples were less than kind. I remember in 1967 Jack Dusay and Claude Steiner standing up stating that there was no such thing as the "unconscious". I remember Eric commenting quietly, "Then what about the defenses?"

Steve Karpman (personal communication, September 26, 2006) wrote that Berne "was finishing up the complete separation of himself and TA from the psychoanalytic world, and brand new identity for him and us without strings attached, ... he would never allow us to use analytic words in the Seminar." Karpman (2006) has written of Berne that, "He often smiled while saying, 'We're [transactional analysts] driving a brand new Mercedes while the psychoanalysts back East are still driving a Model T Ford.' ... Freud was propped up as the 'straw man' whom we eagerly overthrew" (p. 286). Karpman said that "Once I got kicked out of the seminar for twice using the passive, non-transactional word 'identification'" (p. 289). In this article, Karpman describes the rebellious and revolutionary atmosphere of the late 1960s and of his own struggle to try (unsuccessfully) to integrate his psychoanalytic training with his new learning in TA; like Berne, he decided to leave psychoanalysis behind in favor of what he saw as the efficacy of TA.

Marty Groder (personal communication, September 27, 2006) wrote to me in his inimitable style:

> As Eric's thinking imbued the ego states with increasing internal as well as social/transactional reality, the point of ascribing important issues like script to this theoretical black hole of the "unconscious" was becoming moot. TA became increasingly a decisional theory.... The EGO as a schmuck trapped in the orbit of the black hole of unconsciousness was ejected to the outer rim of the galaxy.... Also by then he was isolated (by choice in part) from all of his peers who could have validated and enriched his thinking. He had only us, his disciples, a limited, if intoxicating, source of sustenance.

We can clearly see this shift in tone in Berne's writings during the last few years of his life. All of his early work reflected a deep regard for the power of unconscious motivations balanced by an optimism of the strength of the ego and the impact of healthy social transactions and relations. With the writing of *Games People Play*, Berne set out to write a best-seller and to set himself apart from the psychoanalysts. It does seem, however, that Berne's conflict was more with the psychoanalysts themselves than with psychoanalysis proper. In

Principles of Group Treatment, written two years after *Games*, Berne offers a detailed, thoughtful, and respectful differentiation of transactional analysis from psychoanalysis. But by the time of *Hello* and his last published talk, "Away from a theory of the impact of interpersonal interaction on non-verbal participation" (Berne, 1971), his attitude toward psychoanalysis had become overtly bitter and mocking.

Bitterness, however, does not support the development of sound theory, and I would suggest that the evolution of TA theory has suffered for many years as a result of Berne's final bitterness and the inability of his colleagues of the time to critique his thinking and its limits. And yet, in the midst of his bitterness, Berne was also making important theoretical challenges and offering substantial alternatives to the psychoanalysis of *his* day (which, I must underscore, is not the psychoanalysis of *our* day). In his email in response to my inquiry, Len Campos (personal communication, September 26, 2006) wrote, "I think Berne dropped psychoanalytic metaphors such as 'the unconscious' because the newer metaphors of TA were more conducive to changing people's lives." In his response to me, Claude Steiner (personal communication, October 12, 2006) wrote that Berne's

> definitive statement on the matter was that unconscious was a pa [psycho-analytic] concept which should be used carefully and conscientiously (as other pa concepts like masochism or transference) in the fully psycho-analytic meaning, namely 'dynamically repressed unconscious' rather than all the obvious biological processes that are indeed out of awareness, but not unconscious in the pa sense. Scripts were also not unconscious in the pa sense but merely often (but not always) out of awareness.

Jack Dusay did not respond to my email inquiry, but he did write a fascinating article (1971) on Berne's studies in intuition shortly after Berne's death, in which he addressed some aspects of Berne's shift away from psycho-analysis. Given his place within the original seminar, I thought it important to quote Dusay as well. In his discussion of two landmark papers of Berne's from 1957, "The ego image" (1957a) and "Ego states in psychotherapy" (1957b), involving the cowpoke story in which Berne first differentiated the Adult and Child ego states, Dusay comments:

> Berne felt that the conscious and the unconscious, the ego and the id were involved, but *this was not directly important*. What was observed directly and was most obvious to both the patient and the observer, was the existence of two different *conscious* ego-states: one of an adult, and the other of a child.... This is where Berne parted ways with classical psycho-analysis. Although he did not reject psychoanalytic theory, he saw it was not directly useful for these new considerations.... His evolving system was concerned with the conscious derivatives of the primal images and primal

judgments which had their conscious representation in what he called the Child ego-state.

(1971, p. 40, italics in the original)

Berne's critique of the Freudian conceptualization of the unconscious

I used the phrase "unconscious experience" in my title, rather than the more familiar phrase of *the* unconscious. When first titling this chapter, I wrote "the unconscious" quite automatically, or one might say, "unconsciously." As I began to write this chapter, I realized that I needed to change the title—that what I had written rather automatically did not reflect what I actually wanted to convey. The concept of *the* unconscious, the dynamically repressed unconscious of Freud's theories, is what Berne challenged in classical Freudian theory.

I think Berne's was an important theoretical challenge. Berne's personal psychoanalysts were Paul Federn and Erik Erikson, both representatives of the ego psychology model of psychoanalysis, the model of psychoanalysis in which Berne was also trained. This model stressed the ascendancy of ego function over the ravages of the superego and the irrational, primitive, regressive impulses of the id. Superego, ego, and id were seen as functions within the mind, and *the* unconscious conveyed a sense of a *place* within the mind, a kind of dumping ground and holding tank for repressed and forbidden impulses. In classical Freudian theory, *the* unconscious was understood as the location of regression, irrationality, infantile transference fantasies, and psychopathology. This, I would suggest, is the model of *the* unconscious that Berne, quite rightly, wished to challenge. Berne was arguing that script, defenses, the Child ego state are not inherently irrational or pathological. He offered us a model of functional adaptation and creativity in addition to awareness of psychological defenses and psychopathology. He came to conclude that Freud's model of *the* unconscious was not useful in psychotherapy, more obfuscating than clarifying. But Berne's theoretical challenge became contaminated by his personal bitterness. If a word, a concept, like unconscious, is officially derided and dropped from our professional lexicon, then how can we continue to think about it?

As Berne moved away from notions of the unconscious in his later work, he described intrapsychic experience in this way:

> The Child expresses his wishes in visual images; but what he does about them, the final display through the final common pathway, is determined by auditory images, or voices in the head, the result of a mental dialogue. This dialogue between Parent, Adult, and Child is not "unconscious," but preconscious, which means that it can easily be brought into consciousness. Then it is found that it consists of sides taken from real life, things which were once actually said out loud. The therapeutic rule is a simple derivative

of this. Since the final common pathway of the patient's behavior is determined by voices in the head, this can be changed by getting another voice into his head, that of the therapist.

(1972, pp. 368–369)

In this quote, we see a mode of psychotherapy with which we, as transactional analysts, are very familiar and which deeply influenced the transactional analysts who were most closely affiliated with him at the time. The next major TA book after Berne's death was Steiner's *Scripts People Live* (1974) in which he defined script as

> based on a decision made by the Adult in the young person who, with all of the information at their disposal at the time, decides that a certain position, expectations, and life course are a reasonable solution to the existential position in which she finds herself.

(p. 55)

The Gouldings (1978), in another major text of that era, argued similarly, "Our clients were not 'scripted.' Injunctions are not placed in peoples' heads like electrodes. Each child makes decisions in response to real or imagined injunctions, and thereby 'scripts' her/himself" (p. 213). The Gouldings' work was a synthesis of transactional analysis with Gestalt methodologies; their work was strongly influenced by Gestalt theory, which also rejected Freudian theories of the unconscious. Central to redecision therapy was the client's return in Child ego state to the remembered "scene" of the original decision so as to redecide from one's current Child. The decisional models of transactional analysis always seem to convey a sense of consciousness and intentionality in script formation. While it is clear that some aspects of script formation are consciously made and/or consciously remembered, I would argue that this is not always the case, and I would suggest that Berne did not mean to suggest that either.

Berne's error

Here we find, I think, Berne's important correction to the classical psychoanalytic and ego psychological theories of his day, but one that was marred by his personal invective against *psychoanalysts*, which created a rigidity in his thinking that was passed on to the next generation of transactional analysts.

In taking these positions in his later writing, Berne was both right and wrong. He was, I think, right in that much of racket, game, and script behavior is preconscious and can be brought into consciousness (although I don't know about it being as "easy" a part as Berne suggests it to be). Rackets, games, and much of script are defensive in nature, grounded in some childhood experience of threat and an effort to manage the threats to the wellbeing of oneself and others; this level of experience is often preconscious. But where I differ with Berne, and where I think we need a theory of unconscious experience, is that *not* all of our internal experience is carried in dialogue or was learned from what was *said*. All that motivates people is not so obvious and observable as Berne came to emphasize in his later thinking.

Much of the internal structure and experience of the Child ego state is incorporated from what was *done* during our early relationships and family patterns (Cornell, 2003). There is a level of organization in the Child ego state that is learned at a body level and lived, experienced, and expressed not in the words of an internal dialogue, but in somatic organization, in unconscious fantasies and wishes, and through the styles of our contemporary relationships. This I understand as unconscious experience. It is not adequately described as "preconscious." These days, TA folks often refer to stuff in the head that is "out of awareness," which I think is a kind of linguistic gymnastics to avoid the "bad" word, unconscious. I do not think that "preconscious" or "out of awareness" capture the depth and compelling force of unconscious psychological organization. I want to emphasize in the strongest possible terms that because something is unconscious, it is not necessarily primitive, regressive, or pathological. Unconscious processes are *foundational, fundamental*, and *un-worded* in our internal experience, an inherent and compelling means by which we "know" ourselves in the world of others, the "unthought known" described by Christopher Bollas (1987). This is the realm of experience, of affective and somatic organization, that Berne explored in his original concepts of intuition and protocol, which were decidedly modes of unconscious perception and organization.

The richness and vitality of unconscious modes

Cornell and Landaiche (2005) have described the non-pathological aspect of unconscious processes through their elaboration of Berne's concept of script protocol:

> Protocol based behavior is not a game-like, ulterior form of communication, but a deeply compelling implicit (wordless) memory of primary relational patterns, lived through the immediacy of bodily experience. Protocols function as ongoing, unconscious templates for making judgments about the significant figures and encounters in our lives. Yet protocols are not necessarily pathological; they embody an innate human capacity for making unconscious sense of life with others. They only become problematic when they interfere with the ability to generate new bodily and relational possibilities.
>
> (p. 19)

> Protocol is *not* a set of adaptive or defensive decisions, like a script. Protocol is not remembered in a narrative fashion but *felt/lived* in the immediacy of one's body. ... We are suggesting that with his concept of

protocol Berne was trying to capture the sense of the most fundamental, nonverbal aspects of what it means to relate to someone.

(p. 21)

In my reading of Berne, something fundamental was lost in the richness of most of his thinking when he was overtaken by his need to distinguish himself from psychoanalysts. Also, in my reading of Berne, I see the "can-do" attitude of Americans, driven to accomplish, control, come out on top. Of course, can-do can rather easily be internalized as "must-do," shifting from Adult to Parent ego states. I think transactional analysis has too often incorporated a "must-do" Parental attitude toward "curing" (fixing) clients. Clients do not come to therapists, counselors, and consultants only to "get fixed"; they also come to deepen self-understanding, to discover and explore unexpressed aspects of self-development, and to unfold more complex meanings and understandings of the self, what is sometimes called the "emergent unconscious" (Cornell, 2005). This work is enriched with a theory of unconscious experience and desire.

The understanding of the nature and function of unconscious experience in contemporary theory and research is very different than that described by Freud and classical psychoanalytic theory. In contemporary psychoanalytic thinking, the unconscious is no longer seen simply as the psychic trash bin of repressed impulses and childhood trauma but is seen as a core of unformulated experience (Stern, 2003) and unsanctioned or unacknowledged desire and potential (Bollas, 1989, 1992; Mitchell, 1993; Eigen, 1998; McLaughlin, 2005). As so eloquently stated by Bollas (1992):

> Our inner world, the place of psychic reality, is inevitably less coherent than our representations of it; a moving medley of part thoughts, incomplete visualizations, fragments of dialogue, recollections, unremembered active presences, sexual states, anticipations, urges, unknown yet present needs, vague intentions, ephemeral mental lucidities, unlived partial actions: one could go on and on....
>
> (p. 47)

Infant research and its various models of implicit relational knowing (Holmes, 1996; Karen, 1998; Lyons-Ruth, 1998, 1999; Fivaz-Depeursinge & Corboz-Warnery, 1999; Bremner & Slater, 2004; Beebe et al., 2005) present another perspective on unconscious organization and experience, quite consistent with Berne's foreshadowing in his concept of protocol. Contemporary cognitive and neuroscience research is also replete with models of the centrality (and health) of unconscious processes and "implicit", or "procedural," knowing (Schacter, 1992, 1996; Bucci, 1997; Siegel, 1999; LeDoux, 2002; Schore, 2003; Hassin, Uleman, & Bargh, 2005; Anderson, Resnik, & Glassman, 2005). This research and these theories emphasize that unconscious processes are not only reflections of infant and early childhood experiences but are a part of our ongoing, lifelong development. Like Freud, I do think that split-off aspects of childhood trauma and disturbance (*and* adult life) can be disavowed and so deeply spilt from consciousness that they become a repressed, dynamic component of unconscious experience. These split-off aspects of experience foster defenses and psychological/relational disturbances, the origins of which are not easily brought to conscious awareness. But I would argue that unconscious experience is richer and more complex than that conceptualized by Freud.

It is outside the scope of this chapter to attempt to delineate the rich implications of these models of unconscious experience. Suffice it to say, for the moment, that these new models offer understandings of unconscious, non-conscious processes very different from those developed by Freud and challenged by Berne. Now we need to challenge Berne and keep our theory and practice, our understanding of the meaning of unconscious, open, refreshed, and renewed.

Conclusion

I would suggest, in the strongest possible terms, that unconscious experience is a fact of the human mind and life. Our work as human relations professionals is impoverished if we ignore or deny it. In making this argument, I do not in any way wish to diminish our attention to the conscious experiences and memories of our clients. Many conscious experiences and memories fill our consulting rooms, our own lives, and the lives of our clients with suffering, anxiety, hope, pleasure, love, and fury—all the passions and meanings of life. But all passion and meaning is not conscious.

So the task for us now as transactional analysts is to think anew about the nature of unconscious experience, motivation, and organization and its place in the theory and practice of transactional analysis. We can do this without having to create yet another school of TA. I do not think we need a "relational" TA or a "psychoanalytic" TA or a "constructivist" TA to think about the incorporation of new understandings of the role of unconscious experience in our psychological and emotional functioning. I also want to emphasize that to incorporate an understanding of unconscious processes in TA theory and methodology, we do not have to become psychoanalysts nor mimic their techniques.

Chapter 11

Impasse and intimacy: Applying Berne's concept of script protocol

Co-authored with N. M. Landaiche, III

Eric Berne drew inspiration from his original psychoanalytic training to create a new model of psychotherapy that was both more efficient and more user-friendly than the psychoanalysis of his time. His model—transactional analysis —also proved more comprehensive. It could be used to analyze intrapsychic transactions within the client's mind as well as interpersonal transactions in the client's life. It could be used to treat individuals suffering from problems in addition to helping those seeking personal learning and growth. Transactional analysis could also be applied to understanding the dynamics and difficulties of groups and organizations. These broad traditions continue to underlie the many forms of transactional analysis practiced and taught today. They also continue to make transactional analysis a powerful tool for social learning and change.

Yet there are times when the model functions poorly. In spite of our best efforts, certain interactions with some clients become intractably stuck. What can transactional analysis teach us about resolving such impasses in our therapeutic, educational, and consulting work? How could transactional analysis be modified to increase its usefulness in these difficult encounters?

Looking back, we can see that—along with the many useful traditions inherited by transactional analysis practitioners and trainees—there are also some that seem counterproductive. For example, in spite of Berne's sincere effort to develop a treatment model that was more accessible to clients and based on a mutual, contractual working relationship, he also held himself carefully apart from his clients and his therapeutic engagement with them, much as his psychoanalytic contemporaries did. Berne maintained the role of the external observer, examining and analyzing patterns of intrapsychic and interpersonal interaction in his diagnosis of each client's ego states, transactions, games, and script phenomena. Berne's emphasis on making change through conscious, intentional choice has also fostered a professional culture that can be intolerant of what cannot be changed through insight alone.

We in transactional analysis can trace some of our technical failures to this legacy of the disengagement of the therapist and overemphasis on the cognitive. However, this legacy also continues to exert its influence because of the considerable difficulties that arise when working in a more engaged manner.

When it comes to making contact with states of self and affect that do not readily lend themselves to words or diagrams, many of us are reluctant to experience the disturbances our clients bring to and evoke in us. Yet such disturbances seem an inevitable consequence of the intimacy that develops in every therapeutic and consulting relationship. The very nature of such close contact between any two or more human beings is bound to affect us at levels that operate outside of consciousness and that inform our most fundamental patterns of relating. As a result, we may discover ourselves and our working relationships stalled in habitual ways of being, often accompanied by feelings of frustration, anger, and a sense of inadequacy. Once our work has become so maddeningly stuck, how do we find our way back to productive engagement?

Theoretical perspectives on the nature of impasses

In the early transactional analysis literature, the term "impasse" was used by Goulding and Goulding (1978, 1979), Erskine (1978), Johnson (1978), Mellor (1980), and others to refer to a conflict or stalemate between ego states within the client. The term did not refer to a breakdown in the therapeutic process, *per se*. Therefore, interventions to address impasses intended to facilitate a resolution and were focused on intrapsychic redecisions, not on understanding the relationship dynamics between the professional and client. Gradually, however, the term "impasse" was used to describe the experience of being stuck in the working relationship, as it was initially being explored by Novellino (1984), Moiso (1985), and others. Even Bob Goulding, ten years later, was discussing impasses in terms of the therapist's countertransference contribution (Hoyt & Goulding, 1989).

This shift was consistent with growing interest in the transactional analysis community in understanding the dynamics of the working relationship through such concepts as parallel process, transference and countertransference, and projective identification phenomena, and their contributions to difficulties in treatment. Today, discussions of transference and countertransference are as common in transactional analysis as they are in other schools of psychotherapy. We therefore believe it is important for transactional analysts to be familiar with these and related terms, if only to access the rich literature and ongoing debates pertaining to these complex dynamics in psychotherapy and counseling, which we believe operate as well in teaching and supervision. While most of the literature addressing these issues has been written from a clinical perspective, we see these dynamics operating across the range of psychotherapeutic, counseling, training, supervisory, and educational fields. Throughout this chapter, we will refer to professionals and practitioners in these areas also, so as not to isolate this discussion to clinical fields.

An impasse typically impoverishes the therapeutic or consultative experience. Impasses situated within the client's intrapsychic dynamics (i.e., within script and counterscript) will limit the client's Adult capacities, and autonomous functioning may be severely compromised by childhood influences. In the face of actual client-centered impasses, the professional will most likely be able to observe, think, and relate effectively, functions that will serve as significant resources for the client who is trying to get out of his or her own bind. However, sometimes the client's professional resources are disabled, in that conflicts and inhibitions within the professional's functioning (often addressed in transactional analysis as parallel process) may restrict his or her capacity to observe, think, and relate flexibly. In such situations, professional-centered supervision is necessary to prevent the work from becoming repetitive, superficial, cognitively dominated, and ultimately ineffective or harmful. Once the therapist or consultant has resolved his or her own impasse, the client can return to making use of the professional as a source of help.

Intrapsychic impasse

One means of understanding a point of impasse within the therapeutic/educational process is to focus on a potential impasse within the mind (between the ego states) of the client. The theory of impasses was first developed by the Gouldings (1978, 1979) and further elaborated by Mellor (1980).

According to Mellor, first-degree impasses are the internalization of verbalized and demonstrated parental counter-injunctions and accordingly are carried in language. Second-degree impasses are a result of script-level injunctions, originating much earlier in development, and are encoded and communicated through emotions. Mellor posits third-degree impasses as being related to "primal protocols" (1980, p. 214), originating in "very early experience, perhaps even prenatal" (p. 214). In keeping with the redecision model developed by the Gouldings, Mellor goes on to suggest that treatment interventions focus on remembering/recreating with the client the scenes in which the original parental injunctions were taken in by the child, precipitating the child's making of a script decision, which becomes evident in later life through areas of intrapsychic impasse. In this model, resolution of first-degree impasses between P2 and C2 are made by redecisions from A2 and with second-degree impasses between P1 and C1 by redecision in A1. Third-degree impasses are understood to occur between P0 and C0 with the redecision by A0, but we find it hard to conceive of a "redecision" being made at a level of psychic experience and organization that has no real capacity to observe or think. We suggest, and will elaborate below, that third-degree impasses are rooted in the level of experience Berne called protocol, are enacted within the working relationship, and change as they are *reorganized* (rather than redecided) within the therapeutic relationship. When the understanding of impasses moves from the intrapsychic realm of the client to include the interpersonal realm between client and practitioner (therapist, educator, consultant, etc.), then various forms of transference–countertransference come into play as described below.

Transference and countertransference

The essence of the theories of transference and countertransference is that there is an unconscious communication and interpersonal pressure from the client to the therapist arising from the client's emotional (Child ego state) fusion of the therapist with an early parental figure that causes the therapist to feel and behave like that historical figure. Berne's game theory provides one avenue for analyzing and intervening in the interpersonal communication patterns that sustain the transference–countertransference dynamics. Seen from the perspective of script theory, the client's script is enacted within the transference–countertransference matrix with the unconscious cooperation of the therapist who has been drawn into participating as a character in the client's script. Seen from the perspective of classical transactional analysis, the therapist is hooked into a game that maintains the client's script, and neither is able to think clearly about what is going on. The inability of the two to step outside of what is happening and think about it creates the conditions for an impasse in which the interpersonal behavior becomes repetitive and thus reinforced rather than changed.

In our view, script-centered, historical interpretations that focus primarily on the intrapsychic conflicts and distortions within the client can serve to keep the professional's own intrapsychic experience out of view, thus shielding the professional and client from the intimacies and uncertainties of their working relationship. As Rosenfeld (1987) observed, "If the analyst has many areas which can be described as 'private: no entry'... then the analyst and patient may collude unconsciously to keep those areas out of the analysis and so create a therapeutic impasse" (p. 39).

The literature on transference and countertransference is immense and outside the scope of this chapter. Over time, these terms have come to address the unconscious emotional and psychological patterns between therapist and client, in which the therapist may be drawn into the client's script, or vice versa. Within the transactional analytic literature, readers are referred to thorough discussions in the special 1991 issues of the *Transactional Analysis Journal* (Friedlander, Ed., 1991), as well as Clarkson (1992) and Hargaden and Sills (2002). Transference impasses can be understood as the induction of one participant in the working dyad into the script of the other. Script-level interpretations and interventions with one or both members of the party are needed to dislodge the impasse.

Parallel process

Parallel process is a form of transference in which the practitioner enacts with a third party (typically, a supervisor) dynamics that originally arose with a client. Discussions of parallel process tend to posit the origins of a therapeutic impasse within the functioning of the therapist rather than the client. The central supervisory intervention is to identify an element of the therapist's script that has been evoked in the work; once "in script," the therapist can no longer be effective. Supervisory attention is then shifted to the therapist's intrapsychic experience, away from that of the client. Though little has actually been written in the transactional analysis literature about parallel process, use of the concept has become commonplace within the supervisory models used in transactional analysis training throughout Europe and in North America. In our experience, it seems that the concept of parallel process has been taken up in supervisory contexts without sufficient explication and examination in the published literature.

The concept of parallel process emerged in the psychoanalytic literature with discussions of the supervisory process first put forth by Searles (1955), Ekstein and Wallerstein (1958), and Arlow (1963). Each of these explorations of the supervisory process makes rich reading, quite apart from the specific issues we are addressing here. Searles described what he called the "reflection process," through which a therapist would *show* (enact), rather than *tell*, the patient's behavior with which he or she most struggled.

Ekstein and Wallerstein were perhaps the first to use the term "parallel process," in which the therapist's problems of understanding and learning in supervision are related to the patient's problems in psychotherapy. They emphasize that supervisor and therapist can also create a parallel process that is then conveyed back to the patient, in that supervision is also an emotionally charged process devoted to learning and change, in which both parties can experience personal vulnerability and stuck points.

Arlow emphasized that elements of parallel process are inevitable and educative for all (supervisor, therapist, and client). For Arlow, parallel process is a result of the therapist's identification with the conflicts and struggles of the patient. Parallel process is a result of an over-identification in which the therapist cannot clearly *observe and think* about what is going on and so transmits the problem through actions rather than words in supervision. Arlow stresses that parallel process does not mean that the therapist is stuck in a pathological countertransference (i.e., "hooked in script") but is engaged in a level of experience with the client that is not yet available in words. He emphasizes that supervision is a kind of psychoanalysis *of a psychoanalysis*. It is *not* a psychoanalysis of the psychoanalyst. We strongly concur that the function of supervision, especially when working with points of impasse in treatment and/or parallel process, is to reach an understanding and opening up of the therapeutic process—it is not a form of treatment of the professional.

Projective identification

Projective identification, an aspect of transference (Ogden, 1982; Goldstein, 1991), was first articulated within the Kleinian tradition (Klein, 1946). It involves a deep, unconscious pattern of emotional communication, usually from the client to the practitioner, but also potentially from the practitioner to the client or the supervisor. Kleinians offer a particular understanding of projective identification as "that aspect of the transference that involves the therapist's being enlisted in an interpersonal actualization (an actual enactment between patient and therapist) of a segment of the patient's internal world" (Ogden, 1982, p. 69).

We understand projective identification as an unconscious effort at affect regulation in which the client is experiencing an emotional, intrapsychic disturbance, usually a state of intense affect, which the client cannot tolerate. This affective disturbance is understood to be projected by the client into the professional, who then feels what the client cannot tolerate. In these situations, the professional's feelings, while often intense and uncomfortable, are not a result of his or her own unresolved conflicts (as is understood in parallel process) but are a consequence of the projection of the client's disowned feelings. If the practitioner is able to tolerate and observe these states of projected affect, she or he can contain the disturbance and use those affective states to understand the internal world of the client. Gradually, the feelings can become tolerable to the client and used for self-understanding and conscious communication. When the professional is unable to tolerate these deep states of affective disturbance, an impasse is likely to occur in which there will be a defensive splitting of good and bad—tolerable and intolerable—rendering understanding and conscious communication virtually impossible.

These conceptualizations of intrapsychic impasse, parallel process, transference–countertransference, and projective identification are each a description of the defensive dynamics of script and tend to suggest that impasses reflect the psychopathology of the client, the mental health professional, or both. We have found, over years of training and supervision, that these terms are often useful, but not always sufficient, in understanding and changing points of interpersonal impasse. Moreover, these ideas are often accompanied by attributions of immaturity to all unconscious and unworded phenomena, and a mystification of ordinary modes of nonverbal communication. We wish to emphasize that *such mystification and judgmental attributions of the unconscious and nonverbal do not help professionals or clients understand that we continually live large sectors of our lives outside of conscious awareness and that we conduct many of our most essential, non-problematic, and often intimate transactions without using words.*

We have also found that often at exactly those points of breakthrough from script (that of the client *or* the practitioner)—at those points where one might expect an impasse to be resolved—a stalemate may nonetheless occur. At these points in treatment and change, intense anxiety may emerge *within the working dyad* (in contrast to an intrapsychic disturbance in one or the other of the pair). This anxiety seems to be generated by the simultaneous breaking of the familiarity and predictability of script combined with movement into *un*familiar, *un*mapped modes of relating. These moments are more a matter of falling into health and novelty than into pathology and history.

In addition to our understanding of impasses from the perspectives just described—intrapsychic impasse, transference–countertransference, parallel process, and projective identification—we have gained significant insight from the use of Berne's original concept of protocol (Berne, 1961, p. 117; 1963, p. 228). At these points of potential therapeutic transformation, there are no templates for the future, creating both excitement and anxiety. We have observed that at these times there is often a heightened vulnerability to the re-emergence of our earliest relational patterns, which Berne called protocols, as a means of managing the anxiety of the unknown. When early protocols emerge within the working dyad, impasse is much more likely than transformation and growth. Before discussing Berne's theory of the protocol, we will elaborate the idea of the "working couple" in education, treatment, and consultation.

The working couple

To understand the dynamics of impasses that arise in the course of psychotherapy, education, supervision, and consultation, we have found it useful to frame those dynamics in terms of a working therapeutic or consultative couple.

Obviously, the term "couple" can be highly evocative. It is often associated with sexuality, romance, and the parental dyad, along with images of sexual, romantic, and partnering failure. All of these emotional features and fantasies can arise in professional relationships that form for the purpose of promoting self-understanding and development. Human relationships always operate within erotic fields of varying intensities. In any new relationship, there is frequently a sense of hope and romance associated with what the other might bring to make one's life richer. And once any two of us begin working together, we typically develop a sense of familiarity that can move between trust and mistrust and comfort and irritation, not to mention autonomy and dependence. All of these conditions can stimulate our most fundamental sense of what it means to be in relationship with our intimates.

For these reasons, we believe the word "couple" aptly describes the intimacy characteristic of therapy, consultation, and mentoring. Although a couple usually refers to a dyadic relationship, the emotional characteristics associated with the word apply as well in settings where there are more than two people working together. And while the terms "group" and "family" also can be emotionally charged, they fail to convey the degree of proximity that develops in group contexts and within which all individuals working together must come to some recognition of their own bodily responses and unspoken patterns of interaction. Simply put, the term "couple" points to our most intense, primary, and challenging modes of relating.

Furthermore, the image of the couple underscores a fundamental human process of interaction to which certain professional skills and contractual obligations are brought to bear. The contract in a professional setting may be to address what is not working in the client's life, on what is insufficiently developed, or on the acquisition of new personal or professional skills. Any of these may be the reason a working therapeutic or consultative couple comes into being. Yet the inherent relational asymmetry is also counterbalanced by the fact that neither party is necessarily healthier, smarter, or better educated. Both can contribute as full partners to the task at hand.

As this couple begins to work, the development of intimacy or closeness is unavoidable, even in situations in which there appears to be substantial professional distance. In recognition of this fact of relational life, we use the term "intimacy"—as we do "couple"—for its evocative associations of physical and emotional proximity and for its precision. We are not suggesting a therapeutic goal or ideal.

Intimacy sometimes connotes tenderness and quiet. But for some, it can evoke crowding, suffocation, and noise. Perhaps at its most productive, intimacy is a bodily capacity for sustaining affect, thinking, and working to put experiences into language within an ongoing relationship. Even without physical contact, intimacy describes the way we get into and under the skin of the other person and the way the other gets into and under our skin, too. It is not always pleasurable, although it sometimes can be.

In some situations, intimacy may encourage the capacity for experimentation, exploration, self-reflection, and recognition of differences, as well as the capacity for those involved to think together about the functioning of the couple or the group. It may also encourage the reverse: the avoidance of differences, the collapse of thinking and reflection, and the prohibition of dynamic interplay. Indeed, the intimacy that develops within therapeutic and consultative couples may be characterized by many of the same gratifications, satisfactions, irritations, and blinds spots that attend any of our closest relationships. Such intimacy often touches and disturbs us where we least expect it and, particularly, where we are least prepared to understand what is going on. Even when interactions within the working couple are apparently going well, we are always deeply immersed in modes of being that have been typical throughout our lives with other intimates, both past and present. At the same time, regardless of how things are going, the ground is being laid for the unique interplay and character that develops within each therapeutic or consultative couple. And it is on that rich and unwitting basis—in that complex, often turbulent interpersonal field—that intimacy can so easily lead to impasse.

In a consultative, learning, or therapeutic setting, impasse describes the experience of the work being stuck—unable to move forward or step out of its repetitive loop. An impasse for the therapeutic or consultative couple is characterized by the loss of reflective or free-thinking capacities. It is an induction into an automatic or predictable way of being with self and others, an arrested form of development. In essence, the relationship of the couple stops evolving and maturing. Both members of the couple become stuck in a region of the mind and body that neither can think about. This is typically due to the intensity of affect that resides in our closeness with one another and the passions we inevitably experience in that proximity.

Many impasses take the form of covert contracts or collusions that are negotiated outside awareness of the working couple. These take innumerable forms, as diverse as the quality of the intimacy that can develop between any two people. And although impasses are often seen as a kind of catastrophic or overtly destructive stuckness, there are also impasses of the blissfully stuck kind in which there is an agreement, again made outside awareness, to remain in a state of immovable complementarity.

Whatever the emotional valence of the impasse, it is typically the result of an overload or threat of affect that gets out of hand and mind. However, impasses can also occur in the apparent absence of any affect, within a working relationship that looks and feels utterly dead, especially if an unconscious agreement has been reached within the couple not to stir things up too much. As Hinshelwood (1994) asked:

> What is going on when it seems nothing is going on? The stilling of lively contact by the patient—perhaps with the analyst's collusion—can be understood as a protective endeavor to remain afloat among flooding anxieties.
>
> (p. 193)

The threat of affective intensity can be sufficient to sustain a stillness that is at once reassuring and deadening.

In an intimate impasse, both people are trapped in a mode of relating and both experience it as the only available option. Impasse is a kind of emotional activation that occurs "under the skin" and that is responded to in highly repetitive, sometimes nonproductive ways, as if each party only knew one thing to do under the circumstances. With any luck, some intervention can be made to address this process (often input from a third party) while there is still time to discover what is going on, before the illusion of permanence has a chance to kill the life of the couple. For instance, in a therapist–client couple, hopefully the impasse can be brought to supervision before the desperate professional escalates the diagnosis of his or her own pathology or that of the client.

Impasses *within* the professional couple, however, can threaten the very existence of the work as well as the viability of the relationship. These are the relational impasses in which it is not uncommon for the therapist or consultant to terminate the work prematurely (sometimes under the guise of a making a more appropriate referral) or in which clients feel deeply damaged and may themselves abruptly quit, personally attack, or bring ethics charges. We find it helpful to think of these intimate, seemingly intractable impasses as arising out of the mutual evocation of each person's unconscious, relational protocols, as Berne defined the concept.

Protocol: The relational template for intimate contact and disturbance

Before proposing his idea of "protocol," Berne was deeply interested in what he called intuition, which today we might see as the unconscious organization of sensory, nonverbal experiences. Berne's early writings on this topic were collected posthumously in *Intuition and Ego States* (1977).

In one of these papers, "Intuition IV: Primal images and primal judgments," Berne (1955) discussed the relationship between the infant's early, primal image of a significant other and the infant's primal judgment based on that image. He defined the primal image as the infant's "pre-symbolic, non-verbal representation of interpersonal transactions" (p. 67). In essence, a primal image is an impression made on the child's body by a significant other's "mode of relating" (p. 68). It is a cluster of sensations, organized outside awareness by the child, that reflects his or her experience of another before the child has access to words or symbols. Berne considered the child's organizing role to be an act of primal judgment, similar to the judgments we make about our worlds throughout life and, in particular, about others we see as significant allies or enemies. Berne defined this kind of judgment as "an image of reality which affects behavior and feelings toward reality. An *image* is formed by integrating sensory and other impressions with each other and with inner tensions based on present needs and past experiences" (p. 72).

In Berne's conception, the formation of the image and the action of judging are nearly simultaneous processes. They describe what occurs when we have a flash of intuition about a person or situation we have encountered, an assessment that may or may not be accurate. Berne essentially combined his early ideas about primal images and primal judgments into his later concept of the protocol. With characteristic humor, Berne (1963) conveyed his sense of the simultaneously creative and defensive functions of the protocol:

> Each person has an unconscious life plan, formulated in his earliest years, which he takes every opportunity to further as much as he dares in a given situation. This plan calls for other people to respond in a desired way... The original set of experiences which forms *the pattern for the plan* [italics added] is called the protocol. .... Partly because of the advantages of being an infant, even under bad conditions, every human being is left with some nostalgia for his infancy and often for his childhood as well; therefore, in later years he strives to bring about as close as possible a reproduction of the original protocol situation, either to live it through again if it was enjoyable, or to try to re-experience it in a more benevolent form if it was unpleasant.
>
> (pp. 218–219)

As Berne (1963) goes on to describe, these unconscious patterns for relating then become the basis for later script decisions:

> The original drama, the protocol, is usually completed in the early years of childhood, often by the age of 5, occasionally earlier. This drama may be played out again in more elaborate form, in accordance with the growing

child's changing abilities, needs and social situation, in the next few years. Such a later version is called the palimpsest. A protocol or palimpsest is of such a crude nature that it is quite unsuitable as a program for grown-up relationships. It becomes largely forgotten (unconscious) and is replaced by a more civilized version, the script proper: a plan of which the individual is not actively aware (preconscious), but which can be brought into consciousness by appropriate procedures.

(p. 228)

In essence, Berne suggested that the protocol is a latent level of somatic and relational organization, which precedes the formation of script and operates outside of conscious awareness. Contemporary infant observation research suggests that relational protocols are established well before the age of 5. In the groundbreaking observations of Daniel Stern (1985):

> Our concern... is with preverbal infants and with different happenings such as what happens when you are hungry and at breast, or what happens when you and mom play an exciting game. Moreover, our interest concerns not only the actions but also the sensations and affects. What we are concerned with, then, are episodes that involve interpersonal interactions of different types. Further, we are concerned with the interactive experience, not just the interactive events. I am suggesting these episodes are also averaged and represented preverbally.
>
> (p. 97)

What Berne accounted for initially in his speculations about intuition and subsequently in his observations of the protocol would today be accounted for in the contemporary language of implicit relational knowing (Lyons-Ruth, 1999) or the co-construction of intersubjectivity (Beebe & Lachmann, 2000).

Protocol-based behavior is not a game-like, ulterior form of communication, but a deeply compelling implicit (wordless) memory of primary relational patterns, lived through the immediacy of bodily experience. Protocols function as ongoing, unconscious templates for making judgments about the significant figures and encounters in our lives. Yet protocols are not necessarily pathological; they embody an innate human capacity for making unconscious sense of life with others. They only become problematic when they interfere with the ability to generate new bodily and relational possibilities.

According to Steere (1985), one of the few transactional analysis practitioners and researchers to substantively address the concept of protocol:

> The best explanation for the phenomenon of protocol is that the Child ego state preserves in particular psychomotor patterns an often repeated sequence of events from formative years. Our earliest way of thinking, from birth to 18 month according to Piaget [Piaget & Inhelder, 1954], is in

the form of sensorimotor schemes.... The sensorimotor constructs contain all the cognitive substructures that will serve as a point of departure for later perceptual and intellectual development, as well as the elementary affect reactions that shape emotional life.

(p. 254)

Given how little Berne actually wrote about protocol, it is not surprising that not much else has been written about this key concept in his theory. The term "protocol" has typically been used only in passing by most transactional analysis theorists. As an exception, Greve (1976) proposed a form of intervention for protocol based on the Gestalt redecision models prevalent at the time. Steere (1985), as noted above, explored in greater depth the way protocol elements appear in bodily postures as clients live out their scripts. Hostie (1984) and Müller (2000) discussed protocol in the context of the evolution of Berne's thinking, and Cornell (2003) has elaborated Berne's original concept more explicitly in terms of contemporary interest in somatic process, unconscious communication, and creative interplay in therapy.

Woods (2003) is among the contemporary transactional analysts who believe it is important to focus attention on here-and-now communications between the client and professional, on communications that are occurring outside awareness, and on the unconscious content of games. From that perspective, exclusively historical interpretations of client protocol material can be experienced as distancing from the immediate encounter with that client's active, if unconscious, sense of self in the world and in interaction with the professional today. Caravella and Marone (2003) wrote of this balanced attention in regard to working with psychotic patients, which they do by listening "freely to the patient's pain" and by establishing "an intimate Child–Child communication and a therapeutic alliance with the Adult... even during the psychotic phase" (p. 252).

Protocol is *not* a set of adaptive or defensive decisions, like a script. Protocol is not remembered in a narrative fashion but *felt/lived* in the immediacy of one's body. Protocol is the literal embodiment of the repetitive, often affectively intense, patterns of relatedness, preceding the infant's capacity of ego function. Script, in contrast, is—as Berne emphasized—preconscious, that is, potentially available to conscious awareness. Script can be recognized as an adaptation of the ego, often to the underlying protocol. The situations in which script decisions are made can often be remembered in the context of some sort of story or narrative. Protocol, on the other hand, precedes and underlies the subsequent, narrative-based script.

We are suggesting that with his concept of protocol, Berne was trying to capture the sense of the most fundamental, nonverbal aspects of what it means to relate to someone. Berne is describing an unconscious, fundamental relational experience that underlies many transferential experiences, be they expressed as impasses, enactments, parallel processes, or projective identifications. Protocol is a kernel of nonverbal, somatic experience that may be touched or triggered in intimate relationships. Such moments are often impregnated with both hope and dread. When the experience of a therapeutic relationship evokes protocol, the Child ego state is deeply opened, and the transference dynamics that may then be played out become more anxiety-provoking and more difficult to tolerate, understand, and resolve for both client and practitioner.

Protocol does not exist separate from a person's sense of self but is the very matrix from which we each organize our relational experiences. It is inextricable from our bodies and selves. The most salient aspect of protocol, as distinct from script, is that it cannot be cognitively changed, redecided, or rescripted. Protocol can only be brought into awareness, understood, and lived within. We can only alter how we behave as a consequence of our protocols. In short, we can decide not to act on the sense made with our bodies at one time in life if that sense does not serve us well at this time in life. But we cannot change what the sense feels like as it operates "under our skins." Protocols are with us for life, never fully analyzed or understood, like our experiences of unconscious realms in general. We can never diffuse their intensity but can open them to new experience and action.

The deepening intimacy within a therapeutic or consultative relationship brings us in contact with our passions about others and the world, and that growing contact and intensity can lead us to being stuck. In that sense, an impasse at the level of the protocol is a defense against deepening affect and intimacy within the therapeutic couple. For example, a therapist in supervision described his disgust with a client's lack of hygiene and his frustration in their work together. However, once he explored the situation further, he realized he was actually troubled by sitting with a woman who was living her life in madness. It was the pervasive impact of her deep emotional disturbance, not her actual body odor, that he could not bear to name or take into his physical being. This insight shook his conception of himself as a therapist who believed he could, with skilled interpretations and careful emotional reserve, cure the troubled people who came his way. In fact, his particular client was someone in a psychotic state who desperately needed emotional engagement and containment from her therapist, not interpretation or detachment.

This therapist, through his transactional analysis training and personal therapy, had come to understand that much of his motivation and style as a therapist was script-based. His had been a chaotic family system, one from which he protected himself by increasing layers of emotional distance and finely tuned critical thinking. He remembered his decision as an adolescent to become a psychiatrist, feeling if he could not cure the suffering and chaos within his own family, he could relieve it in the lives of others not so close to him. As he addressed his impasse with this unkempt, psychotic woman, he began to realize that he felt invaded by her. With her smell and her madness, he could not maintain his script-based distancing. He felt moved by her, touched as well as invaded, and he realized how disorganized he felt in her presence. He remembered that he had often felt this way in his mother's presence, though he could not recall specific instances. He also realized that this psychotic client had, for some reason, come to trust him and was committed in her own peculiar way to a real relationship with him. Neither knew quite what to do with themselves or each other. This characterized their impasse.

When given the idea of protocol as a tool with which to think about his experience, in addition to what he knew of his script, the therapist began to *feel* his fear of the invasiveness of his mother's anxiety and disorganization. He then felt less afraid of his client and her madness and began to feel, quite to his surprise, a kind of tenderness toward her. Though he did not share any of this with her, he could see that she *felt* the difference in his way of being with her. He gained confidence that he could accept and contain her deep disturbances. They recovered their capacity to feel, think, and work together.

So, although their coupling began with two separate histories and two sets of unconscious, relational protocols, this therapist and his client were together developing a discomfiting history and protocol mix of their own. Together, they would also need to find a way of being with one another that allowed a gradual closeness and understanding—an emotional sanity and compassion—in the face of madness and habitual recoiling from closeness.

In moments of therapeutic intimacy, professional and client *both* show one another what it means and how it feels to be close. Their encounter starts with a way of being, each with the other. Words may follow, but they do not lead. As Bollas (1999) reflects, "Each patient creates an environment in which both participants are meant to live a psychoanalytic lifetime together. The therapist must be willing to suffer the illness of such a place" (p. 142). As we conceive of the work in therapy, education, and consultation, the word "illness" does not suggest pathology as much as it does a feeling of being deeply ill at ease in a way of being, as if we were feeling sick. Nor is suffering meant to suggest victimization or masochism. As Bollas uses the term, he means the act of being with and informed by a client's way of living such that we know it keenly from inside our own bodies.

With each client, we live a unique encounter in time. Moreover, our openness to understanding our clients' modes of being means that we will develop an intimacy with them that will affect or infect us with many of our strongest feelings and protocols. We, in turn, convey those experiences back to our clients, in a reciprocal and often unspoken dialogue about what it means to be in the world with others. The often subtle interaction of those relational cues and counter-cues can be traced in the following case illustration.

Getting "under the skin": A case of protocol at work

Anna, a therapist in her mid-40s with considerable clinical experience, had been presenting a troubling case for several months in supervision. The work with her client, Catherine, a successful advertising writer in her late 30s, had apparently proceeded well for the first three years. Catherine had entered treatment after a devastating break-up with a lover. She described herself as the one who broke men's hearts by leaving them when the relationship peaked in its excitement. This gave her a great sense of desirability and power. She told Anna that for years she had fucked men, not loved them. This most recent lover, however, she had begun to love, and his leaving left her furious, humiliated, and bereft. Though Catherine spent many of the early sessions raging about what a "pig" this man was, she knew she had actually entered therapy to give up what she saw as her perverse sexual behavior and learn to love someone. She wanted children and a family, and feared she was not capable of such attachments.

Anna felt a deep respect for Catherine's commitment to therapy and found herself growing quite fond of her client. She did not want Catherine to get hurt again and at the same time felt silently judgmental of Catherine's risky sexual exploits. Catherine, on the other hand, had begun to complain of feeling too vulnerable and dependent upon Anna. In some way, Anna's respect and affection had begun to register in Catherine's experience, but she felt disoriented with it and could not recognize it for what it was—one woman (who happened to be a therapist) coming to respect and care for another woman (who happened to be a client). Catherine grew increasingly anxious in her relationship with Anna and started to become silently suspicious of Anna's motives. At the same time, Catherine acknowledged that she was gaining a lot of insight, had stopped leaping from one relationship to another, and—with Anna's active insistence—was spending a period of time alone in her life without a lover to stimulate and distract her.

Catherine told Anna that she felt her interest and investment but did not understand her motives. What she did not tell Anna was that she had begun to project onto Anna many romantic and sexual fantasies to explain Anna's deepening interest in her. Catherine could only understand experiencing their deepening intimacy in the familiar terms of sexual usage. She pressed Anna to explain how she really felt about her. Unable to tolerate or explore Catherine's deepening anxiety and confusion, Anna finally gave into the pressure and explained to Catherine that she was not treating her any differently than any other client, that she was invested in the quality of Catherine's life, and that she did not want to foster a dependent relationship. Catherine felt profoundly shocked and humiliated by this explanation, though she could not risk telling Anna how she felt.

Up to this point, the treatment relationship had been productive, but it had also stayed within the essential elements of both Anna and Catherine's scripts. Anna, due to her own therapy, had subtly begun to change her way of relating to her clients, including Catherine. Anna had begun to discover that being less habitually nurturing to her clients left her feeling more open and deeply engaged with them. The closeness, she found, could also be quite unnerving. The therapeutic relationship between Anna and Catherine, though still influenced by script constraints, was productive enough to begin opening levels of intimacy, shifting each of the women from predictable, script-level styles of relating into more unpredictable realms. Neither was conscious of the shift, but each felt increasingly disorganized and anxious. Neither could tolerate and reflect upon the anxiety, and both shifted into escalated script behavior to ward off their anxiety and the uncertainty of what was emerging between them.

In retrospect, we can speculate about the script and protocol levels of interaction for both Anna and Catherine. Anna was born to a very young mother who had not finished high school and who greeted the birth of her daughter with overwhelming anxiety. Anna "knew" through her body, from her earliest days, that she was a profound source of anxiety to her mother, which her mother enacted with massively intrusive behavior. Her father, immature and frightened of the world (and of his wife), withdrew from his endlessly distressed and inconsolable wife and from the baby. Anna quickly discovered if she calmed herself down, Mom was more at ease and available. Infant Anna probably scanned the environment constantly for signs of anxiety. Anxiety was the defining state of affect at the level of protocol, and separation of one sort or another among the family members was the relational means of reducing anxiety. As she got older, she learned to soothe her mother and entertain her father, in a severe and chronic reversal of roles—and the beginning of her script. Anna's earlier protocol was dominated by anxiety and distancing, while her caretaking and entertaining script provided a more satisfying (if defensive) experience of relationship. When other siblings were born, Anna became the caretaker and buffer for all anxieties—more script. We could say that, by age 3, a "therapist" was already hard at work.

Catherine, in contrast, was an only child, born out of wedlock. Her father did not want the baby and threatened his girlfriend with leaving if she did not have an abortion. Due to pressures from both families, the young couple married and had the baby, or "the little brat," as Catherine's father typically referred to her. Catherine's mother, terrified of losing her reluctant husband, often left "the brat" in the care of grandparents or girlfriends and renewed a vigorous sexual relationship with her husband and served at his beck and call. Catherine never had a chance of breaking into this fused and immature couple. Life in the house was saturated with sexual energy. Her body knew little of tenderness or constancy but a great deal about anxiety, loneliness, and hostility; this was her protocol. Her script was centered in hatred and in living up to her nickname, "the brat." She insisted that her earliest memory was of wishing her father dead. No one could tell her what to do. She was smoking at 10, drinking at 12, having sex and using drugs by 13. She was raped for the first time at 15. In a later adolescent evolution of her script, she became the rapist, and then as an advertising writer she got great satisfaction in writing "bullshit," "getting over on everybody," and making a lot of money.

The deepening involvement and intimacy between Anna and Catherine carried each of them beyond the safety of their scripts. The closeness threatened each, and the resulting anxieties pushed each into affective and bodily experiences at the level of protocol, which for these two women would become bad news. Neither was able to tolerate *either the intimacy or the anxiety*, and no one in the treatment system understood protocol, so as to help either of them understand what was happening. Each reacted to the pain and anxiety of the protocol level of experience by moving back into script defenses with unconscious urgency.

In what seemed to Anna to be an abrupt change, treatment took a turn for the worse. In session after session, Catherine accused Anna of having lied to her, of having seduced her sexually, and of causing her depression and suicidality to worsen. Outside the sessions, Catherine began photographing Anna, her car, and her home. Anna's efforts to explore what had gone wrong were increasingly derailed by Catherine's escalating behavior both during and outside their sessions. Catherine began sending long, rambling letters and cards in which she included passionate poems and spoke of the friendship the two would have once the therapy relationship was over. At the same time, Catherine initiated several calls to the agency where Anna worked, citing ethics violations and incompetence.

Anna tried to absorb these shocks as she attempted to repair what had seemed a positive and productive relationship. Her script-level interpretations to Catherine about her projections and her behavior, when she could hold on to her mind long enough to formulate them, were met with fury. Anna's efforts in her personal therapy to understand past relationship troubles seemed to go in unhelpful, discouraging circles. She was also becoming increasingly confused, anxious, and paranoid in a way that she felt was affecting her work with other clients, many of whom had histories of trauma and numerous failed treatments.

Anna's supervisor, Paul, a seasoned clinician in his late 50s, responded to her case first by listening and asking questions, then by offering more script-level interpretations and advice in the face of her increasing anxiety, and finally by distancing himself from her developing depression. He found himself angered by her presentation of herself as a victim and by her apparent inability to stem what to him was a clear need to interpret the client's behavior and set professional limits. He thought she ought to refer the client for medication (which Anna had done many times before, to no avail) and, if the client refused to be evaluated psychiatrically, Paul strongly believed Anna should terminate the relationship by offering an appropriate referral to another therapist.

As the months of this supervisory process wore on, Paul became increasingly rigid—emotionally, physically, and intellectually. He began to suspect that some of the accusations made by Anna's client might, in fact, be true. He questioned Anna's competence. He began documenting his interventions with Anna to protect himself in case the client's threatened legal actions against Anna would grow to involve him. Additionally, he felt guilty and angry about the fact that, over the years of supervising Anna, he had enjoyed her attractiveness and had always looked forward to their sessions together. This was now replaced by a feeling of being burdened and angry that she could not make use of his advice.

Curiously, he also avoided discussion of this case with the woman he saw for his own consultation on a monthly basis.

Quite understandably, the affective intensity and impasse developing within these interlocking relationships made thinking extremely difficult. What remained was primarily a suffocating mix of anxiety and contempt for all parties, including others being dragged into the situation: friends, partners, professional colleagues, attorneys, and advocates at a local women's sexual assault center. This was not the kind of situation that was likely to turn out well. Indeed, it was eerily reminiscent for all of prior catastrophic situations in school, at work, in families, and among friends. But those reminiscences were operating outside conscious awareness. They were present more in the form of forebodings and compulsions to escape from something that had turned so bad.

The resolution of this complicated impasse began in an unexpected way. Catherine—who sought help and healing from a variety of people—was at that time also consulting a nutritionist named Sarah. Sarah lived on a small farm, outside the city, where she grew vegetables and fruit, some of which she gave to clients as a way of supporting better eating habits. Catherine had been telling Sarah about her unethical therapist, as she had been telling everyone. Sarah, in turn, had been lending a sympathetic and empathetic ear, as she was inclined to do with her clients. One day, Catherine was at Sarah's picking up her nutritional supplements as well as a small bag of tomatoes and peppers from Sarah's garden. Sarah, in response to Catherine's latest report on Anna, made a casual remark to the effect that perhaps Catherine also had a role to play in what was happening with Anna. Without missing a beat, Catherine's face froze; she dropped the bag of vegetables to the ground, and with one move placed her foot squarely on the vegetables. She leaned toward Sarah, saying with quiet fury, "You better stick to what you know about. I don't need you poisoning me, too."

Sarah's response was to step back in shock and fear. Then, although she nearly began to cry, she chose instead to recover by breathing deeply, alternately looking Catherine in the eye and turning away to collect herself. Finally, after what seemed an eternity to both of them, Sarah looked directly at Catherine and said, "I'm not interested in a phony, abusive relationship, Catherine." Sarah was still shaking. "I don't think it's good for either of us. When you are ready to apologize for ruining what I gave you, you are welcome to come back here again." Then she stood facing Catherine, trembling and waiting for her to leave, which Catherine did, in a state of bewilderment and anger.

Catherine spent a week feeling utterly depressed and pained. She could not even function at work, which had not been a problem during the conflict with Anna. Yet Catherine did not join in with her friends when they suggested that Sarah was just another treacherous witch. Instead, she found herself with little enthusiasm for her campaign against Anna. She became terrified of the idea that maybe the whole thing had been a terrible misunderstanding. She made one trip out to Sarah's, with the intent both to hurt her and to apologize, yet when she got out of her car and saw Sarah looking at her from the garden, Catherine began sobbing without knowing why. She fled. She then called Anna the next day to ask for a special appointment, which Anna later said she must have been crazy to accommodate given everything that had been happening.

Yet a corner had been turned. Catherine's encounter with Sarah—to whom Catherine eventually apologized after some months of working with Anna—had precipitated a sequence of painful realizations for Catherine, Anna, and Paul. When Paul first heard what had happened with Sarah and Catherine, for example, he also felt close to tears, then went blank, and found himself thinking of an experience he had had recently with a young male client who had been acting out and missing sessions. For the first time, Paul began talking about his impasse with Anna, both with his consultant and a close friend. Anna, too, shifted how she presented her experience with Catherine and began to recognize how Paul's responses had not been helpful. She ventured some timid suggestions to that effect, which Paul was able to explore with her without either blaming himself or distancing, although he continued to feel uncomfortable with the new intimacy of their relationship. His prior feelings of attraction and disdain for her were being replaced by a new sense of her as a person and as a colleague, feelings that he found even more disconcerting.

Anna and Catherine worked together for another year and a half, trying to sort out what had happened, and eventually decided together that it would be helpful for Catherine to see another therapist. Catherine felt sadness at this decision but believed it was the right one. She found it too difficult to think with Anna about what had happened. She left grateful for what Anna had given her. Anna, on her part, just felt relief when Catherine was gone. She began to consider taking an administrative position at her agency, believing that she could no longer emotionally handle her work as a therapist.

Discussion: Applying the concept of the protocol to move through an impasse

After conducting the interviews from which we assembled this case illustration, we were struck by how the resolution of the impasse was simultaneously productive and saddening. Both of us could identify with the story based on our own clinical experience, and it resonated with the impasses to which we each have been a party. It also left us with the sense that it is impossible to emerge from an intimate encounter without being deeply affected. In particular, it seems impossible to grow within a therapeutic or consultative couple without feeling a sense of both accomplishment and loss.

In hindsight, the crisis or disruptive impasse that occurred for these three individuals likely arose from the disruption of a more confluent, script-level impasse that had been operating for some time between the client–therapist and the therapist–supervisor. As a therapist, Anna had behaved with Catherine in ways that she typically did with others in her life, repeating a script-based, relational role of being supportive, non-confronting, and overly responsible. This had suited Catherine just fine. Anna's therapeutic style was a welcome respite from the hopeless neglect that Catherine experienced in the midst of her parents' intensely fused and rejecting relationship, and so the first three years of treatment seemed to have gone quite well. In fact, there was little room for individuality, surprise, or robust intimacy. Yet Anna had, over those years, continued her own work in personal therapy, supervision, and training and had begun to mature to the point that she was less inclined to follow some of her old script patterns. She had begun to change gradually, and many of her clients had adjusted productively to the change in her style of engagement. Catherine, however, experienced Anna's change as a threat and a betrayal, and so had retaliated in kind, feeling as if her most fundamental trust had been violated.

In this case, the resolution of the impasse did not occur because the therapist and supervisor came to their senses, were able to think again, and helped the client think. Rather, the turning point occurred outside the therapeutic context and was then brought by the client back into the therapeutic setting, whereupon it was relayed into the supervisory situation.

That sequence usefully illustrates two principles. The first is that an intimate, protocol-level impasse cannot be resolved until someone in the relationship is willing to sit with the extreme discomfort of the activated affect, *feel* it, and gradually find words to think about it and communicate it to the other. This brings to mind Bion's (1963) concept of containing, whereby the therapist or consultant willingly receives the client's affect-drenched experience and demonstrates that it is possible to experience the impact of it and find meaning in it, rather than immediately defending against it by acting out of script. We see an example of containment in the response of Sarah, the nutritionist, to Catherine. Once Sarah had demonstrated that she could withstand the strength of her own intense reactions to her client without acting in a rejecting or retaliatory way, her way of being began to have an effect on Catherine's experience. It destabilized a fundamental and unconscious worldview, that is, protocol, that Catherine had been living out in every other area of her life. Sarah's protocol in this case was not hooked; shocked, yes, but permitting of enough perspective to recognize that her relationship with Catherine might yet be salvaged and that her anger and limit-setting were appropriate. She did not blame Catherine or turn her into an overwhelmingly fearful monster. Sarah set a personal boundary and spoke of the relationship in terms that she believed might function more effectively in the future.

Work in a therapeutic or consultative relationship can begin to move again once the therapeutic or consultative couple's history and feeling tones have been contained. As McLaughlin (1994) writes in regard to impasses in the analytic setting:

> I do not wish to assert that growth of personal insight in the analyst invariably disposes of all stalemates, nor that his bettered involvement can

heal all woundings. But I feel confident that seeking to restore one's optimal competence is the best, and sometimes the only, recourse in times of analytic impasse. Without this personal investment in self-scrutiny by the analyst, he is very likely to keep inflicting hurts and abandonment. These can become chronic strain traumata which will erode beyond restoration the aliveness and hope essential for both members of the dyad if they are to sustain their investment in reaching for analytic engagement.

Thus, the professional may be the one to recognize the need for self-analysis.

But the second principle that this case illustrates is that the resolution of an impasse can begin with the initiative of *either* partner in the therapeutic or consultative couple. Things can begin moving when at least one partner can begin to reflect on the affect that both are living within. In this particular case, the client initiated the process of thinking within the therapeutic relationship, which in turn was carried into the supervisory relationship, in an instance of what might be called productive parallel process.

What most characterizes the clinical situation involving Anna, Catherine, and Paul as a protocol-based impasse is the intensity with which certain emotional patterns were activated in what had been long-term working relationships. The intimacy within them had become taken for granted, as habitual and familiar as the ways each person negotiated that intimacy. However, when the impasse occurred, the capacity to think while remaining engaged had simply collapsed and was most likely on the road to fulfilling the highly negative fantasies each person had about their significant relationships.

It is important to note, however, that Catherine's initial response to Sarah was not appreciative or even insightful. She instead felt her interior world and certainties being shaken. She experienced a collapse. She entertained intense fantasies of revenge, nearly leading to action. Yet instead of reacting out of force of habit by attacking Sarah further, which would have been a continuing enactment of script, she chose to take Sarah's goodwill toward her on faith, a goodwill grounded both in their history as nutritionist and client and in Sarah's demonstration of courage in the moment. Catherine could feel the possibility of a new way of relating.

Anna, for her part, could have also chosen to take Catherine's rapprochement as an opportunity simply to cover over the ugliness of the preceding months. She could have pacified Catherine and appeared to be engaged in a process of reconciliation. But she decided, instead, to look at herself and her other relationships. We do not know whether her idea to change careers was the result of reflection, of her typical habit of retreat, or of being burned out. But there is reason to believe that whatever decision she finally came to would be made with considerably more thoughtfulness than if she had not chosen to reflect thoughtfully on what had happened in her work with Catherine.

Paul also took the opportunity to look at some of his usual ways of relating, especially to the women in his life. He showed a bit more emotional availability in both his work and his personal life, to which he reacted at times with renewed distancing, as if the increase in vulnerability also opened him to more intense feelings of pain and pleasure, about which he was ambivalent and tentatively hopeful.

When Anna and Catherine eventually had a chance to talk about what had precipitated the crisis, it seemed that it had been a simple remark made by Anna, similar to the observation that Sarah eventually made to Catherine. When Catherine's response to Anna turned explosive and assaulting, Anna did not have the resources at the time to stand her ground. She felt—more than she was conscious—that her move toward maturity was destructive of her significant relationships. Following protocol, she had become defensive and withdrawn. Her small step toward growth had precipitated such a cataclysm that it did not seem worth the cost to proceed.

Paul also had settled into a comfortable, repetitive role with Anna. He had, in fact, built his supervision practice to relieve himself of the strain he felt seeing clients. The therapists he worked with, although struggling and unaware of their own entrenched protocols, were typically adapted enough not to disturb him too much. Anna, for example, found his attention and attraction to her appealing, although she was not consciously aware of it. Paul had learned to operate with emotional distance in all the areas of his life. He had figured out how not to bring into his own supervision any of the issues that might give his supervisor something with which to stir him affectively. So, when Anna began to use her supervision with Paul in a way that was intense, he had become removed and passively hostile toward her. Yet he had been moved by Catherine's encounter with Sarah, when Anna eventually relayed it, because it corresponded to his own pained hope for more vitality. He deeply, and unconsciously, regretted the loss of connection in his life and work.

Above all, this case illustrates that resolving a protocol-based impasse is never neat. The emotional threads that underlie our most primary relational templates are a part of our history that cannot be undone, even if we learn to live differently with them. Yet these are the very interactions we are drawn to again and again, because, as McLaughlin (2005) notes, "we seek to test and find ourselves in the intimacy of the therapeutic relationship, to become known to and accepted by the other, in whose sum we may more fully assess ourselves" (p. 158).

Therein lies the paradox. The closeness that comes of human relating gets under our skin in a way that can be felt as a fantasy of perfect merger and love or as a nightmare of constricting sameness and hatred. At the same time, it is in this intimacy with others that we finally know that we are capable of living in the world. In their sum, we can then most fully assess our potential for life.

Chapter 12

Nonconscious processes and self-development: Key concepts from Eric Berne and Christopher Bollas

Co-authored with N. M. Landaiche, III

Expediency was one of Eric Berne's guiding principles. He strove to be efficiently and quickly helpful. He likewise developed his theory of human functioning and his practice of helping in a relatively short period of time (from 1957 to 1970). His contribution—transactional analysis—has been remarkably successful around the world in providing an efficient framework for professionals in a wide variety of organizational, educational, and clinical settings. However, given the speed with which Berne worked out his theory and approach to practice, he understandably left gaps in a full understanding of human personality and interaction.

In those gaps, differing schools of thought soon emerged, including the classical, redecision, and Cathexis schools (Barnes, 1977). More recently, integrative approaches to transactional analysis (TA) have been offered by Clarkson (1992) and Erskine (1998). There is also a growing interest in what is known as relational TA (Cornell & Hargaden, 2005; Hargaden & Sills, 2002). There is even a method of transactional psychoanalysis (Novellino, 2005). Increasingly, TA practitioners have recognized the need to expand their understanding of human behavior and their practice methods in order to help clients and groups who are not responsive to traditional TA approaches. This parallels a similar trend in psychoanalytic circles whereby Klein's followers built on classical Freudian ideas in order to treat the psychotic patients Freud considered unanalyzable. Kleinian innovations have in turn been extended and modified by analysts from the British Independent tradition, by followers of Lacan in France, and by analysts affiliated with the American relational schools.

We believe that some of these contemporary psychoanalytic ideas can contribute significantly to an expansion of traditional transactional analysis. But we also think that traditional TA concepts can, in turn, clarify those psychoanalytic ideas by translating them into more ordinary language and by emphasizing their practical use in people's lives. In this Bernean spirit, we will explore some of Berne's (1949, 1952, 1953, 1955, 1962, 1963, 1968, 1972) under-developed ideas related to nonconscious processes and the development of the self. Those ideas correspond to contemporary psychoanalytic thinking, particularly the early work of analyst Christopher Bollas (1987, 1989). We will then link Bollas' analytic concepts back to the practice of transactional analysis. In this way, we hope to remain true to Berne's vision while encouraging ourselves and our TA colleagues, as a community of professionals, to continue learning and growing.

A conversation between transactional analysis and psychoanalysis

Our thinking for this chapter was inspired by an invitation from the Societa' Italiana di Metodologie Psicoterapeutic e Analisi Transazionale in Rome to present a three-day workshop comparing the ideas of Eric Berne with those of Christopher Bollas. One of us (first author) was an expert in transactional analysis, body psychotherapy, and psychodynamic psychotherapy. The other (second author) knew little of transactional analysis but was trained as a counselor, psychotherapist, and organizational consultant with a background in object relations and group analytic theories. The workshop attendees engaged our different yet complementary backgrounds in a way that helped us to appreciate the meaningfulness of what we presented for both their work in diverse fields and their personal lives.

Eric Berne and Christopher Bollas also came from different yet complementary backgrounds. Both trained as psychoanalysts, although a generation apart in very different psychoanalytic cultures. Both were rebellious thinkers among their psycho-analytic colleagues. Berne (1910–1970) was trained in classical psychoanalysis and the American paradigm of ego psychology, which extolled the functions and capacities of the ego. That model infused Berne's thinking as he developed transactional analysis. He saw the ego (especially in its Adult state) as the road to health and autonomy. He also sought to make patterns of communication and beliefs about self and others conscious, with decisions made ideally under the guidance of the Adult ego state. More than a generation later, Bollas (1943–) was trained in London in British object relations theories, with particular emphasis in the Indepen-dent, Winnicottian tradition. Bollas' primary attention has been to patterns of unconscious communication and experiencing. Yet in contrast to Berne, Bollas has not conceived of the ego as ideally in charge but rather as relentlessly—and with great effort—swimming upstream against the forces of early object relations.

In spite of these contrasts, Berne and Bollas each sought to engage the intelligence and generative potential of their patients. Each worked to counter the sometimes authoritarian and rigid frameworks of their contemporaries. The freedom and essential hopefulness of their thinking also offer us an opportunity for dialogue today about what it means to be human and how to make the best use of our lives.

Nonconscious processes: Internal and interpersonal

When we encounter our clients and students, we must make sense of more than they put into words. They "speak" to us with gestures, body language, facial expressions, states of feeling, and unique ways of being. Whether we work individually or in groups, we must process enormous quantities of experiential data about which we and our clients/students may not be fully aware. As we work, we must also account for our own feelings, bodily reactions, intuitive cognitions, and interpersonal interactions, about which we may also be unaware. In short, a great deal of human relations work involves processes that are nonconscious.

Generally, the term "nonconscious" refers to physiological and psychological organization and learning that operate outside of conscious awareness. Nonconscious levels of mental and somatic functioning contain, among other things, the undigested remnants of past experiences, many of which may be haunted by loss, helplessness, rage, shame, or trauma. This is similar to the classical psychoanalytic idea of the dynamic Unconscious, a place within the mind often characterized (and caricatured) as the trash bin of childhood—the dark repository of repressed, split-off, rejected aspects of a "primitive" self and unwanted, unassimilated aspects of childhood. Yet, although the realm of nonconscious experience may well contain elements of developmental history and trauma, our minds and bodies also constantly inform, shape, and enrich our lives in nonconscious, fully healthy ways. We learn to do things such as walk, dance, drive, play sports, cook, care for children, and engage in conversation so that ultimately we do them without much conscious thought. In fact, we successfully live large parts of our lives without being fully aware of everything we are sensing, organizing, or doing.

Mancia (2007) describes this nonconscious aspect of life in terms of implicit memory, which he says "extends the concept of the unconscious and considers a possible non-repressive origin, linked to a child's earliest preverbal and presymbolic experiences that cannot be recalled but nevertheless influence the person's affective, cognitive and sexual life even as an adult" (p. 7). He explains:

> Implicit memory... stores experiences that are not conscious and cannot be described verbally. Here various forms of learning are filed, such as priming (meaning a person's ability to identify an object visually or [auditorily] as a result of having already been exposed to it, possibly not consciously but only subliminally); *procedural memory*, which keeps track of motor and cognitive skills such as the movements needed for certain sports, or to play musical instruments, and the memory of numerous everyday things we do automatically without even being conscious of how; [and] *emotional and affective memory*, where the brain stores its recollections of emotions arousing from affective experiences of the child's earliest relations with the environment, and particularly with the mother.
>
> (p. 32, emphasis in original)

Indeed, without awareness, our bodies receive and process an extraordinary amount of environmental stimuli and accomplish highly complex activities (cardiopulmonary, digestive, motoric, visual, auditory, fight/flight, and immunological, to name a few). Most of us could never process these inputs or sustain these activities with full intention and awareness. As a result, most of what we live occurs nonconsciously.

The term "unconscious" commonly refers to a cognitive/emotional process within the individual. But we think of nonconscious processes as also being interpersonal. Human beings are continually engaged in interactions and communications that are not always fully conscious. We pick up, are influenced by, and utilize nonverbal signals from one another without always knowing that we are doing so. We often choose our friends, lovers, and enemies on the basis of gut reactions, attractions, and intuitions that operate outside awareness. These nonconscious processes also operate in professional relationships and in our transactions with clients and students, as we will discuss in greater detail later.

Thus, to avoid some of the connotations and misunderstandings often associated with the term "unconscious," we will speak here of "nonconscious processes." We want to address more than just a place in the mind; rather, we want to consider an active, interpersonal dynamic that is central to human relations work.

Berne's emphasis on intuition

Early in his career as a psychiatrist, Berne (1949) had the job of assessing the psychological health of young men to determine their fitness for US military service. These assessments had to be performed quickly, and Berne noticed that he began jumping to rapid conclusions about the men based on minimal interaction. When he later attempted to verify these conclusions, he found that many of his spontaneous insights turned out to be accurate. He became curious about how he could know something about a patient without receiving much overt information and without knowing how he came to his conclusions. This led him to wonder more broadly about how people know the things they know.

Berne organized his thinking on this topic in a paper he delivered on October 18, 1947 to the annual joint meeting of the San Francisco and Los Angeles Psychoanalytic Societies. In that paper, he drew on the work of Edward J. Kempf, an early 20th-century physician and psychoanalyst. Berne (1949) wrote:

> E. J. Kempf ... somewhat like Darwin, speaks of understanding emotional states in others by "reflex imitation though similar brief muscle tensions," and states that by this token "in a certain sense we think with our muscles." This method of judgment may be called "intuition through subjective experience."
>
> (p. 3)

Berne was challenging the usual notion of knowing as a purely mental process. When he highlighted phrases such as "reflex imitation" and "think[ing] with our muscles," he was acknowledging that we learn and know things in our bodies.

He could well have been describing what we speak of today as "somatic resonance" or even "countertransference." In a paper published six years later, however, Berne (1955) emphasized that he was not confusing intuition with empathy, as some readers had assumed:

> By intuition, [I am referring] to a spontaneous diagnostic process whose end products spontaneously come into awareness if resistances are lifted. In the case of empathy ... [it] has a connotation of identification. Intuition, as the writer sees it, has essentially nothing to do with such adult forms of identification. It has to do with the automatic processing of sensory perceptions.
>
> (pp. 94–95)

In choosing the ordinary word "intuition," as opposed to coining something more technical, Berne (1949) sought to elucidate what he saw as an ordinary human capacity for processing sensory perceptions:

> Intuition is knowledge based on experience and acquired through sensory contact with the subject [the other], without the "intuiter" being able to formulate to himself or others exactly how he came to his conclusions.... It is knowledge ... acquired by means of preverbal unconscious or preconscious functions.
>
> (p. 4)

> Not only is the individual unaware of how he knows something; he may not even know what it is that he knows, but behaves or reacts in a specific way as if ... his actions or reactions were based on something that he knew.
>
> (p. 5)

Berne was alluding here to the fact that complex cognitive processing and decision-making can occur outside awareness. He considered intuition to be "an archaeopsychic phenomenon" (Berne, 1962, p. 161). This nonconscious aspect of living would, of course, eventually form the basis for his concepts of protocol and script. But in his early writings, Berne did not consider intuitive, nonconscious decision-making to be necessarily problematic. Nor did he seem to believe that it was even essential to make those processes conscious:

> To understand intuition, it seems necessary to avoid the belief that in order to know something the individual must be able to put into words what he knows and how he knows it.
>
> (Berne, 1949, p. 28)

By characterizing these nonconscious cognitive processes as normal and likely pervasive, Berne was challenging the belief that we are consciously in charge of our lives. He was thus laying the groundwork for his analysis of transactions, in which such nonconscious processes can sometimes be understood to be operating at odds with the lives we seek to live with intention.

The concept of protocol

Berne began his professional career deeply influenced by psychoanalysis. He had hoped, early on, that he might eventually become a psychoanalyst himself. But as a rebel in a time that was highly intolerant of nonconformity, Berne ended up rejected by his psychoanalytic colleagues. Some of his later repudiation of psychoanalysis seems to have been a hurt and angry reaction to this treatment by his peers. But some of Berne's criticism of psychoanalysis was similar to that being voiced by other psychiatrists and psychologists of his era, part of an emerging cultural and professional challenge to psychoanalytic dogma. For these reasons, Berne strove to differentiate transactional analysis from psychoanalysis. In his final book, *What Do You Say after You Say Hello?* (1972), he eliminated nearly all references to the unconscious, arguably the most central premise of psychoanalytic theory.

Before that last book, however, Berne's writings were permeated with references to unconscious organization and motivation within individuals and groups. To address this discrepancy between Berne's earlier and later legacies, a two-day conference entitled "Attualità dell'Inconscio" ("The Relevance of the Unconscious Today") was convened in Rome in 2006 to reconsider the usefulness of "the unconscious" for transactional analysts today. (Selected papers from that conference, along with other contributions on the topic, appeared in a special April 2008 edition of the *Transactional Analysis Journal*.)
Berne drew on the idea of unconscious organization when he created his concept of "protocol," a concept he never developed as fully as he did his theory of script. In Berne's (1963) thinking, protocol was the largely unconscious pattern that shaped an individual's later script:

> Each person has an unconscious life plan [or script], formulated in his earliest years.... *The original set of experiences which forms the pattern for the plan is called the protocol....* In later years he strives to bring about as close as possible a reproduction of the original protocol situation, either to live it through again if it was enjoyable, or to try to re-experience it in a more benevolent form if it was unpleasant.
>
> (pp. 218–219, emphasis added)

> The original drama, the protocol, is usually completed in the early years of childhood, often by the age of 5, occasionally earlier.... A protocol ... is of such a crude nature that it is quite unsuitable as a program for grown-up relationships. It becomes largely forgotten (unconscious) and is replaced by a more civilized version, the script proper.
>
> (p. 228)

Cornell and Landaiche (2005) summarized protocol as follows:

> Protocol based behavior is … a deeply compelling implicit (wordless) memory of primary relational patterns, lived through the immediacy of bodily experience. Protocols function as ongoing, unconscious templates for making judgments about the significant figures and encounters in our lives. Yet protocols are not necessarily pathological; they embody an innate human capacity for making unconscious sense of life with others. They only become problematic when they interfere with the ability to generate new bodily and relational possibilities.
>
> (p. 19)

Fast (2006), although not describing protocol, nonetheless illuminates the concept when she writes,

> These familial impressions … [are] patterns established in the activities of family life, the "stereotype plates" that might persist to govern a person's life even in adulthood: patterns of loving and hating, of fears and desires, of interpersonal relationships and action.
>
> (p. 278)

In essence, the protocol is a latent level of somatic and relational organization that operates outside conscious awareness and precedes the formation of script. Protocol is more than implicit memory, however. It is not just a record of the past. Rather, protocol is the result of the child's active effort to make meaning and sense of things, both bodily and pre-verbally.

Protocol shares some characteristics with Berne's conception of intuition. Both operate outside awareness. And both exemplify the human capacity to make complex, nonconscious sense of things. However, Berne used the two concepts differently. Whereas his use of the term "intuition" fits the standard meaning of the word, he adapted the term "protocol" to reference a form of patterning that is not commonly recognized. He spoke of "protocol" in order to indicate that we not only organize our experiences outside awareness, but those organizations also compel the decisions we make about living.

Berne wrote about protocol as forming in the early years of life. That emphasis on the impact of early development is shared by most psychologists, psychotherapists, and psychoanalysts. Indeed, Bollas, in his early work, wrote of the mother–infant relationship as establishing the basis for later relationship patterns. We will explicate some of his ideas later in this chapter. However, we also want to point out that nonconscious processes, intuition, and protocol are not just part of developmental history; they are not just archaic forms of knowing. Rather, they remain an integral aspect of every human being throughout life. Moreover, we establish new protocols as we experience and organize new things in life. Learning a new physical activity, for example, can change our experience of moving through the other areas of our lives. Learning a new way of relating likewise can reshape our nonconscious sense of what it means to be in the world with others.

Unthought knowing

As we began reading Berne and Bollas alongside one another, we had the sense of their texts and ideas in dialogue, back and forth. We were struck by the number of parallels in their work, especially the way Berne's theory of intuition and his writings on how to listen clinically fit with Bollas' theories of unconscious communication and reception. As we noted earlier, Bollas has been a radical thinker in his own time. But he came of age when psychoanalysis had already begun to lose its power in psychiatry, and he thus had room to think more freely. That freedom has likely been a factor accounting for Bollas' greater success in challenging psychoanalytic orthodoxy while retaining the respect of his analytic peers.

Indeed, whereas Berne wrote as if he had to promote and defend his ideas against a more dominant and pervasive theory of human functioning, Bollas writes as if others might find his ideas stimulating. He seems less encumbered than Berne in that respect. In fact, many of Bollas' concepts are more poetic than scientific. He chooses words or terms not for their efficiency, as Berne did, but to stir our imaginations.

Take, for example, Bollas' (1987) frequently referenced idea of "the unthought known" (pp. 277–283), which he elaborated in his first book. This phrase seems almost paradoxical. Its terms nearly cancel each other out. In that way, Bollas captures some of the elusive, paradoxical quality of human mental activity. What we know may not yet exist in thought. What we choose to unthink may yet continue as a potent form of knowledge. Bollas is introducing us to the strange realm of the human mind and body.

And yet Bollas' ideas are common-sensical as well. In his use of "the unthought known," he is suggesting that every individual has a bodily capacity to sense and organize countless impressions of the world and to use that knowing to make nonconscious decisions about life. This bodily way of knowing is available for use by the individual but is not consciously thought in the form of words, images, or symbols. This conception of nonconscious experiencing and knowing differs from the Freudian unconscious in that it is not a product of repression, defense, or pathology. The unthought known is a normal and lifelong function for human beings. Bollas' concept also encompasses much of what Berne meant by intuition and protocol.

Moreover, these nonconscious processes apply to more than just individual behavior and psychology. Groups, families, and organizations also operate with patterns and assumptions that are known without anyone actually giving them conscious thought. Berne (1963) wrote about the primal power of the "group canon," which included the group's not-always-explicit governing constitution, its laws, and the resulting group culture (p. 147). He also wrote about the "group imago" as an individual and collective picture of what the "group is or should be like" (p. 321); he suggested that this imago could be "conscious, preconscious, or unconscious" (p. 321). He even discussed how protocol can affect an individual's group imago, although he was quick to add that there is not always a one-to-one correlation between the group imago and protocol (p. 241).

Anyone who has ever consulted in organizations knows the distinct feel that every organization develops: An atmosphere, a set of unspoken rules, a prevailing belief about what it means to survive as a group in the world. This, too, suggests the workings of protocol and the unthought known. And we pick up these things intuitively from those around us, whether we become aware of doing so or not.

Formative intersubjective experiences

Part of Berne's radicalism as a psychoanalytically trained psychiatrist was his emphasis on interpersonal transactions at a time when the prevailing psychiatric view—so heavily dominated by psychoanalytic thinking—emphasized individual intrapsychic mental processes. Berne believed we need to attend to what happens to people as they relate to one another. He further saw that changing these relationship patterns can contribute significantly to improved psychological health. This has been a foundational insight of transactional analysis.

Berne's thinking in this regard was influenced by object relations theory, particularly the work of Melanie Klein (Harley, 2006). Berne was receptive to this Kleinian way of thinking at a time when Klein's ideas were not widely accepted in psychoanalytic circles, especially in the United States where Berne worked. This same object relations tradition also strongly influenced Bollas' work, although his teachers and mentors had already begun to form a distinct, independent tradition within the British psychoanalytic community. In his writing, Bollas especially shows his indebtedness to Winnicott.

Object relations theorists see the primal interaction between mother and infant as foundational to the growing child's psychology. But this image of the mother and child is not invoked primarily to explain psychopathology. Rather, the interaction within the mother–infant dyad is paradigmatic of the human process of growth and maturation. Yes, elements of the history of that primary relationship remain with us and impact us. But more importantly, that same process of maturing within asymmetric relationships occurs throughout life. It characterizes the forward movement of maturation and growth that we also attempt to facilitate as consultants, teachers, counselors, and psychotherapists.

Just as Berne believed, nonconscious, intersubjective experiences play a fundamental role in how we continue growing as people.

Berne's intuitive function

Berne (1949) conceived of what he called "the intuitive function" (p. 30) as more than just an intrapsychic process. Rather, he saw it as an essential component in an interpersonal process, "part of a series of perceptive processes which work above and below the level of consciousness in an apparently integrated fashion, with shifting emphasis according to special conditions" (p. 30). Many of those "special conditions" pertain to ever-changing relational dynamics. Berne noted how human beings are exquisitely sensitive to one another, as if each of us is continually assessing one another—a fundamental psychological orientation that occurs outside awareness.

> It is apparent ... that there are cognitive processes which function below the level of consciousness. In fact, human beings, when they are in full possession of their faculties, behave at all times as though they were continually and quickly making very subtle judgments about their fellow-men without being aware that they are doing so; or if they are aware of what they are doing, without being aware of *how* they do it.
>
> (Berne, 1952, p. 35)

Berne (1955) contended that "the normal adult, like the infant, understands some fundamental—that is, dynamically predominant—aspects of each person he meets" (p. 84). He linked this keen interpersonal sensitivity directly to the work of human relations professionals, which he often framed in terms of psychiatric or clinical roles:

> The term "intuitive individual" as used here ... [refers] to the clinician who deliberately uses his intuitive faculties when desirable in his diagnostic and therapeutic work. Descriptively, such a clinician is curious, mentally alert, interested, and receptive of latent and manifest communications from his patients.
>
> (Berne, 1962, pp. 159–160)

Beyond that level of perception and assessment, Berne (1953) also observed the nonconscious communicative process in which we are also continually engaged:

> In the case of interpersonal relationships... intended, precise, formal, rational, verbal communications are of less value than inadvertent, ambiguous, informal, nonrational, nonverbal communications.
>
> (p. 57)

> Interpersonal communication generally refers ... [to] communication which influences the development of the relationship between the autonomous portions of the personalities concerned.
>
> (pp. 58–59)

This attitude toward nonconscious communication is admittedly at odds with Berne's theory of games, for which transactional analysis is best known and which emphasizes the split-off, defensive, and manipulative intent of covert communications. In game theory, that which is covert is not simply nonconscious or hidden; it is hidden with an ulterior motive. Yet as the aforementioned passages indicate, Berne also appreciated other kinds of "ambiguous, informal, nonrational, nonverbal communications." Although he did not develop these concepts further, he was talking about the exchanges that occur as a normal part of human relations work. Moreover, in contrast to the usual idea of communication as a transfer of information, Berne was describing communication as an active process that "influences the development of the relationship." This development occurs between the "autonomous portions of the personalities," which are those self-aspects that exist independently and that are not bound by problematic script roles. In other words, we convey and exchange nonconsciously our energy, our passions, our ideas, our idiosyncrasies in order to grow in relation to others.

A shadow of the object

One of the unfortunate aspects of object relations theory is its use of the word "object." It sounds impersonal, even inanimate. It is left over from a legacy within psychoanalysis of attempting to sound scientific and emotionally unentangled. One could just as easily substitute the word "other." Yet "object" is the word we are left to deal with, even in the work of someone who writes as vividly as Bollas does.

For example, one of Bollas' (1987) more evocative phrases, borrowed from Freud, is "the shadow of the object." We can translate this as "the shadow of the other" or, more precisely, "the shadow of the significant other." This phrase is used to indicate that the individual's ego, or sense of self, always forms and functions in the shadow of the significant others who came before her or him (i.e., parents, grandparents, and so on). The word "shadow" suggests a trace or imprint, the felt sense and presence of our parents and their palpable early influence on us, an influence that precedes, and in some cases supersedes, specific messages received later from them. We are shadowed by the lives they lived and by their inadvertent legacies.

In choosing the word "shadow," Bollas (1987) is also suggesting an area of darkness within the ego that is hard to see or decipher. That shadowed area is structured, like protocol, and that structure and its history can likewise be difficult to trace.

Bollas (1987) notes, "The object can cast its shadow without a child being able to process this relation through mental representations or language" (p. 3). We experience our caregivers, teachers, and mentors in ways that may never be fully conscious or that may never be put into words. Bollas is indirectly asking us to appreciate the profound impact we can have on those who come to us for help in learning and growing.

Mother's idiom of care

Bollas (1987) suggests that we are haunted by the shadows of our predecessors. He thus points to an imponderable situation. We may feel the weight or impression of the past, yet never know it in detail. That level of mystery, he implies, is part of the human condition.

On the other hand, Bollas is also suggesting a way out of that area of darkness. He believes it is at least possible to imagine the specificity with which we have each been imprinted. More importantly, he conceives of the care we have received from important others to have been structured like a language, yet a "language" or idiom that was not necessarily put into words and that was in some sense unique or idiosyncratic to those important others. Bollas (1987) invokes the complex interaction between the infant's emerging self and the mother's more developed sense of self:

> We know that because of the considerable prematurity of human birth the infant depends on the mother for survival.... She both sustains the baby's life and transmits to the infant, through her own particular idiom of mothering, an aesthetic of being that becomes a feature of the infant's self. The mother's way of holding the infant, of responding to his gestures, of selecting objects, and of perceiving the infant's internal needs, constitute her contribution to the infant-mother culture.... The language of this relation is the idiom of gesture, gaze, and intersubjective utterance.
>
> (p. 13)

Bollas (1989) writes, "Human idiom is the defining essence of each person" (p. 212). By using the term "idiom," he alludes to each individual's unique nucleus, a kernel that, under favorable circumstances, will grow and articulate itself. Each person's idiom thus unfolds in time. It also refers to our human capacity to speak with a voice that is our own and to create symbols or ways of being that speak uniquely of us as individuals. An idiom, therefore, reveals our "aesthetic of being"—how we respond to our preferences, displeasures, and erotic inclinations in life.

Yet Bollas uses the term "aesthetic" to convey more than just our bodily response to the world or to works of art. He is also talking about the sensuous ways we organize those experiences and, in effect, create new works. An aesthetic sense is more than just one of pleasure; it acknowledges more than what might be considered attractive. After all, we create works of art, in part, to make sense of a world that can be extremely difficult and painful, too. A sense of the terrible informs the ancient concepts of truth and beauty. We seek the aesthetic to rediscover meaning and a sense of satisfactory organization. Bollas is trying to describe how individuals carry their experiential, aesthetic organizations in their bodies, sometimes in an effort to repeat those experiences and sometimes in an effort to convey or communicate them to another. The aesthetic also implies the possibility of finding satisfaction and meaning in our own work as professionals and in our own process of becoming ourselves.

Bollas considers the mother's idiom—her aesthetic or unique mode of expression—to be the source of a paradigmatic imprint on the developing child, an imprint not unlike Berne's idea of protocol in that the imprint is not just passively received but also shaped by the child's unique way of receiving and organizing it. Analogously, the idiom of any important person (e.g., a counselor, teacher, or mentor) will leave a unique, idiosyncratic impression on those whose growth and maturing they facilitate. Yet that impression will also be shaped, in turn, by the uniqueness of those growing and maturing individuals.

Transformational objects

Words like "imprint" and "impression," however, do not quite capture what Bollas believes can be the far more fundamental transformation achieved through our key relationships. He refers to that more radical potential when he writes, "The mother's idiom of care and the infant's experience of this handling is … the most profound occasion when the nature of the self is formed and transformed by the environment" (Bollas, 1987, p. 32). More succinctly, "As the infant's 'other' self, the mother transforms the baby's internal and external environment" (p. 13).

This facilitating, transformative function of the mother—offered in service to the infant's development—is the basis for Bollas' (1987) concept of the "transformational object" (p. 13). The mother is the paradigmatic object, or other, through whom self-transformation takes place. Yet formative relationships of this kind can occur for any of us across the life span, not just in infancy. So, although the transformational object is described in terms of the mother's role, Bollas means that object (or other) to be any person who performs a similar facilitative function in service of another's growth and maturation (e.g., a counselor, teacher, or mentor). That is, a transformational object is a significant other who engages with a child, student, patient, or client such that the engagement leads to fundamental change and growth. Bollas (1987) even says that "*the mother is less significant and identifiable as an object than as a process* that is identified with cumulative internal and external transformations" (p. 14, emphasis in original).

How does this transformative process occur? Bollas derives his idea from object relations theory, in which the mother or significant other takes in, at a bodily level, the unworded, nonconscious experiences of the child, client, or student. We are not describing anything mysterious here. Berne had already discussed this in terms of the intuitive function. As human beings working with other human beings, we simply pick up more information about other people than we can consciously process and usually more than they consciously intend to communicate. And in the arena of human relations work, we are especially receptive to the experiential aspects that our students and clients find problematic. In the same way that a mother or father learns to detect the signs of a child's distress, we come to know what is troubling our students and clients. And in the same way that a parent may not have an immediate solution for a child's upset, we often have to sit with our client's or student's distress for a period of time before we can think what to say or do.

That receptivity is only an initial step in a transformative process. In and of itself, receptivity (like empathy) is not sufficient for change. The human relations professional must find a way to feed back the experience so that the client or student can take it in and use it to do productive psychological work and to make useful changes in her or his life. The transformation, therefore, first takes place in the body of the mother or significant other, and not always consciously. What began as confusion or upset is transformed into something that can be lived within and perhaps thought about. And it is the communication of that attitude toward the problem—an attitude lived nonconsciously in the body—that then allows the child, student, or client to experience a change in her or his body as well. The transformational object is thus an embodied process. Moreover, it is a process we experience as operating on our behalf. And when that internalized process brings us relief from confusion or upset, we may recognize the transformational object first as our own experience of gratitude toward those significant, transformational others—our parents, teachers, and mentors.

In addition to designating an actual person, the transformational object is also an internalization of a transformative interpersonal encounter. It is an often unconscious memory of past maturational experiences. It can even be a nonconscious recognition that through such interactions one can significantly change internal states of affect and cognition. We then sometimes instinctively seek such significant, transformational others to further our growth and development. As Bollas (1987) writes, "In adult life... the [transformational] object is pursued in order to surrender to it as a medium that alters the self" (p. 14).

Bollas is speaking here of the desire that we have to achieve a fuller sense of self over the course of a lifetime and the recognition we have, often outside awareness, that we need others to help us with the difficult and sometimes painful experiences that come with maturing. So although Bollas evokes the maternal image as one of transformation, it is still an interpersonal process of growth that occurs throughout life and one for which we all will require subsequent transformational others.

Countertransference readiness

The ongoing potential for transformation or maturation is what makes human relations work possible, difficult, and ultimately so rewarding. In light of this role we play as professionals, Bollas (1987) introduces the idea of "countertransference readiness" (pp. 201–202).

"Countertransference" is a term used in multiple, sometimes contradictory, ways within the field of psychodynamic psychotherapy. For the purpose of this chapter, we use Bollas' sense of it as a form of nonverbal communication that occurs between the therapist and the client. Countertransference in this context refers to the professional's moment of receiving, bodily, the client's or student's way of being. We have discussed this receptivity in terms of problem areas or distress; but, of course, we also pick up our clients' and students' unique ways of being, their idioms, as Bollas would say. We learn through our intuitive function what it feels like to live in their bodies, how they experience their areas of difficulty, and how they embody their potential for creative change.

Countertransference, as Bollas uses the term, refers to the professional's emotional, somatic, and freely associative resonance with the unworded, unthought known that the client or student relives in the therapeutic, consultative, or educative setting. These experiences of being with a client or student constitute important information about that individual's sense of self and way of relating to others. It is vital information in our work as human relations professionals. As Bollas (1987) writes:

> By cultivating a freely-roused emotional sensibility, the analyst welcomes news from within himself that is reported through his own intuitions, feelings, passing images, phantasies and imagined interpretive interventions. ... To find the patient we must look for him within ourselves.
>
> (pp. 201–202)

We can think of this process of finding the client or student within ourselves as a form of nonconscious communication. Part of that communicative process is instinctive, as Berne noted. Part of it is also nonconsciously intentional on the part of our clients and students, deriving from what Bollas sees as the universal desire to be known in a manner that permits our transformation. As such, the client or student may in effect be saying, without necessarily knowing, "This is how it is to be me." And with that declaration comes the implied plea to be taken in and accepted.

Countertransference readiness describes the willingness of the professional to take in and attend to that form of communication. It is the willingness to be receptive to the client's or student's nonverbal, emotional, somatic, and free-associative states of being. This work occurs in the midst of the ongoing therapeutic contract and work with conscious content. Opening up in this additional way pushes the professional into a particular form, which begins to shape the relationship. "This is what it's like to be *in* this body. This is what it's like to be *engaged* with this body." As professionals, we use such nonconscious communication to begin bending ourselves to the task of working with our unique clients and students.

In contrast, Berne's stated understanding of countertransference was more traditional. He saw it as the professional's unexamined script responses to the client or student. Yet in his final book, *Hello* (Berne, 1972), when he talked about "how to listen" (pp. 321–322), Berne suggested an attitude of receptivity that is quite similar to Bollas':

> The listener ... must free his mind of outside preoccupations. ... [and] must put aside all Parental prejudices and feelings, including the need to "help" ... [He] must put aside all preconceptions about his patients in general and about the particular patient he is listening to. .... [The listener's] Adult listens to the content of what the patient says, while his Child-Professor listens to the way [the patient] says it. In telephone language, his Adult listens to the information, and his Child listens to the noise. In radio language, his Adult listens to the program, and his Child listens to how the machine is working. Thus, he is both a listener and a repairman.
>
> (p. 322)

To some extent, listening without preconceptions is impossible given the way our human minds work, that is, seeking familiar patterns and quickly moving to categorize what we experience. Nearly everything we encounter can be filtered through the protocols we have previously established. But Berne directs us to listen freely and without prejudice because we are also capable of questioning our preconceptions. We can bracket what we already know in order to discover a more valid pattern of meaning. Bollas also considers it an accomplishment *not* to know, *not* to be too certain, but rather to leave room for what actually transpires between the client/student and professional, to leave space for curiosity, for bodily as well as mental responses, for intuition and feeling in addition to thought. Berne, likewise, had moments when he was confident that we can tolerate uncertainty and not knowing long enough to understand reality more clearly.

Berne was also describing how, as professionals, we listen with more than our ears or eyes. We listen to more than words. We listen with our full bodies. We permit ourselves to be emotionally responsive to what we receive in order to understand nonconscious internal and interpersonal processes. By talking about the different roles of our Adult and Child ego states, he was also talking about how we use different aspects of ourselves and so allow ourselves to function in multiple ways to help the growth of our students and clients.

The multiple functions of the analyst/professional

Bollas contends that each person who seeks help does so with a desire for change and with the fervent hope that the person he or she has engaged can be the means to that change. When we are in the role of student or client, we begin that relationship by conveying some sense of who we are. For no matter how we may try to hide, we immediately begin to communicate something of how we relate to ourselves, to others, and to the world. Moreover, no matter how reticent we may behave on the outside, we rather aggressively begin to shape the other person into the person we hope and believe will be the agent of the change we seek. Bollas (1989) writes about this from the perspective of the patient using the analyst: "When an analyst is used to express a paradigm derived from an object relation, he is coerced into an object relation script and given a certain sustained identity as an object" (p. 17).

This closely matches Berne's observation of how clients and students reenact their scripts and recruit others to play roles in those scripts. Bollas would agree that sometimes the template or protocol that guides our quest for change may work against our aspirations. For both Bollas and Berne, one goal of a therapeutic, consultative, or educative relationship would be greater awareness of the way our lives may be problematically governed by script or nonconscious processes. This exists alongside the striving for greater access to our Adult or observing ego state to make more satisfying choices in our lives.

Yet the kind of coercive or aggressive use of the analyst or professional that Bollas describes is not always problematic in the way that Berne saw it. Bollas, after all, is writing from within the Winnicottian tradition that sees aggression as a healthy impulse, especially when such aggressive use of the significant other is not destructive but leads to maturing. Bollas operates from the assumption that human relations work entails a certain ruthless engagement. Depending on the needs of a student or client, the professional will be provoked nonconsciously into a particular kind of interaction. Again, this is frequently the client's or student's way of nonconsciously striving to grow by leading us into the kind of interaction that will matter to him or her. Bollas describes this as a process of eliciting certain elements in our personality. Yet he adds, "When … an element is elicited in [us] to be used by the patient and then abandoned (with no aim to set [us] up as part of the logic) … it is more likely to be a true self movement" (Bollas, 1989, p. 17).

In this passage, Bollas is offering a diagnostic guideline. He acknowledges that some relationships or script patterns have a repetitive, non-productive quality. In such cases, the professional is likely to feel more than just utilized by the student or client. Rather, the professional is likely to feel trapped in a particular role, forced into an unyielding logic, which is emphasized in script theory. In contrast, Bollas suggests that self-aspects or elements can be provoked or elicited in us that, although possibly uncomfortable or unfamiliar, do not have that same immobilizing, repetitive quality. He is alluding to the more fluid process of healthy play in children, whereby an activity is taken up out of a sheer sense of exploration, curiosity, or impulse, and then, when that particular form of play has run its course, is just as easily abandoned for some other generative activity. In fact, Bollas claims that through such a process of active, experimental engagement with a significant other, less-than-optimal relational protocols can be experientially modified.

So when Bollas (1989) writes about "the psychoanalyst's multiple function" (pp. 93–113), he proposes that each client uses the analyst or therapist to achieve a particular experience of self for the ultimate purpose of growing. And since every client or student is trying to express a unique personality or idiom, the professional will end up being used in multiple, idiosyncratic ways. Not only will different individuals evoke different uses, but the same individual may experiment over time with different uses. This process of being used in service of growth is highly dynamic.

Parents may have experienced the different ways of being that their different children have evoked in them or that an individual child has evoked over time as he or she has grown. Teachers, consultants, and therapists have likely also noticed the ways in which they are pushed, stretched, and shaped by the differing needs of their students and clients. Cornell (1988) has described this process of mutual influence in which the growing child has as much influence on the parents' scripts as the parents have on the child's developing script.

As professionals, our openness to such use—our countertransference readiness—creates the conditions by which we can learn our clients' or students' personal idioms. Making ourselves available as whole persons to meet the developmental needs of clients and students, we offer the opportunity for transformative experiences.

Bollas is not, however, suggesting that we simply abandon personal boundaries or individual separateness. Excessive flexibility is as problematic for growth as excessive rigidity. Rather, successful parenting, teaching, and mentoring embody a vigorous process of give and take. They embody a tension, sometimes an intense struggle. Moreover, this dynamic is not simply one of balancing the needs of two individuals. The roles in parenting and professional relationships are not as symmetrical as they might be in, say, an adult couple. The parent or professional will certainly have her or his own unique needs and ways of being, as will the child, student, or client. But the parenting and professional relationship exists in service to the aspirations for growth of the child, student, or client. In fact, all parties sacrifice something of their personal preferences to move toward the hope of such maturation.

Growth and self-formation

In the writings of both Berne and Bollas, there is an ongoing tension between the power of the past—with its constraining childhood experiences and relationships—and the forward-moving, generative forces of the human body and mind. For example, Berne argued, on the one hand, that we are all born "OK," that the Child ego state is the psychological center of vitality and creativity, and that we are driven by *physis* (or aspirations) to seek the best in ourselves and our lives. On the other hand, his clinical model is dominated by ideas about rackets, games, and problematic scripts—all constructions of psychopathology that reference the oppressive power of the past, the negative impact of parents, and the limiting and long-lingering effects of childhood challenges and beliefs.

We see a similar tension in Bollas' writing. In his first book, *The Shadow of the Object* (1987), he emphasizes the mother-infant relationship as foundational in the human psyche and all future relationships. Even its title, *The Shadow of the Object*, suggests how we are constrained and haunted by history or fate. However, in his second book, *Forces of Destiny* (1989), Bollas contrasts that sense of being fated with a sense of moving toward a desired destiny in a hopeful future. In that book, he articulates the generative force of unconscious desires and motivations. He describes an insistence within the unconscious that is not just about repression but that seeks to move forward productively in life.

Interestingly, Berne's subtitle for *Hello* (1972) is "The Psychology of Human Destiny," but he uses the word "destiny" sometimes to mean "fated," exactly the opposite of what Bollas means by destiny as an urgent sense of purpose and promise. Yet Berne's (1972) definition reveals more hopeful aspects as well:

> The forces of human destiny are foursome and fearsome: demonic parental programming...; constructive parental programming, aided by the thrust of life called Phusis [*physis*] long ago; external forces, still called Fate; and independent aspirations.
>
> (p. 56)

Although Berne (1972) would consider some of these more productive aspects of destiny—which we discuss in the following section—still, a sense of fatedness pervades his conception of script:

> Each person decides in early childhood how he will live and how he will die, and that plan, which he carries in his head wherever he goes, is called his script.
>
> (p. 31)

> A script is an ongoing life plan ... the psychological force which propels the person toward his destiny, regardless of whether he fights it or says it is his own free well.
>
> (p. 32)

Physis and aspiration

In his writing, Berne often comes across with a sense of humor that is skeptical, sometimes bordering on the sarcastic. Certainly, that humor and skepticism can be refreshing and enlivening. Some of his sarcasm has enough edge to wake us up to the stalled lives we may be living. But sometimes it seems bitter, a frantic defense against a gloomy view of human life, a view that developed, perhaps, as a result of being hurt. Indeed, one can catch glimpses of Berne's more tender side and, with it, his more hopeful view of life.

In describing this, we are not criticizing Berne. Rather, we are discussing the quality of his idiom. People responded in various ways to him. But for those who felt he changed their lives, his clear thinking, humor, and aggression were curative, transformational factors.

In working with his clients, Berne often focused on elements from the past and parental injunctions that had pressed upon and influenced the growing child's, and eventually the adult's, sense of what it meant to live in the world. Yet he contrasted this more problem-focused concept of script with what he called *physis*, a "force of Nature, which eternally strives to make things grow and to make growing things more perfect" (Berne, 1968, p. 89). Berne saw this force of life as one that survives even the most imprisoning scripts.

Physis is a Greek theological, philosophical, and scientific term that Berne (1968) borrowed and defined as follows:

> PHYSIS – The growth force of nature, which makes organisms evolve into higher forms, embryos develop into adults, sick people get better, and healthy people strive to attain their ideals.
>
> (pp. 369–370)

Although Berne himself made little of this idea, or its implications for human relations work, Clarkson (1992) took its essentially hopeful view of life as key to her approach to transactional analysis:

> Physis is nature, coming from the deepest biological roots of the human being and striving towards the greatest realisation of the good.
>
> (p. 12)

Berne and Clarkson seem nearly utopian in these passages. We may wonder how their conceptions square with the fact of death, with nonliving forces in nature, with organisms that do not evolve into higher forms but die out, with embryos that are not able to survive to adulthood, with sickness, and with failure. Berne, for one, would have been the last to deny these aspects of life. However, he seems to be asking us to recognize that while we are alive, while life persists, it has at its core a wellspring of potential and willfulness.

In choosing a term such as *physis*, Berne was acknowledging a reserve of energy that is available to every living being. It is a source of liveliness, an eternal striving, that exists without our necessarily being aware of it, because it exists in every cell and for every form of life. By implication, Berne is asking us, as professionals, to recognize this nonconscious potential in each client or student who comes to us, no matter how stuck or collapsed. *Physis* is, for each of us, a powerful ally for our development and growth.

Although Berne's concept of script typically refers to transactional patterns that are defensive or that do not serve the individual well, he sometimes wrote about script in a way that suggested that it represents the child's effort to articulate a unique plan for life. In that sense, script can serve the individual's aspirations and hopes for living.

Berne conveyed the thrust of such hopes by incorporating an "aspiration arrow" into the script matrix (see Berne, 1972, p. 128). Clarkson (1992) believed that "the aspiration arrow represents the dynamic force of Physis" (p. 13). As she elaborated:

> Berne postulates that the autonomous aspiration of individual human beings rises from the depths of the somatic Child (oldest ego state) and transcends the limit-inducing downward pressures of the script which is shaped in the matrix of love and death in our earliest relationships.
>
> (p. 12)

The aspiration arrow, driven by physis, moves in the direction of optimal maturing or self-development. We are driven to move, in life, toward our truest, heart-felt desires. In an atypically elegiac mode, Berne (1972) acknowledged:

> All men and women have their secret gardens, whose gates they guard against the profane invasion of the vulgar crowd. These are visual pictures of what they would do if they could do as they pleased. The lucky ones find the right time, place, and person, and get to do it, while the rest must wander wistfully outside their own walls.
>
> (p. 130)

By combining his concept of *physis* (as a force to be reckoned with), with his concept of aspiration (as a longing to be safeguarded), Berne was describing the vulnerability that can attend our efforts to live openly with integrity. In our work as professionals, it is important to respect the protective measures people take to guard their "secret gardens," just as we might say Berne attempted to guard his own with sarcasm. At the same time, something at the core, some force and vision, wants to be freed, wants to find its best expression in the world.

When we facilitate maturational processes, we must analyze not only the defensive scripts but also those scripts that have been created out of a sense of purpose and aspiration. As Berne (1972) rather sweetly put it:

> The object of script analysis is to . . . open the garden of their aspirations to the world.
>
> (p. 131)

Destiny drive

Bollas (1989) describes something similar to the ideas of *physis* and aspiration in his discussion of destiny. He conceives of the "destiny drive" as the urge within each person to articulate and elaborate his or her unique personality, or idiom, through interactions with significant individuals. Given the urgency of this drive, each individual strives to become his or her own true being through experiences with others that release this potential. Bollas describes such formative interactions in terms of the transformational object.

As such, Bollas' destiny drive is an instinct for life, similar to Berne's *physis*. Bollas (1989) also lists "heredity, biology, and environment [as] factors contributing to one's destiny" (p. 33), which is strikingly similar to Berne's (1972) mention of "parental programming," "the thrust of life," and "external forces" (p. 56).

Berne's (1972) fourth force of destiny—"independent aspirations" (p. 56)—is also recognized by Bollas (1989):

> A sense of destiny ... would be a feeling that the person is fulfilling some of the terms of his inner idiom through familial, social, cultural, and intellectual objects.
>
> (p. 34)

Whereas Berne did little with his ideas about *physis* and aspiration, Bollas (1989) devotes full chapters to his conception of destiny as a drive and weaves this attitude toward life's potential into all areas of his work. For Bollas, fortune comes not just to "the lucky ones," as Berne would have it, but as a result of active, determined seeking.

Toward a truer self

Bollas conceives of our sense of destiny as driving each of us toward our unique idiomatic expression or fulfillment of a true self. Borrowing the idea of the "true self" from Winnicott, Bollas (1989) writes:

> Infants, at birth, are in possession of a personality potential that is in part genetically sponsored and ... this true self, over the course of a lifetime, seeks to express and elaborate this potential through formations of being and relating.
>
> (p. 11)

According to Bollas, we each start out our lives with this inherited potential. Yet the "true self" also refers to the *expression* of that potential, which we have discussed in terms of "idiom." A true self is both a possibility and an actuality. Actualizing our true idiom contrasts significantly with expressions or behaviors that are false or adapted, that betray our desire to become most urgently our potential selves. In fact, living falsely can lead to psychological and emotional pain that may show itself in various symptoms. For each of us, when our unique thrust toward life is thwarted, we live something like a death, something that is less than our full capacity for life.

Just as Berne was inclined to analyze problematic, scripty transactions, the psychoanalytic tradition has also tended to analyze and interpret psychopathological formations, typically seen as unconscious. But Bollas is describing a different nonconscious process, one that is not problematic or growth inhibiting. For although he admits that our drive toward destiny will largely operate outside conscious awareness, Bollas (1989) wants us to recognize that this difference has implications for professional practice:

> We cannot analyze the evolution of the true self. We can facilitate it. We can experience its momentary use of our self.
>
> (p. 18)

Berne was able to identify script patterns in his patients because human beings, as learning creatures, tend to repeat what they have learned in the past, even if what they learned is not serving them well. Some certainty, even if painful, can seem better than an uncertain future of possibilities. Bollas is saying, however, that the process of living toward aspirations or a sense of destiny is not inherently repetitive; it is open to creative and novel solutions. So we cannot analyze or identify this evolutionary process because it literally has not yet come into being. And being truly alive and evolving, it will never settle into a pattern or script that can be analyzed, even if we have an image or plan for getting there.

Yet Bollas sees a role for the professional in terms of facilitating that evolution of the self. In particular, he sees us facilitating it through allowing our nonconscious selves to be engaged and used as transformational objects in service to the persistent hopes, however secret and fearful, that our clients and students inevitably bring with them.

Our commitments to reality

In highlighting this tension—which Berne and Bollas both embody—between despair and hopefulness about the human condition, we want to emphasize the critical role such attitudes play in our approach to human relations work.

People come to us for help because they feel constrained by what they have already learned. Such limits can show up as depression, anxiety, over-functioning, marital conflict, substance abuse, or any of the other symptoms from which our students and clients suffer. Behind every symptom is a sense of despair and a belief that life cannot be any better. Even manic beliefs about magical cures belie an underlying sense of impasse and failure. So as professionals, we certainly do not want to meet those difficulties with facile solutions or naïve beliefs about the painlessness of life. Those only feed the sense of despair. Yet neither do we want to meet our clients and students with our own underlying sense of despair or pessimism about being unable to work through life's struggles. It is important that we form an alliance with what Berne saw as each person's core OKness or *physis*, and with what Bollas conceived as the emergence of the true self.

Berne (1968) suggested that, as human beings, we each must make a commitment to seeing our lives more realistically, with their struggles as well as the potential for growth:

> One of the most important things in life is to understand reality and to keep changing our images to correspond to it, for it is our images which determine our actions and feelings, and the more accurate they are the easier it will be for us to attain happiness and stay happy in an ever-changing world where happiness depends in large part on other people.
>
> (p. 46)

Maturation, in other words, is the process of coming to terms with the facts of our lives—in our minds and bodies—in the same way that we begin learning as babies to live with our experiences of hunger, fear, anger, other people, separation, and the world. Yet maturation is not just a process for babies and children. We mature for the whole of our lives to the extent that we want to learn more about the world and ourselves in it. And to help us get there, we often need a parent, friend, teacher, mentor, consultant, or therapist.

In this framework for human relations work, our professional role is to be present in the fullness of our nonconscious beings to this emergence into life and to allow ourselves to be engaged and used viscerally on the sometimes difficult path that attends any developmental challenge. Maturing is the lifelong process for which transformational others are often essential. Let it be our privilege to serve in that capacity. And let it also be our fortune to find those with whom we can each transform toward our own truer, fuller selves.

Part II

When life grows dark

Chapter 13

The Old Stone House: Eric Berne's memories and mourning for his father's life and death

In the short book *A Montreal Childhood* (2010), based on an unfinished memoir, we meet a different side of Eric Berne, who writes here in a voice that is sweet, often poetic, and quietly melancholic. The unfinished manuscript was discovered among Berne's papers by his son, Terry, who then edited it for publication. It is accompanied by a prologue and epilogue by Terry Berne, with a postscript from Claude Steiner.

The original manuscript was titled *The Old Stone House* by Berne, referring to the house on Ste. Famille Street into which the Bernstein family moved when Berne (then Eric Leonard Bernstein) was two years old. Berne describes the street on which he grew up as quite unique in Montreal:

> The street was one of the few in the city which sheltered approximately equal numbers of the three religions, and where the children of the two crosses and the star played together in harmony without jeers or bitterness. ... Their parents, however, maintained complete, but in this case polite, segregation.
>
> (p. 41)

One gets the impression that Berne's father's choice of a house on this street was not an accident, that David Bernstein was already well aware of the prejudices against Jews. The shelter of Ste. Famille Street did not in the long run protect his son from the jeers and hatred too often aimed at Jewish children in this predominantly Christian city. Berne notes, with a bit of irony, that it was not until he was leaving the city that he realized that he had grown up on "Holy Family Street."
The Old Stone House was a proud house, one reflective of the young Dr. Bernstein's professional and economic accomplishments:

> The Old House was built with broad stones if impenetrable hardness. ... No house was ever more solidly fortified and rooted in its long narrow plot of city soil. It was a place where nothing ever happened that was not supposed to happen, except for the ultimate crushing blow from the rusty fist of Fate which finally crumbled it into teeming slummery.
>
> (p. 43)

Here, Berne foreshadows the economic decline of the Bernstein family following his father's very young death to tuberculosis. The decline of the Old Stone
House becomes a metaphor for the gradual undoing of the Bernstein family's
security and ideals.

In this short book, we meet a young Leonard (as he was called in his family)
with a deep and lonely sensitivity, a young man upon whom life vividly
impinged. We meet the boy and young man who is the precursor of the doctor,
psychiatrist, humanist, transactional analyst, outsider, and cynic we meet in his
professional writings. We see the profound impact that his physician father had
on the man Berne wished to become.

The memoir opens with a lovely, deeply moving story of Leonard as a young
boy proudly accompanying his father on his house calls to his patients (back in
the day when doctors actually visited patients in their homes). This opening
vignette is steeped in Berne's admiration for his physician father. He writes in
the memoir's opening segment:

> Father rang the bell and someone's faded mother opened the door into a
> dim house. Father went in with his black satchel and the door closed behind
> him. I looked at the door and the door looked back and said: "I'm a door
> and I stand between you and the mysteries of others' lives."
>
> (p. 17)

This image of the door closed between the young Berne and the private
mysteries of the lives of others is recurrent through the book. We get a
glimpse of the psychiatrist/psychoanalyst in the making, someone who has
earned the official right to look behind closed doors. Over and over again in
this memoir are stories of Berne as a boy and adolescent held outside the
social relations of others, by dint of his personal awkwardness, lack of social
skills, precocious intelligence, and/or being a Jew. In a particularly poignant
scene, Berne writes of his effort at age 10 to start a boys' club in his
basement:

> ... but it was called the Agamemnon Club and none of the other boys knew
> who Agamemnon was and they didn't care when I told them, so the club
> soon disbanded. ... From time to time through the years I tried to start other
> clubs, but they didn't last either, until I discovered the secret, and then I
> was able to start lots of clubs.
>
> (p. 51)

Berne doesn't tell the reader what the secret was that he discovered, but I
couldn't help but read this passage and think of his failed efforts to join the
psychoanalytic club and his retaliation in starting his own, the San Francisco
Social Psychiatry Seminar, and subsequently the International Transactional
Analysis Association.

Berne's accountings of his father's work as a physician are probably the most moving of the memoir. As a boy, and as a man remembering his father, Berne is filled with love and admiration for his father. David Bernstein was deeply concerned about the environmental and economic factors that contributed to the illnesses, especially tuberculosis, that plagued Montreal and his patients. Terry Berne has included a fascinating appendix of Berne's commentary on some of his father's papers and his place in the medical establishment of Montreal.

David Bernstein wrote a paper on "Home treatment of tuberculosis," arguing that for many patients, like his own, who were too poor to go to sanatoriums in the countryside, adequate treatment could be provided at home under the careful supervision of the family physician. In his last published paper, "The relation of physical exhaustion to chronic ill health," he argued:

> There is no substitute for the large practice, the repeated home visits, the continuous observations of birth, life, death, and pathology over a long period in the living family tissue, all passing through the alert, sophisticated, and intelligent brain of the creative and purposeful physician.
>
> (1921, p. 158)

Berne then comments on his father's philosophy and ethic of medical practice, "For true clinicians, there is no substitute for themselves; not in the superior, but in the existential sense" (p. 159). Reading Berne's reflections about his father, I was richly reminded of Berne's determined efforts to bring his training as a psychiatrist and psychoanalyst into the realities of the lives people actually lived, of his profound regard for the intelligence of his patients, and the deeply ethical stance that he outlined in *Principles of Group Treatment*. I was reminded, too, of listening to his own children—Janice, Robin, and Terry—speaking at the Montreal 2010 Berne Centenary Conference of their experiences of Berne as a father, of their deep regard for him, and of the pleasure Berne took in being a father.

But in the midst of this pride, there was to be tragedy. Berne's father contracted tuberculosis, the very disease he had been so dedicated to fighting. David Bernstein continued to practice and write until the very end. It is here that Eric Berne's writing aches with loving admiration and loss:

> Father soon began to experience little fevers, and his X-rays showed the sinister opacities in the tissues of his lungs. ... Perhaps the hardest brunt he bore was that he had to refrain from kissing those closest to him, and through this sacrifice none of them ever became ill from his infection.
>
> (p. 63)

One Friday I came home for lunch and Mother met me, looking very grave. She said that Father had had a hemorrhage. "What's a hemorrhage?," I asked.

"Blood from the lungs," she said. She talked to me oddly as though I were a grown-up, and told me to go greet Father. Father was lying very still in bed looking straight up at the ceiling. When I came in, he turned his head.

"Hello," I said.

"Hello," said Father, and took my hand. We looked at each other for a few seconds, and then Father said, "A little boy should take good care of his mother and sister,"

I nodded and Father dropped my hand. "Good-bye, Father," I said.

"Good-bye, Leonard," said Father.

(p. 95)

The following Sunday night, Father died. "Then they took me to stand beside the coffin and recite the prayer with them. *Yisgadal Veyiskadash*. Take one step back at the end. I was not yet eleven years old" (p. 97).

Here, the tone of Berne's memoir changes. After the burial, young Leonard, his mother, and sister returned home:

Back home, Mother and Sister and I climbed up the outside stairs of the old stone house and closed the door behind us. Mother gave us some milk and crackers and told us to play quietly. Then she went upstairs to the bedroom and shut the mahogany door. We drank our milk and ate our crackers slowly. The house was very quiet now, quieter than it had ever been.

(p. 98)

Here, we read again of doors closing—a closing off and leaving out, a secreting away of life's deepest vulnerabilities at this crucial moment.

In the next section of the memoir, which he titles "All aboard for widowville," Berne suddenly uses the sarcastic tone that became all too common in his later writing. Now he tells the story of his family's dance at the edge of poverty—terminating the maid, his mother struggling to earn enough income to support her small family, taking in tenants, the family living in smaller and smaller areas of the Old Stone House until finally forced to sell it to a contractor with the family then living crowded together in just two rooms. I was left with the impression of a quiet disdain for his mother. We never get the sense of Berne experiencing the kind of respect and intimacy toward his mother that he had felt so deeply for his father. As he moves into adolescence, we find now stories of his increasing awkwardness with women and of his isolation and loneliness. I could not help but wonder, had Berne's father lived, how differently Berne's adolescence may have been, accompanied and guided by this man who seemed so wise and determined in the world.

In another of his simply written and sweetly moving passages, Berne writes:

I said my prayers in Hebrew every night, but I didn't know what they meant. Mother told me that I could add things in English, like, "Bless my dear grandma," who was in Heaven, and "Bless us all." Later I added other things, like "Bless my dear Father," "Let Esther find a job," and "Don't let me have bad dreams." Eventually I tried to cover the board with, "Make everything turn out all right."

(pp. 111–112)

Things did not always turn out all right for Leonard Eric Bernstein or for the family that he loved. But I suspect his simple prayer motivated and infused much of his work and wishes as a psychiatrist, psychoanalyst, and transactional analyst.

I thank Terry Berne for his efforts in making his father's wonderful memoir available to us. With it, he gives us a new light on the man whose life's work so many of us have studied and benefited from.

Chapter 14

Grief, mourning, and meaning: In a personal voice

Eric Berne was a young boy when his beloved father died of tuberculosis. In his memoir, Berne describes the family's return from his father's funeral:

> Mother gave us some milk and crackers and told us to play quietly. Then she went upstairs to the bedroom and shut the mahogany door. We drank our milk and ate our crackers slowly. The house was now quieter than it had ever been.
>
> (p. 98)

The theme of doors closing was a frequent one in Berne's memoir. In my review of the book (Cornell, 2010), I wrote, "Here we read again of doors closing—a closing off and leaving out, a secreting away of life's deepest vulnerabilities at this crucial moment" (p. 307). The family's unresolved grief and mourning echo through the remainder of Berne's book.

When I read Berne's memoir, I felt a deep identification with him. When my father was 7, his father went into hospital with a minor illness. He died suddenly and unexpectedly in the hospital. Within a month, my father's mother had remarried; there was no time or room for mourning. My father never told me of his father's death. I learned of it from his older sister many years after he himself had died.

My mother was 40 when hemorrhages in her brain left her deeply regressed and unable to speak. In a few weeks, she was dead. She had been ill with leukemia, but the brain hemorrhages were the result of a medical error. My parents were so overwhelmed by her illness that they never even told my younger brother and sister that she was sick until she could no longer speak. Our father was just 39, I was 19, my brother 15, and my sister 13. My father was 50 when he died, relieved to be spared any more of the relentless and unforgiving suffering and guilt he had experienced since his wife died. Other than his mother and his children, no one from his family attended his funeral. As the deaths of my young parents loomed, I tried to accompany each of them as best I could, but there was no one to accompany me or my siblings or to help us mourn the tragedies of our parents' unlived lives (Cornell, 2013).

When I first heard of a special issue of the *Transactional Analysis Journal* in 2014 devoted to discussions of death and loss, I knew I wanted to write on this topic because it had permeated my life. I returned first to Berne's clinical writing and found virtually no discussions of loss, grief, or mourning. Given what happened in his own youth, perhaps it is not surprising that this was territory that Berne did not want to visit. However, in his last book, he did write about death. In a chilling passage, he commented, "A recent study of causes of death concluded that many people die when they are ready to, and that coronary thrombosis, for example, can be brought about almost by an act of will" (Berne, 1972, p. 188). Berne died of a heart attack while finishing the manuscript of that book, which was published posthumously as *What Do You Say after You Say Hello?* Berne went on to discuss death within the context of script theory, but there is nothing about loss or mourning. Checking the index for "loss," I found multiple entries for "loser" but nothing for "loss."

The transactional analysis literature after Berne

In reviewing the transactional analysis literature on loss, death, and dying, I discovered that there were few articles addressing these issues. This may well be a legacy from Berne: That his own writings provided no basis for transactional analysts to build on in exploring the experiences of loss, death, and grief.

The first issue of the *Transactional Analysis Journal* published a few months after Berne's death, in 1971, had his photo on the cover and included many reflections about him and celebrations of the success of transactional analysis. Ten years later, O'Hearne (1981), identifying himself as both a transactional analyst and a psychoanalyst, described the different levels of intervention made possible through Berne's model of TA while noting that even though some people completed their treatment contracts, "They were mechanical, wooden; their voices were muted, often sad. They seldom celebrated life. TA alone was not enough" (p. 85). He argued that Berne had failed to make use of the psychoanalytic concept of "working through" (p. 85), although he suggested that Berne knew of it. O'Hearne linked the psychoanalytic concept of working through to the process of grieving childhood losses, especially the loss of childhood dreams. He concluded, "This working through may involve anger, awe, fear, anxiety; it will always involve grief" (p. 87).

The next major offering on the topic of grief came another decade later with Childs-Gowell's book *Good Grief Rituals: Tools for Healing* (1992). She was motivated in part to write the book because of the lifelong suffering of her husband, a veteran of World War II:

> He was never able to stop the flashbacks or deal with the pain of the experience until shortly before he died. The legacy of the unspeakable traumas he experienced, which he passed on to his family in a myriad of ways, remain ingrained in all of us.
>
> (p. 3)

Written in a self-help format, *Good Grief Rituals* built on the work of Kübler-Ross and Native American rituals. Childs-Gowell described the common defensive reactions to loss, including those that are script-based, and outlined a range of self-reflective exercises and rituals to facilitate mourning. Her prescriptions were solitary, self-healing procedures.

Another decade passed until Clark's "Psychotherapy as a mourning process" (2001) drew parallels between Kübler-Ross's model of the stages of mourning and Erskine's model of the stages of psychotherapy. Clark warned, "Failure on the part of the clinician to understand the mourning process can lead to arrested mourning that leaves losses unresolved" (p. 160). From Clark's perspective, mourning requires the engagement and accompaniment of others. Solomon (2003) discussed common reactions to the loss of a love relationship and presented strategies for coping with the complex constellation of feelings that accompany both the loss and moving forward. She illustrated how early script decisions can interfere with the resolution of these losses. Steinberg (2010), building on the work of Goulding and Goulding (1997), presented a therapeutic model from a redecision perspective for resolving post-divorce impasses and losses. At the center of this therapeutic process is the expression of resentments, appreciations, unfinished business, and good-byes as the means of resolving impasses in the face of loss. In keeping with Solomon's observations, Steinberg suggested that early script decisions can foster adverse post-divorce adjustments, so it is important for therapists to address such early decisions as well as the mourning and letting go that needs to occur in the here and now. Garcia (2012) offered a model and tools for "learning and growing from painful endings and transitions" (p. 53).

Allen (2006) described the community-wide tragedy of the Oklahoma City bombing, in which 38 percent of the city's population knew someone who had been killed. He presented a comprehensive approach from a psychosocial model of community response to devastating violence and loss, and concluded that the:

> successful resolution of the long-term effects of the Oklahoma bombing seems to have involved three overlapping phases: (1) abreaction and stress modulation; (2) contextualization, construction, and coconstruction of meaning and identity transformation with an acceptance of the irreversible; and (3) growth of a realistic sense of self-efficacy and a willingness to use one's strengths actively in meaningful social engagement.
>
> (p. 131)

In a personal voice

In preparing to write this chapter, I decided to read first-person narratives by those who have lost loved ones under sudden and tragic circumstances (Deraniyagala, 2013; Didion, 2006; Orr, 2004) to see what their accounts might offer to our theoretical and therapeutic models.

Gregory Orr (2004) was 12 when he shot and killed his little brother Peter. Gregory's father was taking him and his older brother out for the first day of deer hunting. When the younger brothers became upset at being left behind, their mother talked her husband into taking all four boys. The result was tragedy beyond the family's capacity to endure. His father carried his dead son's body back to the house, and Gregory was left alone:

> I needed arms to catch me. I needed some voice to tell me I was not alone. But the voices and human presences I yearned for so desperately could not be there when I needed them. My father and mother must each have retreated into their own sense of horror, despair, and guilt.
>
> (p. 20)

Orr lived his grief and guilt in silence for many years, struggling to find the right and the means to live. Only as an adult was he able to find people with whom he could begin to speak about that terrible day.

Sonali Deraniyagala (2013) was on Christmas holiday in Sri Lanka with her husband, parents, and two young sons when the tsunami struck, sweeping away her entire family and leaving her—somehow—alive. Alive and wishing she were dead:

> I must stop remembering. I must keep them in a far away place. The more I remember, the greater my agony. These thoughts stuttered in my mind. So I stopped talking about them, I wouldn't mouth my boys' names, I shoved away stories of them. Let them, let our life, become as unreal as was the wave. . . . I must be watchful, I told myself. I must shut them out.
>
> (p. 51)

Joan Didion (2006) was getting ready to join her husband at the dining room table for dinner when he dropped dead. Even though she accompanied his dead body to the hospital, she often found herself convinced he was still alive. She felt on the edge of madness:

> Grief has no distance. Grief comes in waves, paroxysms, sudden apprehensions that weaken the knees and blind the eyes and obliterate daily life.
>
> (p. 27)

In an effort to make sense of her unending grief and relentless torment, she turned to psychiatric and psychoanalytic literature. She found what she read patronizing and absurd:

> There were, I also learned from the literature, two kinds of grief. The preferred kind, the one associated with "growth" and "development," was "uncomplicated grief," or "normal bereavement." . . . The second kind of

grief was "complicated grief," which was also known in the literature as "pathological bereavement" and was said to occur in a variety of situations.

(p. 48)

Grief was not "uncomplicated" in these first-person accounts. Orr, Deraniyagala, and Didion each at times felt on the edge of insanity:

I liked mixing alcohol with the pills. It made me hallucinate. I watched plump black worms crawl out from the air conditioner and slide down the wall. Hundreds of them, slowly as they crawled. .... This was good. I felt crazy, and that's how I thought I should be. My world gone in an instant, I needed to be insane.

(Deraniyagala, 2013, p. 55)

On the day of Peter's death, I heard every thread in my web snap in a single instant. I didn't know how to repair it, or to make new connections to the world.

(Orr, 2004, p. 135)

We might expect if the death is sudden to feel shock. We do not expect this shock to be obliterative, dislocating to both body and mind. ... We do not expect to be literally crazy, cool customers who believe their husband is about to return and need his shoes.

(Didion, 2006, p. 188)

Didion's struggle reflected what Freud (1917) described:

This opposition [to accepting the reality of the loss] can be so intense that a turning away from reality takes place and a clinging to the [lost] object through a medium of a hallucinatory wishful psychosis. Normally, respect for reality gains the day. Nevertheless, its orders cannot be obeyed at once. They are carried out bit by bit ... and in the meantime the existence of the lost object is psychically prolonged.

(pp. 244–245)

Madness and inconsolable agony permeate these memoirs. As I read them, I could see myself, recall my own moments of breakdown into near insanity and self-destructive risk-taking that might have been one way out of it all. Each of these writers was haunted by memories, wishing at first to kill off memory as a way of arriving at peace of mind. Memories swept in unbidden, unwanted, throwing them into periods of despairing disorientation. It took great courage to write these frank, nearly naked memoirs of anguish, despair, and insanity.

Ian Craig (1994), in his reflections on the nature and necessity of mourning, speaks forcefully of the multitude of ways by which people seek to avoid a collapse into unending, unremitting grief:

> [Some] might prevent such a collapse by continuing to work, staying home from work, talking or keeping silent; … [some] by smashing things, by screaming, by getting drunk; by leaving their wife or husband for their lover; by wearing the dead person's clothes or burning them. I don't think I have ever come across anything so intensely personal as grieving, and it often seems to me that the only attitude to adopt towards it is one of respect.
>
> (p. 29)

A death met differently

Unacknowledged and unresolved grief overwhelmed and fractured my family and my psyche. Following my parents' deaths, there was no place in which to grieve, no other with whom to cry or rage. I did not learn how to feel, face, and integrate the inevitable losses and tragedies of living until well into my adult life. I was in my early 40s when I started my analysis; my analyst was 70. He warned me as we began that he was planning to retire at 80, so the analysis might have to be cut short! I had fully expected to be well and gone long before the man turned 80. I was mistaken. I took all 10 of those years.

As in any productive therapy, there were several pivotal experiences. One was most central to finally addressing the profound loneliness I had endured following my parents' deaths and that had permeated my young adult life. I had just recently separated from my wife when on the eve of the Thanksgiving holiday I received a call from Rose, the women who had stepped into my life as a second mother after my mom died. A healthy and vigorous woman in her mid-70s, she called to tell me that she had been diagnosed with terminal pancreatic cancer and had been given a month to live. All of my family and close friends and my analyst were out of town for the holiday. I was as close to madness as I had ever been. I wanted to die, but I had three sons to raise. I left a message on my analyst's answering machine telling him of Rose's phone call. Three days passed. I couldn't sleep. And I could not imagine going to see my beloved Rose and letting her see me in that deranged state of mind.

On Sunday I got a call from my analyst saying he had landed at the airport, that he was driving directly to his office, and that I was to meet him there. As I was seeing him that Monday morning at 8 am, I said, "No, I'll be all right until tomorrow." He insisted. I went. I was not alone in my despair. When I got home, I crawled into bed, and, as usual, I could not sleep. The phone rang. It was my analyst: "I thought you might be having trouble sleeping and it might be easier to rest tonight with my voice in your ear. This is not a good time to be alone." I slept. And he called me each night that week at bedtime. In two weeks' time, I was able to fly across the country to be with Rose as her death grew near.

After a few years of working together, my analyst said that he had a favor to ask of me. He had seen too many of his colleagues work well past their prime, at the expense of their patients. These therapists had been too proud or too scared to face the encroachments of age and illness and the nearness of death. He did not want to do that. He trusted me to be honest with him, and he asked that when I saw signs of his age encroaching on his competence that I would tell him.

At 79, he announced to his patients that he would be retiring in a year. Most of them, to his shock and dismay, terminated abruptly rather than face his retirement and their feelings about the ending of their relationship. I was not about to do that. I knew I finally had the opportunity to face loss and work it through with someone for whom I cared deeply and who would not shy away from all we had to face.

He asked me to read Freud's (1916) eloquent and deeply personal essay "On transience," a remarkable piece of writing all of three pages long. It, like several of Freud's most personal and complex essays, was written haunted—by the horrors of World War I. This brief essay became a kind of touchstone for our process of reaching an end of the work in which we had been so deeply engaged. In that essay, Freud observed that in the face of "the decay of all that is beautiful and perfect, there tends to be two different impulses"—one an "aching despondency" and the other a "rebellion against the fact asserted" (p. 305), through fantasies of infinity and endless time that defy loss. Freud observed, "We possess, as it seems, a certain amount of capacity for love—what we call libido" (p. 306), which we attach to certain objects. We wish to keep those attachments at all costs. Freud cautioned that when we lose a loved object, it feels as though we are losing our capacity to live and love. In our defensive reactions, there can be a ferocious refusal to relinquish the lost one so as to live and love anew. He argued that it is through the process of mourning—a profoundly painful process—that we can release the lost loved one. Freud wrote that once our mourning is over, we learn that we have, in fact, lost nothing from our discovery of life's fragilities, and we gain the capacity to live fully again.

With Freud's essay as a backdrop, my analyst and I reflected on what we had each gained through our work together and what we were about to lose. I was, at the same time, mourning the end of my marriage and of my fantasies of growing old together with my wife. I was mourning the end of my relationship with this man, my therapist, who had brought me so much and who in the richness of the later years of his life provided me with such a contrast to my father, who had spent his life avoiding life. We dealt with my fears of going it alone. Could I sustain all that I had learned without his presence in my life?

Meaning in mourning

I represented the end of his career just at a time when mine was truly taking off. Together we faced the meaning of my being his last analysand. We spoke directly of his envy that I had many years of professional life ahead of me and that I had been so much bolder in my professional life than he had been in his. My analyst was mourning the end of his career and the many regrets he had about not been bolder and more personal in his practice as an analyst, of how for decades he had submitted to the deadening restraints of following proper technique, fearful of the scrutiny and disapproval of his peers. Only in that last decade of his practice had he allowed himself to be himself, and I profited from that.

Quinodoz, in her eloquent and moving book *Growing Old* (2010), vividly describes how some elderly people, to ward off their anxieties about death, close off from their internal worlds. The memoirs I have quoted express the impact of sudden deaths for which there was no warning, but the people in Quinodoz's book also describe the shrinking of their internal worlds in a desperate effort to deaden their grief, agony, and disorientation. My analyst and I did not shy away from our ending or his declining years. We lived an internal world together. He offered me a process of a deeply personal and mutual reflection that will forever change the meaning for me of what it is to grow old. As Quinodoz frames it, my analyst and I revisited and reinhabited memories of our lives and our work together in a process of mourning and a construction of meaning.

And then the therapy didn't end. As he was about to turn 80, my analyst told me that he was closing his office but that he wanted to continue seeing me at his home. I objected and assured him that I would be fine. He said, "Your character is founded on loss. Premature losses. Endings determined by others, not yourself. I do not want to add your analysis to that list. My mental and physical health is fine. I will continue seeing you until you decide to terminate or you tell me I am not competent to continue." There was a fundamental truth in what he was saying, but I insisted that I could finish. After all, we had just spent an entire year terminating! I felt I had to be ready to stop. He insisted that I not stop. He won. And in his winning I found my anxiety at accepting his offer overwhelming. I was far better prepared to stop than to accept such a generous offer. He may have been old, but he was still smart. He knew exactly the impact his offer would have on me. Three more years of a very productive analysis followed. I did, in the end, have to tell him he was no longer competent to continue.

As we now faced the absolute end of our work together, he asked that we continue a friendship. I said, "No." It felt essential to me that I now experience the loss of our working intimacy. This time my "no" held. This time, it was a healthier one. I needed to know and feel that all I had gained and internalized from our work together was now truly mine: solid and cohesive.

As I re-read "On transience" in preparing this chapter, I saw something new in Freud's essay. In the context of Quinodoz's book, I saw Freud's reflections of incipient loss and the decay of "all that is beautiful and perfect" as a kind of meditation on loss not only in relation to others, but also in relation to one's self: The loss of health, personal agency, mental function, unquestioned vitality —all that is "beautiful and perfect."

How do we face and mourn the loss of our capacities, our identities— conscious and unconscious—that we hold as essential and dear to ourselves? Implicit in Quinodoz's book is an understanding of an internal process of mourning in relation to one's self. We must be able to face, as Freud (1916) put it, "how ephemeral were many things that we have regarded as changeless" (p. 307). And we need a place where we can be furious about it. I think this confrontation with an unwelcome reality and the mourning that must follow is made easier by the understanding and accompaniment of another, be it an analyst, therapist, counselor, partner, friend, lover, sibling, son, or daughter. These are places where we are not meant to venture alone.

When I terminated my analysis, I did ask my analyst for one more thing—that I could be with him when he died. He agreed. A few years passed, and then he called inviting me to lunch, adding, "Don't come alone. Please bring Mick with you." He told me that he had a rare, terminal form of brain cancer. As the disease progressed, we met often. We spoke a great deal about life and my future, little of his illness. He read the papers I was working on. He spoke of what it was like to watch his capacities slip away. He hoped for a death without pain. He was granted that wish as he slipped into a coma before he died. This was our final intimacy, our final work together. As he approached his death, he remained my analyst, and I remained his patient, even in this most unusual intimacy.

When we have the time to see death approaching, we can mourn together in the face of the unwanted and the unavoidable. We can hold on close and tight, to speak of and to one another, before we must let go. My analyst and I had that opportunity. There was extraordinary meaning and intimacy in our having the courage to do this.

Conclusion

Orr, Didion, and Deraniyagala were deprived of the luxury of the time and anticipation I had with Rose and my analyst. Yet each was able, at last, to find a voice of mourning and meaning through their extraordinary memoirs. Each book describes the slowly emerging experience of being able to accept the irreversible loss of their loved ones and to hold a place for them within their internal worlds.

Until now I had only been able to grieve, not mourn. Grief is passive. Grief happened. Mourning, the act of dealing with grief, required attention.

(Didion, 2006, p. 143)

But I have learned I can only recover myself when I keep them near. If I distance myself from them, and their absence, I am fractured. I am left feeling I've blundered into a stranger's life. ... Now I sit here in this garden in New York, and I hear them, jubilant, gleeful, on our lawn.

(Deraniyagala, 2013, pp. 227–228)

When someone you love dies suddenly, the process of surviving them is complex. Part of the difficulty is separating out your entangled identities. Grieving, you celebrate the love bond between you and the dead one, but also, as you grieve, you are distinguishing yourself from the dead one.

(Orr, 2004, p. 75)

Freud wrote "On transience" in the midst of writing his classic essay "Mourning and melancholia," begun in 1915 and finished in 1917. While "On transience" had the feel of a literary essay, in "Mourning and melancholia" Freud elaborated his ideas in the clinical sphere. He considered melancholia to be the outcome of an inability or refusal to mourn, and he saw the consequences of such failure as dire. To Freud, in melancholia there is a turning of one's back on reality, the lost object is not released, the internal world becomes frozen in time, and one's capacity to love cannot open to new appetites, attachments, and meaning. Pain is imperative in the process of mourning. Reading the memoirs by Orr, Deraniyagala, and Didion is, at times, a harrowing experience (I cannot imagine what it was like to have written them), but each in its own way captures the hard and essential work of mourning that Freud sought to convey in his article.

Freud's essays are now nearly 100 years old. And yet today the process of mourning is so often forestalled, medicated, or pathologized. It so often seems easier to hope for a quick recovery, to look away and avoid the anguish. Two recent books, *The Loss of Sadness* (Horwitz & Wakefield, 2007) and *The New Black* (Leader, 2008), articulate powerful critiques of the medicalization of grief and loss: Medication replaces the human domain.

It is my hope that this chapter and the personal voices it conveys will be a contribution to re-establishing respect for the impact of the loss of loved ones and the possibility of a descent into despair that can reach the edge of insanity. Mourning is painful, essential, and requires the presence of others.

My father was an absolute atheist. There was to be no minister and no religious music at his funeral. He refused to have the American flag draped over his coffin. So, how to say good-bye? He loved the singing of Joan Baez, so it was her gorgeous voice that soared over the small group of people who gathered to wish him farewell.

Chapter 15

The inevitability of uncertainty, the necessity of doubt, and the development of trust

This chapter, revised here, was originally presented as a keynote speech at the World TA Conference in Istanbul, Turkey, the theme of which was "Trust and Uncertainty in the 21st Century."

It was nearly a year ago that I came up with the title for this speech. I was under a tight deadline from the ASAM (the Turkish group that helped organize the 2006 World TA Conference in Istanbul), which was in the early stages of preparing the program and needed a title and descriptive paragraph fast. I came up with "The inevitability of uncertainty, the necessity of doubt, and the development of trust," probably under the influence of either too much coffee or too much wine—I can't recall which. A lot has transpired during the year since, both in my own life and in the world at large, so if I were to title this speech now, it would be "Trust and distrust/hope and hatred."

I had come to Istanbul from Kosovo, where I was visiting my son Seth and daughter-in-law, Ghadah. Seth works for the Organization for Security and Cooperation in Europe (OSCE) at their headquarters in Pristina. It would seem, in spite of its name, that the OSCE is forced to spend much more of its resources providing security than promoting cooperation. In addition to staying in Pristina, we drove to Prizren, a predominantly Muslim community near Albania. Our route took us to Gracanice, a Serbian enclave and Roma (gypsy) village where Ghadah, a Sunni Muslim, worked for a foundation promoting education for Serbian and Roma children, and to Mitrovice, a Serbian-identified city near the Serbian border. On our journey, we drove in a white, clearly marked OSCE vehicle, and the welcome—or lack thereof—was palpable as we moved from one area to another. We were welcomed in the Muslim, Kosovarian territories but not in the Serbian/Orthodox Christian communities. We passed war memorials guarded by United Nations (UN) tanks, the UN facilities surrounded by bomb walls and razor wire, and the Christian churches surrounded by walls and razor wire, often guarded by UN soldiers and tanks.

Kosovo was relatively stable at that time, but the tension, distrust, and hatred simmered just below the surface. It was a stark reminder of the compelling need for us to learn to work more effectively with hatred and violence through political, social, economic, educational, and therapeutic means.

I left Kosovo filled with a father's pride and—given the continuing disintegration of Iraq, the renewed destruction of Lebanon, and the obvious tensions in Kosovo—a quiet despair. As I flew to Istanbul, the prime ministers of Serbia and Kosovo were meeting face to face for the first time since 1999, when NATO bombed Serbia to bring the ethnic cleansing of (Muslim) Albanians to an end. The talks ended in a stalemate.

My speech that day would be more about hatred than hope, more about distrust than trust, for I believe if we do not learn to face our hatreds, there will be no true hope or trust. We are thrown into deep uncertainty and doubt at times of war and profound cultural conflicts, like those we are now facing throughout the world. We are thrown back to re-examining the nature of our cultural and social structures. It was probably no accident that the theme of the previous year's International Transactional Analysis Conference in Edinburgh was "Freedom and Responsibility" and that the next year's theme was "Trust and Uncertainty in the 21st Century." The April 2006 issue of the *Transactional Analysis Journal* was devoted to papers from the previous year's conference, and in my introductory editorial to that journal, I wrote that "these articles bring new meaning and spirit to Berne's vision of transactional analysis as a social psychiatry" (Cornell, 2006, p. 76). As was evident from that year's conference program, Berne's vision continued to inspire us.

Pearl Drego's article "Cultural Parent oppression and regeneration," published in the *Transactional Analysis Journal* in 1996, is based on her treatment of and research into the oppression of women in India. In the article, she observed that:

> while the culture of the group requires analysis outside the individual, understanding the Cultural Parent involves introspection and self-awareness. The culture of a group is carried by individuals, and it is possible to become aware of it within the [individual] personality.
>
> (p. 59)

Drego's (1983, 1996, 2005) writings on the Cultural Parent build on Berne's work in *The Structure and Dynamics of Organizations and Groups* (1963). She seeks to provide a means for examining and changing the impact of culture and cultural oppression on the individual's psychology. At the conference in 2006, I was speaking to intercultural tensions and the necessity of understanding distrust and hatred in the movement toward intergroup and cultural change.

Before the conference, I watched the documentary film by Martin Scorcese (2005) on the beginnings of Bob Dylan's career. Dylan has been a hero of mine since I was a teenager, and Scorcese made a brilliant presentation of Dylan's early years. The film was, however, more than Dylan's story, as it wove his life into the cultural revolutions of the civil rights and anti-war movements of the 1960s. It was a time in the United States of turmoil, idealism, and hope. As the documentary came to an end, I wept. But mine were not tears of joy or appreciation. They were bitter tears, tears of rage and despair. What had happened to my country? How had my generation created the United States of 2006? How had we elected George W. Bush as president? How had those of my generation allowed these wars, cultural arrogance, unbridled hostility, religious ignorance, and prejudice? Scorsese captured the cultural and political landscape of the 1960s vividly. It was in this cultural spirit that transactional analysis was born. Eric Berne and his rabble-rousing colleagues were part of the heart of the 1960s in the San Francisco Bay Area. It was the era in which I grew up and with which I deeply identify.

At the beginning of 2006, I went back into therapy after a very difficult 2005. The man I chose as my therapist was a forensic psychiatrist. I agreed to see him after hours at his office in the African-American center in the midst of one of Pittsburgh's now poorest neighborhoods, an area that was once a vibrant jazz and cultural center in the city. After several weeks, I was leaving a session and found the doors locked. It was late, dark, and I had no idea how to get out. Eventually, a man came up to me and said, "Do you want to get out?" I told him I did. "Well, I'll let you out," he said, "if you look at me." "What do you mean?" I asked. He replied, "You've been coming here for several weeks, and you've never looked at me. You act like I don't exist." I was stunned, filled with shame, and mumbled something like, "I'm sorry. I don't really know what you mean. I've been coming to see my therapist, so I'm rather preoccupied when I get here. I don't think I see anybody really." "Maybe, but you walk by me every night and you don't see me, never bother to say 'hello.' So maybe, but you're a white guy, I'm black, and black people are used to white people looking past them. You're not going to look past me. Look me in the eye." I did. "My name is James, what's yours?" James asked. "Bill." "OK, Bill, next week you look me in the eye, say 'Hi James, how's it going?' and we'll start getting to know each other." Thereafter we always greeted each other and we got to know each other, even as I still arrived preoccupied and often left even more so.

I have since given that encounter with James a great deal of thought. At the end of the previous year, I had sold my family home in the country and moved into the city into a predominantly poor, African-American neighborhood, one that was beginning to be revived. There was a great deal of tension in this neighborhood. There, I did see my neighbors, but I didn't know how (or if) to greet those who were black. I didn't know the body language, the social protocol on the street. A few days after the confrontation from James, I was walking to my house and passed two African-American men in a deep, animated conversation. I stepped to the side as I passed them. One of the men turned around and approached me angrily, "We don't bite, you know. You stepped away from us like we scared you. We don't bite, mister." This time, though, I did not feel ashamed. I had consciously stepped aside so as not to intrude on their conversation, as I would with anyone. This time I felt some understanding of the man's reaction, and I was able to talk with the guy comfortably. And yet I knew, here again, was an experience of men accustomed to being avoided, even shunned (Lewin, 2000), so the man's assumption of my avoidance was not ungrounded. We had misread one another, with distrust and tension on both sides.

I tell these stories here because they are everyday examples of uncertainty, of cultural and racial distrust. In these instances, we can see both the subtlety and the depth of cultural misunderstandings. I am trying to understand my own racism, my anxieties, my ways of insulating myself from unpleasantness and differentness, and I don't like this process very much.

I am accustomed to welcoming theoretical differences, challenges, and even conflict in my various roles as therapist, professional colleague, trainer, writer, and editor. In these familiar arenas, the experience of differentness and conflict is exciting and enjoyable. In my work as a psychotherapist, I know that conflict —even hatred—is meaningful.

For example, many of my clients have had exceedingly difficult lives, and they are in various ways rather difficult people. Often their work with me is their third or fourth effort at psychotherapy. They have little reason to be hopeful or trusting, little motivation to be pleasant or reasonable. When I sit with a client in the face of hatred or despair, I see a body that is scarred and battered. I can usually feel a link, and I can bring some comprehension to the hostility and distrust. Sometimes I am an effective partner in the face of deeply distressed affect. Sometimes I am not so effective, but together we eventually work things out. I feel a meaning to these disturbances and some confidence that our work will make a difference. But I find it incredibly difficult to feel hope or trust when I cast these issues onto a societal and political scale.

In my recent writing, I have argued for a theoretical and therapeutic attitude that is neither too certain of the therapist's knowing nor too comforting in what is provided to the client. It can be quite seductive and gratifying to the human relations professional to be seen as the good and understanding parent, the provider of the "secure base" (Bowlby, 1979; Kohlrieser, 2006). Secure base—it is nearly impossible for me to speak this term these days without thinking of the gross injustices carried out by the United States government in the name of Homeland Security, a seductive if empty and deceptive promise promulgated by George W. Bush and the current US administration. As a psychotherapist, I can comprehend how so many Americans have been willing to sacrifice their thinking and autonomy, not to mention the rights and autonomy of other peoples, in exchange for the illusion of protection and security. But as a citizen of the United States, I am also frightened and appalled.

A psychologically secure base is a necessary foundation for our work, but I do not think it is a sufficient model for working with distrust, violence, and hatred. As professionals using transactional analysis to promote personal, group, and organizational change, we need to think very carefully when we imagine that we can offer our clients a secure base. What is it we think we are providing? What is it our clients imagine we are offering? I think the ideal of a secure base needs to be changed to that of a "vital base" within which we offer a challenging, experimental, often conflicted, and rather uncomfortable relationship through which both people must shift their familiar frames of reference. Whether the work is between individuals or groups, both parties must shift their frames of reference if trust of any substance is to develop.

I think that, as a community, it has often been difficult for transactional analysis practitioners to face squarely the degrees of shame, hatred, and irrationality of which we are all capable. Berne (1972) warned us most bluntly when he wrote of the Little Fascist in each of us:

> If the Little Fascist comes out openly, he is a cripple-kicker, a stomper, and a rapist, sometimes with some excuse or other such as toughness, objectivity, or some justification. But most people suppress these tendencies, pretend they are not there at all, excuse them if they show their colors, or overlay and disguise them with fear. [These] form the basis for third-degree or "tissue" games that draw blood. He who pretends these forces do not exist becomes their victim. His whole script may become a project to demonstrate that he is free of them. But since he is most likely not, this is a denial of himself. ... The solution is not to say, as many do, "This has nothing to do with me" or "It's too frightening," but rather "What can I do about it and what can I do with it?"
>
> (pp. 269–270)

We can, perhaps, more easily make arrangements (games) within our dyadic relationships to avoid anxiety, hostility, and differentness, but within and between groups the experience of anxiety, unpredictability, hostility, and differentness is far harder to avoid (Schermer & Pines, 1994). It is probably no accident that Berne addressed the darker side of human relations more frequently and directly in his writings on groups. In *Principles of Group Treatment* (1966), for example, Berne outlined the satisfaction in groups of the basic human hungers for stimulation, recognition, and structure, stressing that "people will pay almost any price to have time structured for them, as few are capable of structuring their own time autonomously for very long" (p. 230). He warned that a derivative of structure hunger is leadership hunger and that, in turning oneself over to a leader, there is enormous compromise in one's willingness to think. Ultimately, all too often, the idealized leader then imposes restrictions or prohibitions on one's right to think for oneself.

It is no accident that it was after World War I that a deeply troubled Sigmund Freud (1921) wrote "Group psychology and analysis of the ego," in which he described the nature of group regression into what he called "mobs and hordes." A group's identification with the leader creates a sense of closeness and belonging. Freud warned of the idealized and dependent transferences to The Leader, the subsequent distortions of superego and ego functions, and the dynamics of such groups as the military, the church, and the state. His conclusions are mirrored in Berne's writings on groups. Neither Freud nor Berne were very optimistic men by temperament—their writings were often infused with a deep pessimism and even cynicism—but both were, nonetheless, often idealistic in their visions for the work they founded.

Freud, for example, was deeply affected by the horrors and utter irrationality of World War I, and he determined that psychoanalysis had a responsibility to its communities. He initiated the creation of free clinics in every major city with a psychoanalytic institute, requiring that all practicing analysts devote at least one day per week to offering free treatment (Danto, 2005). Vienna, Berlin, Frankfurt, Budapest, Paris, and London all witnessed the creation of free psychoanalytic clinics that offered in-depth psychoanalysis, libraries, and mental hygiene classes, a profound expression of Freud's ideals and leadership. All these clinics except those in London were closed down within a few years by the Nazis. Freud was one of the last Jewish analysts to flee Europe for safety elsewhere. I cannot imagine the despair he must have endured in the last year of his life in England as he witnessed, yet again, his idealism overrun by hatred and irrationality.

It might seem on the surface paradoxical that of the many Jewish psycho-analysts who fled the Nazis and established psychoanalysis in the United States, most turned their backs on the social and political aspects of psychoanalysis. They enshrined ego psychology in the United States, a model that returned to the psychology of the individual and emphasized the rational. Many became deeply conservative in their practice and hungry for the sanction and approval of authorities. Erich Fromm and Erik Erikson (one of Berne's analysts), among a very few, maintained the social and more radical perspective in psycho-analysis in the United States.

I try to imagine the profound despair of those emigrating analysts, fleeing for their lives, often leaving family behind to die. I can understand their inward turning and imagine the subtle cynicism underlying their return to, wish for, and idealization of the rational and the power of the ego.

It was within this socially cleansed psychoanalytic environment that Berne was trained, and it was this he challenged in creating transactional analysis as a social psychiatry, with groups at the heart of his work. In the October 2006 issue of the *Transactional Analysis Journal*, Steve Karpman writes of the spirit of that time in the birth of transactional analysis. Here again, in Berne's work, we witnessed a re-establishment of an ideal, a rebirth of hope. Now, nearly half a century later, we struggle with despair, surrounded by hostility and irration-ality around the world. How do we hold our values and pursue our ideals, without idealization and without turning our therapeutic values into saccharine but hollow slogans?

I will focus here primarily on racism, but in so doing I ask the reader to be thinking about misogyny, homophobia, religious fundamentalism, ethnic and nationalistic superiority, and all forms of institutionalized hatred. Race, like culture, is a complex intermingling of psychological and social factors. It is not simply about the color of one's skin any more than culture is about one's country or ethnicity of origin. One's racial or ethnic identity includes such factors as physical characteristics, geographical location, family structure, income, history, and politics as well as economic, educational, and developmental opportunity. Donald Moss edited *HATING in the First Person Plural* (2003), assembling the essays in this book by sending a group of psychotherapists three words—nigger, cunt, and faggot, among the ugliest words in the English language—and asking each author to write an essay on one of those words. It is a powerful collection of writings from which I learned a lot, a book that has helped me to think about and work more clearly with the multiple meanings and sources of bias and hatred. Alan Bass (2003), in an essay in *HATING*, speaks to my experience with James and in my new neighborhood as he observes:

> When racism is part of the everyday environment, there is a particular tendency to disavow its traumatic effects, while of course peremptorily re-creating a traumatic environment. And there can be the tendency on the part of an allegedly neutral observer ... to disavow that all these dynamics are at work.
>
> (p. 41)

Maurice Apprey, an African-American psychoanalyst, examines the suffering of African Americans in particular but writes with a voice that echoes among all populations that are oppressed, assaulted, marginalized, or held in contempt. He uses the image of "transgenerational haunting" (Apprey, 1996a, 1996b, 1998, 2003), by which he means the victim is host to the ghosts of the original aggressors, a haunting passed unconsciously from one generation to the next. He writes that an individual's "interior space is filled with shadows, ghosts, and silhouettes where past and present, inside and outside, are ill-defined ... [and so] urgently strives [without conscious awareness] to repeat historical injury, choosing an inappropriate object to attack" (Apprey, 1998, p. 34).

Berne and Drego, in their writings on the deep influences of cultural and group character, repeatedly demonstrate the split—often a total contradiction—between the professed etiquette of the cultural Parent ego state and the emotional and bodily realities of the character of the group. In *The Structure and Dynamics of Organizations and Groups* (1963), Berne observed that "group character" provides the mechanisms for handling individual anxieties and patterns of emotional expression. Drego (1996) elaborated Berne's concept to include emotionally charged attitudes and deeply inscribed ways of feeling, sensing, expressing, loving, and relating. I would add hating to this list. In describing the dynamics of group cultures, Berne (1963) wrote:

> Character is more "primitive" than etiquette. Etiquette requires a restraint, and understanding and knowledge of social behavior. ... Character is a more direct expression of instinctual life. The group character is chiefly an expression of that aspect of the personality which will later be called the Child.
>
> (pp. 151–152)

Drego refers to group character as the cultural shadow that envelops and contaminates the Child ego state. The term "character" has its origins in Greek, meaning "branded, cut into the skin"; character cuts deep. Apprey (2003) stresses:

> Into this cut [character], as it were, may be inserted a world of lived experience where the oppressed has lost sight of the original enemy. Influenced by this absence, a people may attack its own, as in Black-on-Black crime.
>
> (p. 9)

In transgenerational haunting, then, a contemporary generation is unwittingly possessed by an earlier generation. Such possession preserves history, but in a poisonous, unmetabolized version (p. 12).

For Apprey (2003), "In violent ethnonational conflicts, the pivotal issues are difference and identity" (p. 6), where the dread of differentness—the Other, in his language—is avoided at all costs so as to preserve identity (structure and recognition hungers in Berne's terms). Transgenerational hauntings are drenched in histories of violence, injury, shame, powerlessness, and economic deprivation —the "brandings" of previous generations then carried in the group character (Gilligan, 2000). We must not underestimate the enduring and irrational force of intergenerational injury, hatred, and violence. Uncertainty and doubt inhabit the domain of the tensions between the familiar and the different, between Self and Other. Apprey is not speaking of self and other as we typically do in object relations theory, but of Self and THE OTHER, where the Other represents a threatening, alien identity or way of life. It is a differentness that cannot be explored or made a part of one's own life and identity, so it is rendered inferior, disgusting, evil, or dead. This is the domain of a fundamental experience of differentness in which the experience of "I'm Not OK, You're Not OK" is a very real tension that must be acknowledged. This tension is not to be bridged by some saccharine application of "I'm OK, You're OK" as an unthinking idealization of the human spirit.

In working with distrust, hatred, prejudice, and violence, we must look first at ourselves, honestly. All will not be pretty. If we cannot look honestly at ourselves and our professional and ethnic cultures, we will be of little value to those we wish to help. In working with prejudice and violence, shame and distrust, we need to look together with the person at him- or herself as an individual and the history of that individual and also at the histories of the familial, racial, and ethnic groups to which the individual belongs. As therapists, teachers, trainers, and members of the remarkably international community of transactional analysts, we must face and make room for distrust and dissonance in our work. To develop real trust, we must first acknowledge and express distrust.

In his discussion of the Little Fascist, Berne stated that the answer to these vicious and hateful aspects of ourselves is first to acknowledge them and then ask, "What can I do about it and what can I do with it?" What can we do? In Drego's (1996) article on her work with Indian women, she stresses:

To bring about a change, the oppressive Cultural Parent and its injunctions, myths, and reinforcements must be cleansed at the individual level as well as at the group level. Therapy with individuals needs to be supported by group discussions among mothers, group support systems among women, retraining programs for families, and new kinds of relationships between mothers and their children—in short, a form of cultural therapy similar to one Erikson (1963) described: "'group therapy' of a kind which would not aim at psychiatric improvement of the individual participant but at an improvement of the cultural relations of those assembled" (p. 127).

(pp. 74–75)

This is transactional analysis as a truly social psychiatry, with group work, education, and counseling at its very foundation.

Drego addresses the cultural oppression of the individual by families and groups. Apprey addresses intercultural conflict and violence. He brings his experiences from African-American communities to work in conflict resolution with various groups faced with ethnonational violence. He delineates a process necessitating the involvement of outside facilitators through which Self and Other, as individuals and groups, can begin to open up new opportunities.

The first stage of the work, as outlined by Apprey, is the acknowledgment of polarized views and the space for this polarization to be fully expressed. In the polarization phase, each side defines its own identity while demonizing the differentness of the Other. The second phase is one of differentiation within each of the polarized groups, which allows participants to see that even within the group with which they identify, there are a multiplicity of positions. The third phase involves the "crossing of mental borders" (p. 23) through which each side attempts to enter the Other's frame of reference through meaningful dialogue and "propelled by an ethic of responsibility" (p. 23; see also Bond, 2006; Kohlrieser, 2006). The Bush administration and the leaders of many of the regions currently engaged in armed conflict seem completely unwilling to engage in this process. As I said earlier, meaningful trust is possible only when both parties shift their frames of reference. The fourth and most crucial phase is the one within which the emerging ethics are grounded in joint projects of concrete and mutual benefit. There is little evidence on the world stage today of opposing groups undertaking these last two processes, which we have witnessed in our time in the work of the Truth and Reconciliation Commission in South Africa. The South African efforts have not eliminated poverty or erased racism, but they have allowed enough healing so that functional social structures based in nonviolence can begin to be established. Apprey outlines a process that I believe is consistent with our process of group work in transactional analysis, a process that conveys realistic ideas and ideals that can deepen and enrich our work with cultural and intergroup conflict, violence, and prejudice.

In our work—be it as therapists in individual or group treatment, teachers, trainers, or consultants—we must create the space and the opportunity for the realities of our individual and collective anxieties, shamings, and hatreds to be aired (Nitsun, 1996). We must not avert our gaze. In looking at ourselves and each other within the space of despair, shame, distrust, polarization, and hostility, we create a container, an environment in which interchange, under-standing, and informed, quiet trust can gradually develop. This work takes time. It requires great determination and the willingness to remain engaged during periods of doubt, uncertainty, distrust, and polarization.

In conclusion, I turn to the words of two artists. More than any other members of our societies, I think it is our artists who are able to work within their cultural histories and traditions, and at the same time stand outside the social and cultural norms in critical reflection and representation. I close with a brief quote from an essay by Adrienne Rich (1979) entitled "Women and honor: Some notes on lying":

> An honorable human relationship—that is, one in which two people have the right to use the word "love"—is a process, delicate, violent, often terrifying to both persons involved, a process of refining the truths they can tell each other. It is important to do this because it breaks down human self-delusion and isolation. It is important to do this because in so doing we do justice to our own complexity. It is important to do this because we can count on so few to go that hard way with us.
>
> (p. 188)

Written in the early stages of the Vietnam War, Bob Dylan's anti-war anthem, "With God on Our Side," challenges America's precious notion that ours is a nation with God on its side. Through six stanzas, Dylan (1963) outlines the wars of the United States, each carried out with God on our side, ending the song with a wish (a prayer?) that were God truly on our side, he would stop the next war. It has been more than 60 years since Dylan wrote those words. Dylan's God did not stop the next war, nor has anyone else's, but in the names of various gods, several wars have been started.

As I was leaving the conference, Diane Salters (2006) gave me a parting gift, a book, *A Human Being Died that Night* by Pumla Gobodo-Madikizela (2003). She is a clinical psychologist who served on South Africa's Truth and Reconci-liation Commission's Human Rights Violations Committee. The book is Gobodo-Madikizela's complex and moving account of her interviews with Eugene de Kock, who is serving 212 years in prison for crimes against humanity in his capacity as the commanding officer of apartheid death squads. She describes the complicity of the Dutch Reformed Church in apartheid policies and the South African Army's killings of enemies of the state, a reminder of Freud's linkage of the group psychology of hordes, the state, and the church. Soldiers were issued a special edition of the Bible, each copy of which was inscribed on the first page with a message in Afrikaans by State President P.W. Botha (as cited in Gobodo-Madikizela, 2003):

This Bible is an important part of your calling to duty. When you are overwhelmed with doubt, pain, or when you find yourself wavering, you must turn to this wonderful book for answers.... You are now called to play your part in defending our country. It is my prayer that this Bible will be your comfort so that you can fulfill your duty, and South Africa and her people will forever be proud of you. Of all the weapons you carry, this is the greatest because it is the Weapon of God.

(p. 53)

Chapter 16

In conflict and community: A century of turbulence working and living in groups

War: The rending and reviving of societal relations

There has been a powerful and rather surprising sequence of outbreaks of major wars followed by experiments in group and community treatment. Although international violence over the past century has often severed civilized ties, these periods of violent slaughter have often engendered efforts of redress and restoration through group and community life. Leaders in the evolution of group analysis and group psychotherapy have often stood at the margins of their professional groups and social norms and suffered the pains and losses of societal and professional sanction and rejection.

Through many years of teaching and training in the mental health field, I have come to see the importance of studying the historical contexts within which the theories that inform our practices developed. I have also come to believe that the theories that form our work are efforts of marginalized individuals and their communities to create spaces and places of belonging and to make the unbearable more bearable.

Sigmund Freud and the free clinics

World War I shattered most of Europe. During the years surrounding that war, Freud was consolidating his theories and methods of psychoanalysis, but during the war, his attention shifted to include the societal level as well as that of the individual psyche. Many of his most personal and troubled writings were products of the impact that the Great War had on him, his family, and his colleagues. In an essay entitled "Timely reflections on war and death," written in 1915, Freud lamented:

> It [war] tramples in blind fury on all that comes in its way, as though there were to be no future and no peace among men after it is over. It cuts all the common bonds between the contending peoples, and threatens to leave a legacy of embitterment that will make any renewal of those bonds impossible for a long time to come.
>
> (1915, p. 279)

Freud had opposed his sons fighting in the war. In 1918, the International Psychoanalytic Association met in Budapest. The war was still ongoing. Freud's son Martin was interred in a prisoner-of-war camp, his condition unknown. It was within that context that Freud delivered his paper "Lines of advance in psycho-analytic therapy." He sought to remind his colleagues of the psycho-analytic project and reasserted the urgency of their work. He closed his talk in a remarkable fashion:

> It is possible to foresee that at some time or other the conscience of society will awake and remind it that the poor man should have just as much right to assistance for the mind as he now has to the life-saving help offered by surgery; and [it will be seen] that the neuroses threaten public health as much as tuberculosis.
>
> (Freud, 1919, p. 167)

He then proposed that free analytically oriented clinics be established so that

> men who would otherwise give way to drink, women who have nearly succumbed to privations, and children for whom there is no choice but between running free and neurosis, may be made capable, through therapy, of resistance and of efficient work.
>
> (p. 167)

At Freud's insistence, after the war, all psychoanalytic institutes were required to establish clinics to provide free treatment to the poor and working classes (Danto, 2005). All analysts were required to contribute time in these programs. These clinics were among the first things demolished by the Nazis as they began to move against psychoanalysis, Jews, and all others who lived outside Nazi-prescribed social norms.

Freud (1921) wrote extensively on the psychology of groups but never developed a specific methodology of group treatment. In his reflections on group psychology, he emphasized the regressive impact of groups on the individual ego. For example, he argued, "A group is an obedient herd, which could never live without a master" (p. 81). Nevertheless, through his powerful advocacy for the free clinics after World War I, he demonstrated a deep commitment to community and left an ethos that informed most subsequent developments in group psychotherapies, including the work of Trigant Burrow, Wilfred Bion, S.H. Foulkes, and Eric Berne, among others.

Trigant Burrow and group analysis

Between the world wars, the American social psychiatrist Trigant Burrow (1927) wrote extensively about the social basis of human behavior, arguing that "individual discord is but a symptom of a social discord. The reactions of the neurotic are the direct issue of our so-called normal society" (as cited in Ackerman, 1964, p. x).

Burrow is one of the cast-off radicals of psychoanalytic history. An American psychiatrist practicing in Baltimore, in 1909 Burrow heard lectures by Freud and Jung during their infamous tour of America. He was so impressed that he moved his family to Zurich to undertake analysis with Jung as well as beginning an active correspondence with Freud. On his return to Baltimore in 1911, he co-founded the American Psychoanalytic Association with Ernest Jones. Burrow worked as a psychoanalyst, writing numerous papers during the following decade. Then, in 1921, he accepted the challenge of one of his patients to switch places with him. Through this reversal of roles, Burrow—now the patient—confronted his own resistances to the analytic process and began to recognize the social forces at play in the analytic relationship. He created an experiment in which the members of the study group included himself and his patients and students, colleagues, and members of their families, all of whom engaged in an ongoing mutual examination of the unconscious dynamics of participation in the group.

Burrow called this a *process group* or *social analysis*. He argued that in group analytic work, the analyst could not hold a privileged position. He stated explicitly that "group analysis is not my analysis of the group, but it is the group's analysis of me or of any other individual in the group" (as cited in Pertegato & Pertegato, 2013, p. 138). Everyone in the group was an observer of his or her own processes and was observed and analyzed by everyone else (see Pertegato & Pertegato, 2013).

These group analyses were undertaken strictly in the here and now by discussing the social and group-level pressures on the meanings and behaviors created through membership in the group. Burrow moved away from the exploration of infantile and childhood experiences as the primary explanations for adult neurotic behavior. Gradually, he left his psychoanalytic orientation behind to develop a socially grounded theory of human development. Burrow argued that normality must be distinguished from health, that it is a brand of the shared sickness of the social structure.

This proved a bit too radical for his psychoanalytic colleagues. While still president of the American Psychoanalytic Association in 1926, Burrow (1958) wrote to Paul Federn (who later became Eric Berne's analyst): "At the last meeting of the American Psychoanalytic Association I read a paper on 'Speaking of Resistances' in which I endeavored to point out the resistances existing socially *among ourselves as psychoanalysts*, and I assure you this endeavor met with a most cheerless response on every hand" (p. 141). When his methods were called into question by his psychoanalytic colleagues, who were still invested in the analyst maintaining the position of a neutral, outside observer, Burrow offered to run a group analytic process for the association leadership. It is perhaps not surprising that Burrow's invitation was turned down. Instead, he was asked to resign from the American Psychoanalytic

Association in 1933. His work was nearly erased, not only in the psycho-analytic literature but in the group therapy literature as well (Pertegato & Pertegato, 2013). Nevertheless, Burrow's group analytic model foreshadowed the group and community experiments of Wilfred Bion and S.H. Foulkes during World War II.

Although Burrows's career spanned both world wars, he was never himself directly involved in combat. He was, however, affected such that much of his writing sought to understand the roots of racial, social, and national conflicts (Burrow, 1941, 1950). Writing at the end of World War II, Burrows (1950) offered a hopeful contemplation:

> While war inevitably entails extreme confusion and disorganization, while it causes the disruption of many personal and conventional ties, its mere massing of men in a common endeavor brings them a sense of far deeper, far more elemental bonds. It causes them to feel their common blood, their common need, their identity as one vast human organism.
>
> (p. 45)

Wilfred Bion and the Northfield experiment

World War I shaped Bion in profound ways (Bleandonu, 2000). In the autobiography of his early life (Bion, 2005), he devoted 180 gruesome pages to the account of his service, when at 19 he became an officer in the Royal Tank Corp. Only he and two others in the entire regiment survived the war. By the time World War II rolled around, he was a psychiatrist, again in military service. All of his early work with groups occurred in the context of his service with psychologically damaged soldiers in England and France.

In the Northfield "experiments" he undertook with John Rickman (who had been a conscientious objector serving as an ambulance driver with a Quaker unit in Russia), Bion began a series of experimental groups with soldiers in psychiatric care. Although the experiment lasted only a few weeks and was abruptly terminated by his military superiors (Bleandonu, 2000, pp. 61–63; Bridger, 1992), Bion's (1961) reflections in his now classic *Experiences in Groups* have been foundational for group analytic work. He was a military officer who was also a psychiatrist, a psychiatrist who worked in the midst of war. He described the psychiatric unit this way:

> Under one roof were gathered 300–400 men who in their units already had the benefit of such therapeutic value as lies in military discipline, good food, and regular care; clearly this had not been enough to stop them from finding their way into a psychiatric hospital.
>
> (p. 12)

He continued:

> An officer who aspires to be a psychiatrist in charge of a rehabilitation
> wing must know what it is to be in a responsible position at the time when
> responsibility means having to face issues of life and death. ... A psychia-
> trist who knows this will at least be spared the hideous blunder of thinking
> that patients are potential cannon fodder to be returned as such to their
> units. He will realize that it is his task to produce self-respecting men
> socially adjusted to the community and therefore willing to accept its
> responsibilities, whether in peace or war.
>
> (p. 13)

After the war, a panel of five American psychiatrists were commissioned to
undertake a study tour of the psychiatric care provided to soldiers in Europe and
Great Britain. The result was a collection of papers published in the *Bulletin of
the Menninger Clinic* in 1946. Among those was Bion's (1946) article on "The
leaderless group project," which reflected on the experiences in his war-related
groups:

> It was essential first to find out what was the ailment afflicting the
> community, as opposed to the individuals composing it, and next to give
> the community a common aim. In general all psychiatric hospitals have the
> same ailment and the same common aim—to escape the batterings of
> neurotic disorder. Unfortunately, the attempt to get this relief is nearly
> always by futile means—retreat. Without realizing it doctors and patients
> alike are running away from the complaint.
>
> (p. 79)

In that paper, he outlined the basic principles of the Northfield experiment:

1 The objective of the group/community is to study its own internal
   tensions
2 No problem is tackled until its nature and extent are made clear as part
   of the larger group
3 The remedy had to be shared and understood by the full group
4 The study of the group's tensions never ceased and was a 24-hour
   project
5 It was our objective to send the men out with at least some understanding of the nature of intra-group tensions and, if possible, with
   some idea how to set about harmonizing them
6 The study group had to be seen as a benefit to the majority and has to
   occur in the context of real life situations

(Bion, 1946, pp. 80–81)

It is interesting to note that after the war, Bion went into a personal psycho-analysis with Melanie Klein that lasted from 1945 until 1953. During that period, his interests shifted from groups to individual psychoanalysis, with a particular focus on psychotic processes. His last published paper on groups was in 1952, a review of Freud's theory of group dynamics. Although he wrote little explicitly about groups after that, these papers collected in *Experiences in Groups* (Bion, 1961) have had a lasting legacy in models of group treatment (Lipgar & Pines, 2003a, 2003b; Pines, 1992). Bion (1961) himself expressed surprise at the enduring interest in papers on groups: "The articles printed here aroused more interest than I expected" (p. 7). He agreed to have most of his group-centered papers republished in 1961 under the title *Experience in Groups*. He concluded that collection of papers with a revision of his 1952 review of Freud's theories, at that point placing Klein's theories at the heart of his account of the primitive defense mechanisms that he saw dominating life in groups. In a more personal comment on Freud's perspective, Bion (1961) remarked, "Freud's view seems not to make explicit the dangerous possibilities that exist in the phenomenon of [group] leadership. His view of the leader ... is not easily reconciled with my experience of leadership as it emerges in practice" (p. 178).

S.H. Foulkes and the evolution of group analysis

Foulkes, a Jew who had fought for Germany in World War I, fled Germany with his family in 1933 and moved to England. Like Bion, he became a psychiatrist in the British military in World War II. He came to the Northfield Military Hospital after Bion had left and initiated another round of experiments in group and community-based treatment.

In "Group analysis in a military neurosis centre," Foulkes (1965) argued:

> The emphasis was laid still further on the group as a whole. The main aim was to prevent the conductor from hampering the spontaneous expression and activity of the group. Thus he has to learn to tolerate anxieties and tensions within himself, to resist the temptation to play the role of the authoritarian leader but rather to submit all problems to the group, facing them fairly and squarely with the group.
>
> (p. 189)

This is an extraordinary statement that captures the paradox of group analytic leadership. The leader is a group member who must simultaneously join the group, observe the group, observe his or her own' reactions, and make use of them as a means of grasping what is emerging in the group.

Writing in the same issue of the *Bulletin of the Menninger Clinic* as Bion, Foulkes (1946) suggested, "If the psychotherapist resists the temptation to be made a leader, he will be rewarded by their growing independence, spontaneity and responsibility and personal insight into their social attitudes" (p. 85).

Foulkes (1965) came to describe the group analyst as a *conductor* of the group process: "The conductor puts emphasis on the 'here and now' and promotes tolerance and appreciation of individual differences" (p. 57).

> The group analyst accepts whatever position the group chooses to confer on him. ... He must accept this position as a leader in order to be able to liquidate it later on. He could not wean the group from something which had not been previously established. ... He does not step down, but lets the group, in steps and stages, bring him down to earth. The change which takes place is that from a leader of the group to a leader in the group. The group, in turn, replaces the leader's authority by that of the group.
>
> (p. 61)

Foulkes asked, as did Trigant Burrow, what if we were all, more or less, on the same playing field? The group facilitator never fully relinquishes his or her role—there is always work to do. But to work in a genuinely group analytic style requires those in the leadership role to relinquish such beloved, idealized, and narcissistically gratifying roles as the authoritative, all-knowing leader; the quietly reflective interpreter; and/or the compassionate/empathic good parent.

Eric Berne and group treatment

Bion's and Foulkes's approaches to group analysis were, at their core, experimental social environments within which it was possible to experience and examine the unconscious forces of group process and social life. They were deeply formed and informed by the crucibles of war. It is likely no accident that the group analytical models have a long history of involvement and investigation of social conflict (Dalal, 2002; Friedman, 2010; Nitsun, 2015; Pines, 2010).

A closing chapter of Berne's *The Structure and Dynamics of Organizations and Groups* (1963, pp. 212–222) makes it clear that he had read and was familiar with the works of Burrow, Bion, and Foulkes. In his chapter in *Principles of Group Treatment* addressing methods of treatment, Berne (1966) discussed and contrasted transactional analytic groups with those based in the models developed by Foulkes and Bion. But transactional analysis was grounded in Berne's analytic training in the post-war ego psychology model of American psychoanalysis, so the result was a model of group treatment radically different from those proposed by Bion and Foulkes. Berne's was a model of individual treatment in the group, often as an adjunct to ongoing individual psychotherapy, rather than a form of therapy and social inquiry in and of itself. In Berne's model, the leader was clearly defined as the doctor and the outside observer of the individuals' dynamics enacted within the group.

Berne grew up in Montreal in a Jewish family in a Catholic neighborhood. Berne's father, a doctor, was rejected by his medical colleagues and died when Berne was just 10 from the very disease, tuberculosis, he had dedicated his life to treating (Berne, 2010). As a boy and adolescent, Eric was a misfit. He repeatedly formed clubs with other boys to try to have a group where he belonged. Those clubs always fell apart. Even as an adult, he continued to face rejection and struggled to fit in with groups. He was rejected from membership among his psychoanalytic peers, an experience that both hurt him and spurred him on to articulate his own ideas and methods, eventually giving birth to transactional analysis. The San Francisco Social Psychiatry Seminars and ultimately the International Transactional Analysis Association became his successfully lasting club.

In his discussion of scripts in *The Structure and Dynamics of Organizations and Groups*, Berne (1963) offered the story of Davy, "a therapist whose protocol had to do with 'curing lots of people'" (p. 167). Davy's protocol "was based on a beloved family physician and much illness in the family" (p. 167). Berne went on, "The script proper was active for a while during his grade-school years when he would invite various clubs to 'meet at my house,' hoping in this way to become a leader" (pp. 167–168). Davy became a group psychotherapist, so "this 'meeting at my house' was the first act of a long script which led to a satisfactory professional career when it was properly adjusted" (p. 168). The story of Davy bears a remarkable resemblance to Berne's own. I think there was a perfect match between the role of the doctor/leader as conceived in Berne's classical psychoanalytic training and the call of his protocol and script to be the leader of groups meeting at his house.

Berne in a time of war

Berne, like Bion and Foulkes, worked for the military during World War II, evaluating incoming draftees for their fitness for military service. It was during this time that Berne undertook his thought experiments with the soldiers he had to evaluate in short periods of time. These thought experiments resulted in his series of published papers on intuition (Berne, 1977).

But what was the impact of both the war itself and the Holocaust on Berne's thinking and his work as a psychotherapist? After the war, he undertook an extensive exploration of the practices of psychiatry in countries and cultures all around the world. Traveling at his own initiative and expense, he studied various psychiatric cultures and published several articles based on his travels. Then it stopped. We might never have known why had not his son, Terry Berne (2010), told of the FBI coming to Berne's house and office, seizing many of his papers and foreign correspondence, and revoking his passport. This was post-war America, the early 1950s, and Berne found himself suspected of being a Communist sympathizer. His political and social consciousness seems to have collapsed after that. Berne's definition of social psychiatry was radically different from the society-centered, group analytic perspectives of Burrow, Bion, and Foulkes. Berne came to strip his version of social psychiatry of any social and political critique.

Berne's first book, *The Mind in Action* (1947), was written immediately after the war while he was in psychoanalytic training. He concluded with reflections on "Man as a political animal" and sections discussing "How do evil men gain followers?" and "How does an evil leader hold his followers?" Berne was not oblivious or indifferent to the after-effects of the war, as was evident in his brief comments in *The Mind in Action*. But in the 1968 edition, retitled *A Layman's Guide to Psychiatry and Psychoanalysis* and revised to promote transactional analysis, Berne deleted that section on "Man as a political animal." I cannot help but think that it was his 1950s encounter with the FBI and the government intrusion into his professional work that led him to depoliticize the presentation of his work as he sought to gain public and professional acceptance for transactional analysis.

Although Berne never published formal reflections on his experience as a military psychiatrist or as a Jew during World War II, material in the Eric Berne Archive at the University of California, San Francisco, provides glimpses into his attitudes during and after the war. Included in the archive are his letters applying for deferral from the draft in 1942. When his application was denied, he appealed, outlining a series of professional and personal factors that he thought justified a deferment from Army service. He offered a "clarification of my attitude," writing:

> I hope it will not be thought that I, as a full-blooded Jew, am anxious to evade an opportunity to oppose the Nazi army, or that as a member of a potential minority group I would shirk the defense of a democratic form of government.
>
> (1942, p. 2)

Berne was drafted and served as a military psychiatrist stationed in the United States.

From the materials in the archive, it is clear that Berne was deeply troubled after the war and sought to be of service to veterans. He proposed to the Committee Appointed by Veterans Aid Council (Berne, 1945) for follow-up care for veterans that included educational, advisory, and medical services. He taught a course entitled "Human Nature in Peace and War" (Berne, n.d.) for veterans through the Salinas Evening School and gave public talks throughout the area. "Patience is the Key Word in Helping Returned Soldiers to Adjust to Home Life, Captain Eric Berne Tells AAUW," was the headline of a 1945 article in the local Carmel, California, newspaper. The archive also contains an unpublished, book-length manuscript entitled *A Primer for Peace*, with authorship attributed to one of Berne's many pseudonyms, Eric Servitor. In the preface, he wrote passionately:

> The average man will not have a seat at the peace table, nor a room at the hotel in Geneva where he can shrewdly slip the right words into the coffee

of the proper diplomat; but the steel and the chemical man and the machine man will be there with Benedictine and cigars. ... They will be interested in trade and exports, and we in men, women, and children.

The ideas written here have been presented at various times to groups of young men whose enemy is death and not deficits. The author has had the privilege of trying to help them understand the world and people, and themselves, as well as they understand blood, mud, bullets, and orders.

(Berne, n.d., p. iv)

By the time Berne had published *Transactional Analysis in Psychotherapy* in 1961, his political passion—for whatever reasons—had become hidden from public view.

The Vietnam War and the birth of community mental health

During the time Berne was developing and promoting transactional analysis, the United States was blowing apart. Externally, there was the war in Vietnam. Internally, there was the racial violence of the civil rights movement. John and Robert Kennedy and Martin Luther King, Jr., were assassinated. Violence and war permeated the United States, the images inescapable.

During World War I and World War II, there had been no escape from violence and death. During the 1960s and early 1970s in the United Sates, images of the deaths of innocent African Americans at the hands of racist whites and the slaughter of Vietnamese civilians and American soldiers saturated television, newspapers, and magazines. Once again, the violence of war could not be ignored. But Berne held transactional analysis apart from it all in a resolutely apolitical public/professional position.

As it was after World War I and World War II, there was a resurgence in the United States during the late 1960s and early 1970s of group and community experimentation. Classical psychoanalysis seemed archaic and irrelevant during that period of social upheaval. The United States witnessed the birth of the human potential movement (Bugental, 1967; Rogers & Stevens, 1967) and the Esalen Institute (Anderson, 1983). Norman O. Brown (1966) and Herbert Marcuse (1966) sought to inform and inflame psychoanalytic thought with contemporary left-wing political vitality. There was a resurgence of interest in the work of Wilhelm Reich, especially his sexual-political writings (Reich, 1970, 1972), and Claude Steiner and Hogie Wyckoff challenged Berne's apolitical positioning to found the radical psychiatry movement, inspired in part by Reich's writings (Steiner et al., 1975). There were encounter groups (Rogers, 1970) and groups of every imaginable sort (Schutz, 1971).

The Kennedy administration funded the community mental health movement, which sought to move mental health services out of private offices and hospitals into the communities where people lived and worked; group treatment was an essential element of community-based services. In that era, transactional analysis groups flourished throughout the United States, taught and led in clinics, schools, and churches.

Nixon's election witnessed the undercutting of community mental health services (Torrey, 2014), perversely channeling much of the mental-health-related funding into the "war on drugs," as Nixon positioned himself as the "law and order" president. Nixon had also run for president on the promise of ending the war in Vietnam; history has shown us what actually happened (Weiner, 2015).

President Jimmy Carter and his wife Rosalynn had an abiding interest in mental health related services, so Carter attempted to reestablish federal funding for community-based services. However, he lost the next election to Ronald Regan:

> With President Reagan and the Republicans taking over, the Mental Health Systems Act was discarded before the ink had dried. .... President Reagan never understood mental illness. Like Nixon, he was a product of the Southern California culture that associated psychiatry with Communism.
>
> (Torrey, 2014, pp. 87–88)

Reagan had campaigned under the slogan, "Are you better off now than you were four years ago?," re-establishing the cult of the American individual.

Engaging conflict and trouble

Each of these periods of war seems to have precipitated a time of social/cultural reactions that attempted some sort of healing through efforts at group and communal life. But none of them were to be sustained. Group psychotherapy proved to be a complex and rather demanding modality of treatment. Living and working in groups is not easy.

In their introduction to a collection of essays on analytic groups, *Ring of Fire*, British group analysts Schermer and Pines (1994) cautioned this:

> The group therapist who does not attend to the primitive layers either engages in "whistling in the dark", ignoring and not treating defects and deficits in the self and object relations which underlie the presenting symptoms, sets up the group for catastrophic situations of acting out, loss of group cohesion and failure to thrive as a group. ... To be effective psychotherapists, we must be able to accompany such patients and groups through these very painful layers of experience.
>
> (p. 3)

In recent years, there has been growing recognition in the transactional analysis literature, both in organizational and therapeutic contexts, of the need for more attention to the more conflictual and unconscious aspects of working in groups. Group life, whether in the contexts of therapy, counseling, consulting, teaching, community work, and so on, contains reservoirs of conflict, shame, and anxiety that ultimately need to be surfaced and addressed if the group is to work effectively and represent all of its members. Working within the organizational field, Petriglieri and Wood (2003) argued that

> a consultant makes contact with the complexity of a group through a largely irrational matrix of conscious and unconscious individual and collective psychological factors—thoughts, feelings, and images. Consultants cannot avoid getting their hands dirty. To pretend they can restricts their potential effectiveness unnecessarily.
>
> (p. 333)

Within the transactional analysis literature, van Beekum (2006, 2009, 2012) has consistently represented a voice for working directly with the less conscious and more conflictual and corrosive aspects of group processes. In "The relational consultant," for example, he outlined three central qualities of attention and attitude in working with unconscious foundations and motivations of a group's life:

1   Accepting chaos and unpredictability, listening for the organizational myths, observing such phenomena as splitting and projective identification
2   Accepting that unconscious phenomena reveal themselves slowly and indirectly, suggesting that there is likely much of great interest lurking beneath the stated, conscious contracts
3   Creating a transactional space in which the consultant and the organization together are able to reenact, bring to awareness, make sense of, and ultimately transform and integrate the organization's and representatives' destructive and unhelpful ways of relating to self and others.

> (van Beekum, 2006, pp. 325–326)

For his part, Landaiche (2012, 2013, 2014) has articulated the darker sides of working in groups. There is a powerful honesty in his writings on groups, in part because he switches back and forth from his experiences as a group member to those of group leader. Neither position is necessarily pretty. In "Learning and hating in groups," he described his experience:

> Rather than talking generally about the hatefulness of groups, I will describe what I hate about them. ... [what] I fear and detest ... [including] the boredom of the group's resolute avoidance, the tensions, the threat of being killed or humiliated (social death), the passivity, the entrenchments,

the slowness of deliberation (compared to the quickness and surety of my own mind), the magnification of meanness. ... Frustration, uncertainty, contagion, threat—at such times, groups seem hardly worth the effort.

(Landaiche, 2012, p. 191)

Having written this, he then noted that in a quick count of that week in his work at a university counseling center, he participated in 19 groups of one kind or another. Love them or hate them, groups are hard to avoid.

There are deep echoes of Bion in Landaiche's (2013) writing about his commitment to "Looking for trouble in groups":

I see the areas of trouble as the areas of greatest potential growth. They are the impasses to be resolved, often the areas any of us would least like to look at. So I think of it as my job to venture into these forbidden zones— venturing as a form of inquiry, exploration, lying in wait for the trouble rustling in the nearby brush. My strong sense of going there is in strong conflict with detesting that aspect of my job.

(p. 306)

The richness and depth of these experiences in groups can (sometimes) out-weigh one's anxiety and avoidance. In his reflections on looking for trouble in groups, Landaiche (2013) commented, "If we are fortunate as a group, we come through this disorder and alarm; we move from nonlearning to learning, which is a relief, yes, but also a wonder, an occasion for another kind of gratitude" (p. 306).

Toward the generative capacities of life and work in groups

As we face the disorder and alarm of living in groups, we can discover places of extraordinary generativity. In my study and learning of group analytic models, I have found means by which to engage with disorder and alarm. It is in rather marked contrast with my original training in transactional analytic groups. Berne's intention in the structuring of a transactionally centered treatment group was clear and in certain ways highly effective. The leader's position was that of any outside observer. In my own early years as a psychotherapist, I found the leadership role in traditional transactional analysis groups comforting and in keeping with my script and functions in my family of origin. Given the specific goals of transactional analysis treatment groups, that structure makes sense and serves a definite purpose.

But the transactional analysis structure does not facilitate the kind of learning that the group analytic process seeks to provide. I have questioned Berne's model, arguing for more openness to unconscious experience:

Awareness of unconscious experience necessitates an encounter with other-ness, differentness. ... The gifts of interpretation and differentness are that

> they afford opportunities to create the space that disrupts conscious experience, opening it to the light and insight of unconscious experience.
>
> (Cornell, 2013, p. 282)

Mistrust, anxiety, and aggression are common to the experience of many in groups. Otherness, differentness, and conflict loom as harbingers of potential rupture, shame, or ostracism. Deaconu (2013) also focused on the shift in a group from conscious to unconscious dynamics:

> Such communication about the group's psychological landscape is largely unconscious. This is what contributes to the emergence of uncomfortable or disturbing situations that need to be addressed. In a psychotherapeutic setting, the group might need to deal not only with the wounded aspects but also the wounding counterparts that derive from being human.
>
> (p. 292)

There needs to be space to experience and express these, be they toward the leadership or the group itself. There is an exquisite paradox that in welcoming and respecting mistrust, the basis of trust begins to be established.

Learning to participate in groups in this style has been challenging to me, but I have seen what happens when a group really thinks and works together in the midst of the tensions and freedoms provided in the group analytic models. I had to give up my script-based tendency to over-function so as to allow the silences and anxieties to emerge and create the tensions, confusions, and space for self-confrontation and interpersonal insight within the group. It has not been my experience, as was suggested by Berne (1966, p. 133), that analytic groups have much in common with supportive therapies that do not create real change. To the contrary, I have found working in this model, as both participant and leader, to be profoundly unsettling and promoting of significant change.

Over the years, as I have come to manage my own anxiety and distrust in groups, I have also come to relish the generative capacities of fighting, working, discovering, learning, and living in groups. I have come finally to know my own relief and gratitude as I grow older and make my way into the life of groups in ways that were not possible when I was younger. These group experiences have allowed me to step into and then through the deeply painful and troubled relationships with my siblings and the repeated, awkward rejections by my peers that permeated my childhood and adolescence, so as—finally—to belong among others and to truly relish the vitality of life in groups.

References

Abram, J. (1997). *The Language of Winnicott: A Dictionary and Guide to Understanding His Work*. Northvale, NJ: Jason Aronson.

Adler, A. (1956). *The Individual Psychology of Alfred Adler* (Ed. H.L. Ansbacher & R.R. Ansbacher). New York: Basic Books.

Akerman, N.W. (1964). Foreword to T. Burrow, *Preconscious Foundations of Human Experience*. New York: Basic Books.

Allen, J.R. (2000). Biology and transactional analysis: Integration of a neglected area. *Transactional Analysis Journal*, 29: 250–259.

Allen, J.R. (2001). Biology and transactional analysis II: A status report on neurodevelopment. *Transactional Analysis Journal*, 30: 260–268.

Allen, J. R. (2006). Oklahoma City ten years later: Positive psychology, transactional analysis, and the transformation of trauma from a terrorist attack. *Transactional Analysis Journal*, 36: 120–135.

Allen, J.R., & Allen, B. (1972). Scripts: The role of permission. *Transactional Analysis Journal*, 2(2): 72–74.

Allen, J.R., & Allen, B. (1987). To make/find meaning: Notes on the last permission. *Transactional Analysis Journal*, 17: 72–81.

Alvarez, A. (1992). *Live Company: Psychoanalytic Psychotherapy with Autistic, Borderline, Deprived and Abused Children*. London: Routledge.

Anderson, F.S. (Ed.) (2008). *Bodies in Treatment: The Unspoken Dimension*. New York: The Analytic Press.

Anderson, S.M., Resnik, I., & Glassman, N.S. (2005). The unconscious relational self. In R.R. Hassin, J.S. Uleman, & J.A. Barch (Eds.), *The New Unconscious*. New York: Oxford University Press.

Anderson, W.T. (1983). *The Upstart Spring: Esalen and the American Awakening*. Reading, MA: Addison-Wesley.

Anthony, E.J. (1974a). A risk-vulnerability intervention model. In E.J. Anthony & C. Koupernik (Eds.), *The Child in His Family: Children at Psychiatric Risk* (International Yearbook, Vol. 3). New York: Wiley.

Anthony, E.J. (1974b). The syndrome of the psychologically invulnerable child. In E.J. Anthony & C. Koupernik (Eds.), *The Child in His Family: Children at Psychiatric Risk* (International Yearbook, Vol. 3). New York: Wiley.

Anthony, E.J. (1978). A new scientific region to explore. In E.J. Anthony, C. Koupernik, & C. Chiland (Eds.), *The Child in His Family: Vulnerable Children* (International Yearbook, Vol. 4). New York: Wiley.

Anthony, E.J. (1983). Infancy in a crazy environment. In J.D. Call, E. Galenson, & R.L. Tyson (Eds.), *Frontiers of Infant Psychiatry* (pp. 97–107). New York: Basic Books.

Anthony, E.J. (1987). Risk, vulnerability, and resilience: An overview. In E.J. Anthony & B.J. Cohler (Eds.), *The Invulnerable Child* (pp. 3–48). New York: Guilford Press.

Anthony, E.J., & Cohler, B. (1987). *The Invulnerable Child*. New York: Guilford Press.

Apprey, M. (1996a). Broken lines, public memory, absent memory: Jewish and African Americans coming to terms with racism. *Mind and Human Interaction*, 7: 139–149.

Apprey, M. (1996b). *Phenomenology of Transgenerational Haunting: Subjects in Apposition, Subjects on Urgent/Voluntary Errands*. Ann Arbor, MI: UMI Research Collections.

Apprey, M. (1998). Reinventing the self in the face of received transgenerational hatred in the African American community. *Mind and Human Interaction*, 9: 30–37.

Apprey, M. (2003). Repairing history: Reworking transgenerational trauma. In D. Moss (Ed.), *HATING in the First Person Plural* (pp. 3–28). New York: Other Press.

Apprey, M. (2006). Difference and the awakening of wounds in intercultural psychoanalysis. *Psychoanalytic Quarterly*, 75: 73–93.

Arlow, J.A. (1963). The supervisory situation. *The Journal of the American Psychoanalytic Association*, 11: 576–594.

Aron, L. (1991). The patient's experience of the analyst's subjectivity. *Psychoanalytic Dialogues*, 1: 29–51

Aron, L. (1996). *A Meeting of the Minds: Mutuality in Psychoanalysis*. Hillsdale, NJ: The Analytic Press.

Aron, L., & Anderson, F.S. (Eds.) (1998). *Relational Perspectives on the Body*. Hillsdale, NJ: The Analytic Press.

Atlas, G. (2016). *The Enigma of Desire: Sex, Longing, and Belonging in Psychoanalysis*. London: Routledge.

Babcock, D., & Keepers, T. (1976). *Raising Kids OK* (revised edition). New York: Grove Press.

Bargh, J., & Chartrand, T. (1999). The unbearable automaticity of being. *American Psychologist*, 54: 462–479.

Barnes, G. (Ed.) (1977). *Transactional Analysis after Eric Berne: Teachings and Practices of Three TA Schools*. New York: Harper's College Press.

Bass, A. (2003). Historical and unconscious trauma: Racism and psychoanalysis. In D. Moss (Ed.), *HATING in the First Person Plural* (pp. 29–44). New York: Other Press.

Bauer, P.J. (1996). What do infants recall? Memory for specific events by one-to-two-year-olds. *American Psychologist*, 51: 29–41.

Beebe, B., & Lachmann, F. (2000). *Infant Research and Adult Treatment: Co-Constructing Interactions*. Hillsdale, NJ: The Analytic Press.

Beebe, B., Knoblauch, S., Rustin, J., & Sorter, D. (2005). *Forms of Intersubjectivity in Infant Research and Adult Treatment*. New York: Other Press.

Benjamin, J. (1995). *Like Subjects, Love Objects: Essays on Recognition and Sexual Difference*. New Haven, CT: Yale University Press.

Berne, E. (1947). *The Mind in Action: A Layman's Guide to Psychiatry*. New York: Simon & Schuster.

Berne, E. (1949). The nature of intuition. In E. Berne, *Intuition and Ego States: The Origins of Transactional Analysis* (Ed. P. McCormick; pp. 1–31). San Francisco, CA: TA Press, 1977.

Berne, E. (1952). Concerning the nature of diagnosis. In E. Berne, *Intuition and Ego States: The Origins of Transactional Analysis* (Ed. P. McCormick; pp. 33–48). San Francisco, CA: TA Press, 1977.

Berne, E. (1953). Concerning the nature of communication. In E. Berne, *Intuition and Ego States: The Origins of Transactional Analysis* (Ed. P. McCormick; pp. 49–65). San Francisco, CA: TA Press, 1977.

Berne, E. (1955). Intuition IV: Primal images and primal judgment. *The Psychiatric Quarterly*, 29: 634–658. [Reprinted in *Intuition and Ego States*, 1977.]

Berne, E. (1957a). The ego image. In E. Berne, *Intuition and Ego States: The Origins of Transactional Analysis* (Ed. P. McCormick; pp. 99–120). San Francisco, CA: TA Press, 1977.

Berne, E. (1957b). Ego states in psychotherapy. In E. Berne, *Intuition and Ego States: The Origins of Transactional Analysis* (Ed. P. McCormick; pp. 121–144). San Francisco, CA: TA Press, 1977.

Berne, E. (1961). *Transactional Analysis in Psychotherapy: A Systematic Individual and Social Psychiatry*. New York: Grove Press.

Berne, E. (1962). The psychodynamics of intuition. In E. Berne, *Intuition and Ego States: The Origins of Transactional Analysis* (Ed. P. McCormick; pp. 159–166). San Francisco, CA: TA Press, 1977.

Berne, E. (1963). *The Structure and Dynamics of Organizations and Groups*. Philadelphia: J.B. Lippincott.

Berne, E. (1964). *Games People Play: The Psychology of Human Relations*. New York: Grove Press.

Berne, E. (1966). *Principles of Group Treatment*. New York: Oxford University Press.

Berne. E. (1968a). Staff-patient-staff conferences. *The American Journal of Psychiatry*, 125: 286–293.

Berne, E. (1968b). *A Layman's Guide to Psychiatry and Psychoanalysis* (third edition). New York: Simon & Schuster.

Berne, E. (1969). Standard nomenclature. *Transactional Analysis Bulletin*, 8: 111–112.

Berne, E. (1970). *Sex in Human Loving*. New York: Simon & Schuster.

Berne, E. (1971). Away from a theory of the impact of interpersonal interaction on non-verbal participation. *Transactional Analysis Journal*, 1: 1.

Berne, E. (1972). *What Do You Say after You Say Hello?: The Psychology of Human Destiny*. New York: Grove Press.

Berne, E. (1977). *Intuition and Ego States: The Origins of Transactional Analysis* (Ed. P. McCormick). New York: Harper & Row.

Berne, E. (2010). *A Montreal Childhood* (Ed. T. Berne). Seville, Spain: Editorial Jeder.

Billow, R.M. (2000). From countertransference to "passion." *Psychoanalytic Quarterly*, 69: 93–119.

Bion, W.R. (1946). The leaderless group project. *Bulletin of the Menninger Clinic*, 10: 77–81.

Bion, W.R. (1952). Group dynamics: A review. *International Journal of Psycho-Analysis*, 33: 235–247.

Bion, W.R. (1957). Differentiation of the psychotic from the non-psychotic personalities. *International Journal of Psycho-Analysis*, 38: 266–275.

Bion, W.R. (1961). *Experiences in Groups*. New York: Basic Books.

Bion, W.R. (1963). *Elements of Psycho-Analysis*. In *Seven Servants: Four Works*. New York: Jason Aronson, 1977.

Bion, W.R. (2005). *The Long Weekend 1897–1919: Part of a Life*. London: Karnac.

Blackstone, P. (1993). The dynamic child: Integration of second-order structure, object relations, and self psychology. *Transactional Analysis Journal*, 23: 216–234.

Bleandonu, G. (2000). *Wilfred Bion: His Life and Works 1897–1979*. New York: Other Press.

Bloom, K. (2006). *The Embodied Self: Movement and Psychoanalysis*. London: Karnac.

Boadella, D. (1997). Embodiment in the therapeutic relationship. Main speech at the First Congress of the World Council of Psychotherapy, Vienna, 1–5 July 1996. *International Journal of Psychotherapy*, 2: 31–43.

Bollas, C. (1987). *The Shadow of the Object: Psychoanalysis of the Unthought Unknown*. New York: Columbia University Press.

Bollas, C. (1989). *Forces of Destiny: Psychoanalysis and Human Idiom*. Northvale, NJ: Jason Aronson.

Bollas, C. (1992a). *Being a Character: Psychoanalysis and Self Experience*. New York: Hill and Wang.

Bollas, C. (1992b). Why Oedipus? In C. Bollas, *Being a Character: Psychoanalysis and Self Experience* (pp. 218–246). New York: Hill and Wang.

Bollas, C. (1999). *The Mystery of Things*. London: Routledge.

Bollas, C. (2000). *Hysteria*. London: Routledge.

Bollas, C. (2009). *The Infinite Question*. London: Routledge.

Bollas, C. (2013). *Catch Them before They Fall: The Psychoanalysis of Breakdown*. London: Routledge.

Bond, T. (2006). Intimacy, risk, and reciprocity in psychotherapy: Intricate ethical challenges. *Transactional Analysis Journal*, 36: 77–89.

Bonovitz, C. (2006). The illusion of certainty in self-disclosure: Commentary on paper by Helen K. Gediman. *Psychoanalytic Dialogues*, 16: 293–304.

Bowlby, J. (1979). *The Making and Breaking of Affectional Bonds*. London: Tavistock Publications.

Bremner, G., & Slater, A. (Eds.) (2004). *Theories of Infant Development*. Malden, MA: Blackwell Publishing.

Bridger, H. (1992). Northfield revisited. In M. Pines (Ed.), *Bion and Group Psychotherapy* (pp. 87–107). London: Routledge.

Brown, N.O. (1966). *Love's Body*. New York: Random House.

Bucci, W. (1997a). *Psychoanalysis and Cognitive Science: A Multiple Code Theory*. New York: Guilford Press.

Bucci, W. (1997b). Symptoms and symbols: A multiple code theory of somatization. *Psychoanalytic Inquiry*, 17: 151–172.

Bucci, W. (2001). Pathways of emotional communication. *Psychoanalytic Inquiry*, 21: 40–70.

Bucci, W. (2002). The referential process, consciousness, and the sense of self. *Psychoanalytic Inquiry*, 22: 766–793.

Bucci. W. (2007). The role of bodily experience in emotional organization. In F.S. Anderson (Ed.), *Bodies in Treatment: The Unspoken Dimension* (pp. 51–76). New York: The Analytic Press.

Bucci, W. (2010). The uncertainty principle. In J. Petrucelli (Ed.), *Knowing, Not-Knowing, and Sort-of-Knowing: Psychoanalysis and the Experience of Uncertainty* (pp. 203–214). London: Karnac.

Bugental, J.F.T. (Ed.) (1967). *Challenges of Humanistic Psychology*. New York: McGraw-Hill.

Burrow, T. (1927). *The Social Basis of Consciousness*. New York: Harcourt, Brace.

Burrow, T. (1941). Neurosis and war: A problem of human behavior. *The Journal of Psychology*, 12: 235–249.

Burrow, T. (1950). *The Neurosis of Man*. New York: Harcourt, Brace.

Burrow, T. (1958). *A Search for Man's Sanity: The Selected Letters of Trigant Burrow*. New York: Oxford University Press.

Call, J.D. (1984). From early patterns of communication to the grammar of experience and syntax in infancy. In *Frontiers of Infant Psychiatry*, Vol. 2, Ed. J.D. Call, E. Galenson, & R.L. Tyson (pp. 15–28). New York: Basic Books.

Campos, L. (2006). Personal communication, 26 September.

Caravella, M., & Marone, A. (2003). Acute psychotic states: A clinical interpretation. *Transactional Analysis Journal*, 33: 246–253.

Chess, S. (1989). Defying the voice of doom. In T.F. Dugan & R. Coles (Eds.), *The Child in Our Times: Studies in the Development of Resiliency* (pp. 179–199). New York: Brunner/Mazel.

Chess, S., & Thomas, A. (1984). *Origins and Evaluation of Behavior Disorder: From Infancy to Early Adult Life*. New York: Brunner/Mazel.

Chess, S., & Thomas, A. (1986). *Temperament in Clinical Practice*. New York: Guilford Press.

Childs-Gowell, E. (1992). *Good Grief Rituals: Tools for Healing*. Barrytown, NY: Station Hill Press.

Churchland, P.M. (1995). *The Engine of Reason, the Seat of the Soul: A Philosophical Journey*. Cambridge, MA: The MIT Press.

Clark, F. (2001). Psychotherapy as a mourning process. *Transactional Analysis Journal*, 31: 156–160.

Clarkson, P. (1992a). *Transactional Analysis Psychotherapy: An Integrated Approach*. London: Tavistock/Routledge.

Clarkson, P. (1992b). Physis in transactional analysis. *Transactional Analysis Journal*, 22: 202–209.

Clarkson, P., & Fish, S. (1988). Rechilding: Creating a new past in the present as a support for the future. *Transactional Analysis Journal*, 18: 51–59.

Clarkson, P., & Gilbert, M. (1988). Berne's original model of ego states: Theoretical considerations. *Transactional Analysis Journal*, 18: 20–29.

Coles, R. (1964). *Children of Crisis*: Vol. 1. Boston: Little, Brown.

Coles, R. (1986a). *The Moral Life of Children*. Boston: The Atlantic Monthly Press.

Coles, R. (1986b). *The Political Life of Children*. Boston: The Atlantic Monthly Press.

Cook, R. (2012). Triumph or disaster?: A relational view of therapeutic mistakes. *Transactional Analysis Journal*, 42: 34–42.

Cornell, W.F. (1988). Life script theory: A critical review from a developmental perspective. *Transactional Analysis Journal*, 18: 270–282.

Cornell, W.F. (1997). If Reich had met Winnicott: Body and gesture. *Energy and Character*, 28(2): 50–60.

Cornell, W.F. (2000a). Transference, desire, and vulnerability in body-centered psychotherapy. *Energy and Character*, 30: 29–37.

Cornell, W.F. (2000b). If Berne met Winnicott: Transactional analysis and relational analysis. *Transactional Analysis Journal*, 30: 270–275.

Cornell, W.F. (2003a). Babies, brains, and bodies: Somatic foundations of the Child. In C. Sills & H. Hargaden (Eds.), *Key Concepts in Transactional Analysis: Contemporary Views—Ego States*. London: Worth Publishing.

Cornell, W.F. (2003b). The impassioned body: Erotic vitality and disturbance in psychotherapy. *British Gestalt Journal*, 12: 92–104.

Cornell, W.F. (2005). In the terrain of the unconscious: The evolution of a transactional analysis therapist. *Transactional Analysis Journal*, 35: 119–131.

Cornell, W.F. (2006). Letter from the editor. *Transactional Analysis Journal*, 36: 74–76.

Cornell, W.F. (2008a). What do you say if you don't say unconscious? *Transactional Analysis Journal*, 38: 93–100.

Cornell, W.F. (2008b). Self in action: The bodily basis of self-organization. In F.S. Anderson (Ed.), *Bodies in Treatment: The Unspoken Dimension* (pp. 29–49). Hillsdale, NJ: The Analytic Press.

Cornell, W.F. (2009a). Defying the odds: Lessons from a remarkable man. *The Script*, 39 (9): 1, 6.

Cornell, W.F. (2009b). A stranger to desire: Entering the erotic field. *Studies in Gender and Sexuality*, 10: 75–92.

Cornell, W.F. (2009c). Why have sex?: A case study in character, perversion and free choice. *Transactional Analysis Journal*, 39: 136–148.

Cornell, W.F. (2010a). Whose body is it? Somatic relations in script and script protocol. In R. Erskine (Ed.), *Life Scripts: A Transactional Analysis of Unconscious Relational Patterns* (pp. 101–126). London: Karnac.

Cornell, W.F. (2010b). A Montreal childhood [Book review]. *Transactional Analysis Journal*, 40: 305–307.

Cornell, W.F. (2011). SAMBA, TANGO, PUNK: Commentary on paper by Steven H. Knoblauch. *Psychoanalytic Dialogues*, 21: 428–436.

Cornell, W.F. (2012). This edgy emotional landscape: A discussion of Stuthridge's "Traversing the fault lines." *Transactional Analysis Journal*, 42: 252–256.

Cornell, W.F. (2013a). Lost and found: Sibling loss, disconnection, mourning and intimacy. In A. Frank, P.T. Clough, & S. Seidman (Eds.), *Intimacies: A New World of Relational Life*. London: Routledge.

Cornell, W.F. (2013b). Relational group process: A discussion of Richard Erskine's model of group psychotherapy from the perspective of Berne's theories of group treatment. *Transactional Analysis Journal*, 43: 276–283.

Cornell, W.F. (2014). The intricate intimacies of psychotherapy and questions of self-disclosure. In D. Loewenthal & A. Samuels (Eds.), *Relational Psychotherapy, Psychoanalysis and Counselling: Appraisals and Reappraisals*. London: Routledge.

Cornell, W.F. (2015). *Somatic Experience in Psychoanalysis and Psychotherapy: In the Expressive Language of the Living*. London: Routledge.

Cornell, W.F., & Bonds-White, F. (2001). Therapeutic relatedness in transactional analysis: The truth of love or the love of truth. *Transactional Analysis Journal*, 31: 71–83.

Cornell, W.F., & Landaiche, N.M., III (2005). Impasse and intimacy in the therapeutic or consultative couple: The influence of protocol. *Rivista Italiana di Analisi Transazionale e Metodologie Psicoterapeutiche*, 11: 9–34.

Cornell, W.F., & Landaiche, N.M., III (2006). Impasse and intimacy: Applying Berne's concept of script protocol. *Transactional Analysis Journal*, 36: 196–213.

Cornell, W.F., & Landaiche, N.M., III (2007). Why body psychotherapy?: A conversation. *Transactional Analysis Journal*, 37: 256–262.

Cornell, W.F., & Landaiche, N.M., III (2008). Nonconscious processes and self-development: Key concepts from Eric Berne and Christopher Bollas. *Transactional Analysis Journal*, 38: 200–217.

Cornell, W.F., & Olio, K. (1992). Consequences of childhood bodily abuse: Affect, ego states, and therapeutic implications. *Transactional Analysis Journal*, 22: 131–143.

Cornell, W.F., & Olio, K. (1993). Therapeutic relationship as the foundation for treatment of adult survivors of sexual abuse. *Psychotherapy: Theory, Practice and Research*, 30: 512–523.

Cornell, W.F., de Graaf, A., Newton, T., & Thunnissen, M. (2016). *Into TA: A Comprehensive Textbook of Transactional Analysis*. London: Karnac.

Corrigan, E.G., & Gordon, P.-E. (1995). The mind as object. In E.G. Corrigan & P.-E. Gordon (Eds.), *The Mind Object: Precocity and Pathology of Self-Sufficiency* (pp. 1–22). Northvale, NJ: Jason Aronson.

Cowles-Boyd, L., & Boyd, H.S. (1980a). Play as a time structure. *Transactional Analysis Journal*, 10: 5–7.

Cowles-Boyd, L., & Boyd, H.S. (1980b). Playing with games: The game/play shift. *Transactional Analysis Journal*, 10: 8–11.

Cox, M. (1999). The relationship between ego state structure and function: A diagrammatic formulation. *Transactional Analysis Journal*, 29: 49–58.

Craig, I. (1994). *The Importance of Disappointment*. London: Routledge.

Crossman, P. (2006). Personal communication, 31 October.

Dalal, F. (2002). *Race, Colour, and the Process of Racialization: New Perspectives from Group Analysis*. Hove: Brunner-Routledge.

Danto, E.A. (2005). *Freud's Free Clinics: Psychoanalysis and Social Justice, 1918–1938*. New York: Columbia University Press.

Davies, J.M. (1994). Love in the afternoon: A relational reconsideration of desire and dread in the countertransference. *Psychoanalytic Dialogues*, 4: 153–170.

Davies, J.M. (1998). Between the disclosure and foreclosure of erotic transference–countertransference: Can psychoanalysis find a place for adult sexuality? *Psychoanalytic Dialogues*, 8: 747–766.

Davis, M., & Wallbridge, D. (1990). *Boundary and Space: An Introduction to the Work of D. W. Winnicott*. New York: Brunner/Mazel.

De Masi, F. (2006). *Vulnerability to Psychosis: A Psychoanalytic Study of the Nature and Therapy of the Psychotic State*. London: Karnac.

Deaconu, D. (2013). The group quest: Searching for the group inside me, inside you, and inside the community. *Transactional Analysis Journal*, 43: 291–295.

Deci, E.L. (1972). Intrinsic motivation, extrinsic reinforcement, and inequity. *Journal of Personality and Social Psychology*, 22.

Deci, E.L., & Ryan, R.M. (2008). Facilitating optimal motivation and psychological well-being across life's domains. *Canadian Psychology*, 49.

DeMasio, A.R. (1999). *The Feeling of What Happens*. New York: Harcourt Brace.

Deraniyagala, S. (2013). *Wave*. New York: Knopf.

Didion, J. (2006). *The Year of Magical Thinking*. New York: Vintage International.

Dimen, M. (1999). Between *lust* and libido: Sex, psychoanalysis, and the moment before. *Psychoanalytic Dialogues*, 9: 415–440.

Dimen, M. (2001). Perversion is us? Eight notes. *Psychoanalytic Dialogues*, 11: 825–860.

Dimen, M. (2003). *Sexuality, Intimacy, Power*. Hillsdale, NJ: The Analytic Press.

Dimen, M. (2005). Sexuality and suffering, or the Eew! factor. *Studies in Gender and Sexuality*, 6: 1–18.

Dimen, M. (2011). Lapsus linguae, or a slip of the tongue?: A sexual violation in an analytic treatment and its personal and professional aftermath. *Contemporary Psychoanalysis*, 47: 35–79.

Director, L. (2009). The enlivening object. *Contemporary Psychoanalysis*, 45: 120–141.

Downing, G. (1996). *Korper und Wort in der Psychotherapie*. Munich: Kosel Verlag.

Drego, P. (1983). The cultural parent. *Transactional Analysis Journal*, 13: 224–227.

Drego, P. (1996). Cultural parent oppression and regeneration. *Transactional Analysis Journal*, 26: 58–77.

Drego, P. (2005). Acceptance speech on receiving the 2004 Eric Berne Memorial Award. *Transactional Analysis Journal*, 35: 7–30.

Dugan, T.F. (1989). Action and acting out: Variables in the development of resiliency in adolescence. In T.F. Dugan & R. Coles (Eds.), *The Child in Our Times: Studies in the Development of Resiliency*. New York: Brunner/Mazel.

Dugan, T.F., & Coles, R. (Eds.) (1989). *The Child in Our Times: Studies in the Development of Resiliency*. New York: Brunner/Mazel.

Dusay, J. (1971). Eric Berne's studies of intuition 1949–1962. *Transactional Analysis Journal*, 1: 34–44.

Dylan, B. (1963). With God on our side. In B. Dylan, *Lyrics: 1962–1985* (p. 93). New York: Alfred A. Knopf, 1985.

Eagle, M.N. (2003). The postmodern turn in psychoanalysis: A critique. *Psychoanalytic Psychology*, 20: 411–424.

Edelman, G.M. ((1992). *Bright Air, Brilliant Fire: On the Matter of the Mind*. New York: Basic Books.

Edwards, J. (Ed.) (2001). *Being Alive: Building on the Work of Anne Alvarez*. Hove, East Sussex: Brunner-Routledge.

Eigen, M. (1996). *Psychic Deadness*. Northvale, NJ: Jason Aronson.

Eigen, M. (1998). *The Psychoanalytic Mystic*. London: Free Associations.

Ekstein, R., & Wallerstein, R.S. (1958). *The Teaching and Learning of Psychotherapy*. New York: Basic Books.

Emde, R.N. (1999). Moving ahead: Integrating influences of affective processes for development and psychoanalysis. *International Journal of Psycho-Analysis*, 80: 317–339.

Emde, R.N. (2009). From ego to "we-go": Neurobiology and questions for psychoanalysis. Commentary on papers by Trevarthen, Gallese, and Ammanti & Trentini. *Psychoanalytic Dialogues*, 19: 556–564.

English, F. (1977). What shall I do tomorrow? In G. Barnes (Ed.), *Transactional Analysis after Eric Berne* (pp. 287–350). New York: Harper's College Press.

English, F. (2006). Personal communication, 19 October.

English, F. (2008). What motivates resilience after trauma? *Transactional Analysis Journal*, 38: 343–351.

Epstein, S. (1991). Cognitive-experiential self-theory: Implications for developmental psychology. In M.R. Gunnar & L.A. Sroufe (Eds.), *Self Processes and Development. The Minnesota Symposium on Child Development* (Vol. 23, pp. 79–123). Hillsdale, NJ: Erlbaum.

Erikson, E.H. (1959). *Identity and the Life Cycle*. New York: International Universities Press.

Erikson, E.H. (1963). *Childhood and Society*. New York: W.W. Norton.

Erikson, E.H. (1968). *Identity: Youth and Crisis*. New York: W.W. Norton.

Erikson, E.H. (1975). *Life History and the Historical Moment*. New York: W.W. Norton.

Erskine, R.G. (1978). Fourth-degree impasse. In C. Moiso (Ed.), *Transactional Analysis in Europe* (pp. 33–35). Geneva, Switzerland: European Association for Transactional Analysis. [Reprinted in *Theories and Methods of an Integrative Transactional Analysis: A Volume of Selected Articles* (pp. 147–148). San Francisco: Transactional Analysis Press, 1997.]

Erskine, R.G. (1980). Script cure: Behavioral, intrapsychic, and physiological. *Transactional Analysis Journal*, 10: 102–106.

Erskine, R.G. (1988). Ego structure, intrapsychic function, and defense mechanisms: A commentary on Eric Berne's original theoretical concepts. *Transactional Analysis Journal*, 18: 15–19.

Erskine, R.G. (1998). *Theories and Methods of an Integrative Transactional Analysis*. San Francisco, CA: TA Press.

Fast, I. (2006). A body-centered mind: Freud's more radical idea. *Contemporary Psychoanalysis*, 42: 273–295.

Federn, P. (1952). *Ego Psychology and the Psychoses*. New York: Basic Books.

Felsman, J.K., & Vaillant, G.E. (1987). Resilient children as adults: A 40-year study. In E.J. Anthony & B.J. Cohler (Eds.), *The Invulnerable Child*. New York: Guilford Press.

Ferenczi, S. (1932). *The Clinical Diary of Sandor Ferenczi* (Ed. J. Dupont, Trans. M. Balint & N.Z. Jackson). Cambridge, MA: Harvard University Press, 1988.

Fischer, K.W., & Hogan, A.E. (1989). The big picture for infant development: Levels and variations. In J.J. Lockman & N.L. Hazen (Eds.), *Action in Social Context: Perspectives on Early Development* (pp. 275–305). New York: Plenum Press.

Fivas-Depeursinge, E., & Corboz-Warnery, A. (1999). *The Primary Triangle*. New York: Basic Books.

Fogel, A. (2004). Remembering infancy: Accessing our earliest experiences. In G. Bremmer & A. Slater (Eds.), *Theories of Infant Development* (pp. 204–230). Oxford: Blackwell.

Fonagy, P. (1999). Points of contact and divergence between psychoanalytic and attachment theories: Is psychoanalytic theory truly different? *Psychoanalytic Inquiry*, 19: 448–480.

Fonagy, P. (2001). *Attachment Theory and Psychoanalysis*. New York: Other Press.

Fosshage, J.L. (2010). Implicit and explicit pathways to psychoanalytic change. In J. Petrucelli (Ed.), *Knowing, Not-Knowing, and Sort-of-Knowing: Psychoanalysis and the Experience of Uncertainty* (pp. 215–224). London: Karnac.

Foulkes, S.H. (1946). Principles and practice of group therapy. *Bulletin of the Menninger Clinic*, 10: 85–89.

Foulkes, S.H. (1965). *Therapeutic Group Analysis*. New York: International Universities Press.

Frank, J.D. (1963). *Persuasion and Healing*. New York: Schocken Books.

Frank, R. (2001). *Body of Awareness*. New York: Gestalt Institute Press.

Freud, A. (1936). *The Ego and the Mechanisms of Defense: The Writings of Anna Freud*, Vol. II. New York: International Universities Press, 1966.

Freud, S. (1915). Thoughts for the times on war and death. In J. Strachey (Ed. and Trans.), *The Standard Edition*, 14 (pp. 273–300). London: Hogarth Press, 1957.

Freud, S. (1916). On transience. In J. Strachey (Ed. and Trans.), *The Standard Edition*, 14 (pp. 303–307). London: Hogarth Press, 1957.

Freud, S. (1917a). *A General Introduction to Psychoanalysis* (Trans. J. Riviere). New York: Garden City Publishing, 1938.

Freud, S. (1917b). Mourning and melancholia. In J. Strachey (Ed. and Trans.), *The Standard Edition*, 14 (pp. 243–258). London: Hogarth Press, 1957.

Freud, S. (1919). Lines of advance in psycho-analytic therapy. In J. Strachey (Ed. and Trans.), *The Standard Edition*, 17 (pp. 157–168). London: Hogarth Press, 1955.

Freud, S. (1921). Group psychology and the analysis of the ego. In J. Strachey (Ed. and Trans.), *The Standard Edition*, 18 (pp. 69–143). London: Hogarth Press, 1955.

Freud, S. (1924). The dissolution of the Oedipus complex. In J. Strachey (Ed. and Trans.), *The Standard Edition*, 19 (pp. 173–182). London: Hogarth Press, 1961.

Freud, S. (1937). Analysis terminable and interminable. In J. Strachey (Ed. and Trans.), *The Standard Edition*, 23 (pp. 216–253). London: Hogarth Press, 1964.

Freud, S. (1938). *An Outline of Psychoanalysis* (Trans. J. Strachey). New York: Norton, 1949.

Friedlander, M. (Ed.) (1991). Special issues of the *Transactional Analysis Journal*, 21: 62–111, 122–123, 127–183.

Friedman, R. (2010). The group and the individual in conflict and war. *Group Analysis*, 43: 281–300.

Gallese, V. (2009). Mirror neurons, embodied simulation, and the neural basis of social identification. *Psychoanalytic Dialogues*, 19: 519–536.

Garcia, F. (2012). Healing good-byes and healthy hellos: Learning and growing from painful endings and transitions. *Transactional Analysis Journal*, 42: 53–61.

Gediman, H.K. (2006). Facilitating analysis with implicit and explicit self-disclosures. *Psychoanalytic Dialogues*, 16: 241–262; Reply to commentaries, 16: 305–316.

Gerson, S. (2003). The enlivening transference and the shadow of deadliness. Paper delivered to the Boston Psychoanalytic Society and Institute, May 3.

Gerson, S. (2005). Ghosts from the stage to the consulting room: The family unconscious in classics of 20th century theatre. Paper given to the Western Pennsylvania Forum for Relational and Body-Centered Psychotherapies, Pittsburgh, PA, November 6.

Gilbert, M. (1996). Ego states and ego state networks. Paper presented at the International Transactional Analysis Conference, Amsterdam, Netherlands.

Gildebrand, K. (2003). An introduction to the brain and the early development of the Child ego state. In C. Sills & H. Hargaden (Eds.), *Key Concepts in Transactional Analysis, Contemporary Views: Ego States* (pp. 1–27). London: Worth Publishing.

Gilligan, C. (1982). *In a Different Voice: Psychological Theory and Women's Development*. Cambridge, MA: Harvard University Press.

Gilligan, J. (2000). *Violence: Reflections on our Deadliest Epidemic*. London: Jessica Kingsley Publishers.

Giuli, M. (1985). Neurophysiological and behavioral aspects of the P-0, A-0, C-0 structures of the personality. *Transactional Analysis Journal*, 15: 260–262.

Gobodo-Madikizela, P. (2003). *A Human Being Died that Night*. Claremont, South Africa: David Philip Publishers.

Goldstein, W.N. (1991). Clarification of projective identification. *American Journal of Psychiatry*, 148: 153–161.

Good, M.D. (1992). Work as a haven from pain. In M.D. Good, P.E. Brodwin, B.J. Good, & A. Kleinman (Eds.), *Pain as Human Experience: An Anthropological Perspective* (pp. 49–76). Berkeley: University of California Press.

Goulding, R.L., & Goulding, M.M. (1978). *The Power is in the Patient: A TA/Gestalt Approach to Psychotherapy*. San Francisco: TA Press.

Goulding, R.L., & Goulding, M.M. (1979). *Changing Lives through Redecision Therapy*. New York: Brunner Mazel.

Gowling, D., & Agar, J. (2011). The importance of experience. In H. Fowlie & C. Sills (Eds.), *Relational Transactional Analysis: Principles in Practice* (pp. 81–90). London: Karnac.

Green, A. (1996). Has sexuality anything to do with psychoanalysis? *International Journal of Psychoanalysis*, 77: 345–350.

Green, A. (1997). The dead mother. In A. Green, *On Private Madness* (pp. 142–173). London: Karnac.

Green, A. (2000). Science and science fiction in infant research. In J. Sandler, A.-M. Sandler, & R. Davies (Eds.), *Clinical and Observational Psychoanalytic Research: Roots of a Controversy* (pp. 41–72). Madison, CT: International Universities Press.

Green, A. (2005). *Play and Reflection in Donald Winnicott's Writings*. London: Karnac.

Greenberg, J. (1995). Self-disclosure: Is it psychoanalytic? *Contemporary Psychoanalysis*, 31: 193–205.

Greve, B. (1976). Protocol fantasy and early decision. *Transactional Analysis Journal*, 6: 220–223.

Groder, M. (2006). Personal communication, September 27.

Guglielmotti, R.L. (2008). The quality of the therapeutic relationship as a factor in helping to change the client's protocol or implicit memory. *Transactional Analysis Journal*, 38: 101–109.

Hadley, J.L. (1989). The neurobiology of motivational systems. In J.D. Lichtenberg (Ed.), *Psychoanalysis and Motivation* (pp. 337–372). Hillsdale, NJ: The Analytic Press.

Hargaden, H., & Sills, C. (2001). Deconfusion of the child ego state: A relational perspective. *Transactional Analysis Journal*, 31: 55–70.

Hargaden, H., & Sills, C. (2002). *Transactional Analysis: Relational Perspective*. London: Routledge.

Harley, K. (2006). A lost connection: Existential positions and Melanie Klein's infant development. *Transactional Analysis Journal*, 36: 252–269.

Harlow, H.F. (1953). Motivation as a factor in the acquisition of new responses. In *Current Theory and Research in Motivation*. Lincoln, NB: University of Nebraska Press.

Hartley, L. (Ed.) (2008). *Contemporary Body Psychotherapy: The Chiron Approach*. London: Routledge.

Hartman, S. (2006). Disclosure, dis-closure, diss/clothes/sure: Commentary on paper by Helen K. Gediman. *Psychoanalytic Dialogues*, 16: 273–292.

Hassin, R.R., Uleman, J.S., & Bargh, J.A. (2005). *The New Unconscious*. New York: Oxford University Press.

Hine, J. (1997). Mind structure and ego states. *Transactional Analysis Journal*, 27: 278–289.

Hine, J. (2001). Personal communication, October 18.

Hinshelwood, R. D. (1994). *Clinical Klein: From Theory to Practice*. New York: Basic Books.

Hoffman, D.H. (2015). Independent review report to the special committee of the Directors relating to APA ethics guidelines, national security interrogations, and torture, July 2. Chicago: Sidley Austin LLP.

Hoffman, I.Z. (1998). *Ritual and Spontaneity in the Psychoanalytic Process: A Dialectical Constuctivist View*. Hillsdale, NJ: The Analytic Press.

Holmes, J. (1996). *Attachment, Intimacy, Autonomy: Using Attachment Theory in Adult Psychotherapy*. Northvale, NJ: Jason Aronson.

Horwitz, A.V., & Wakefield, J.C. (2007). *The Loss of Sadness: How Psychiatry Transformed Normal Sorrow into Depressive Disorder*. Oxford: Oxford University Press.

Hostie, R. (1984). Eric Berne in search of ego states. In E. Stern (Ed.), *TA: The State of the Art—A European Contribution*. Dordecht: Foris Publications Holland.

Hoyt, M.F., & Goulding, R.L. (1989). Resolution of a transference–countertransference impasse using Gestalt techniques in supervision. *Transactional Analysis Journal*, 19: 201–211.

Izard, C.E. (1993). Four systems for emotion activation: Cognition and noncognitive processes. *Psychological Review*, 100: 68–90.

Jacobs, T.J. (2013). *The Possible Profession: The Analytic Process of Change*. New York: Routledge.

Johnson, L.M. (1978). Imprinting: A variable in script analysis. *Transactional Analysis Journal*, 8: 110–115.

Kagan, J. (1984). *The Nature of the Child*. New York: Basic Books.

Kagan, J. (1998). *Three Seductive Ideas*. Cambridge, MA: Harvard University Press.

Karen, R. (1998). *Becoming Attached: First Relationships and How They Shape Our Capacity to Love*. New York: Oxford University Press.

Karpman, S. (1968). Fairy tales and script drama analysis. *Transactional Analysis Bulletin*, 7(26): 39–43.

Karpman, S. (2006a). Lost in translation: Neo-Bernean or neo-Freudian? *Transactional Analysis Journal*, 36: 284–302.

Karpman, S. (2006b). Personal communication, September 26.

Kegan, R. (1982). *The Evolving Self: Problem and Process of Human Development*. Cambridge, MA: Harvard University Press.

Kelley, C.R. (1988). *Body contact in Radix work*. Vancouver, WA: Kelley/Radix.

Kelley, C.R. (2004). *Life Force... the Creative Process in Man and in Nature*. Victoria, BC: Trafford.

Kihlstrom, J.F. (1990). The psychological unconscious. In L.A. Pervin (Ed.), *Handbook of Personality: Theory and Research* (pp. 445–464). New York: Guilford Press.

Klein, M. (1946). Notes on some schizoid mechanisms. *International Journal of Psychoanalysis*, 27: 99–110.

Knoblauch, S.H. (1996). The play and interplay of passionate experience. *Gender and Psychoanalysis*, 1: 323–344.

Kohlberg, L. (1984). *The Psychology of Moral Development: The Nature and Validity of Moral Stages*. San Francisco: Harper & Row.

Kohlrieser, G. (2006). *Hostage at the Table: How Leaders Can Overcome Conflict, Influence Others, and Raise Performance*. San Francisco: Jossey-Bass.

La Barre, F. (2000). *On Moving and Being Moved: Nonverbal Behavior in Clinical Practice*. Hillsdale, NJ: The Analytic Press.

Lachmann, F. (2001). Some contributions of empirical infant research to adult psycho-analysis: What have we learned? How can we apply it? *Psychoanalytic Dialolgues*, 11: 167–187.

Landaiche, N.M. (2009). Understanding social pain dynamics in human relations. *Transactional Analysis Journal*, 39: 229–238.

Landaiche, N.M. (2012). Learning and hating in groups. *Transactional Analysis Journal*, 42: 186–198.

Landaiche, N.M. (2013). Looking for trouble in groups developing the professional's capacity. *Transactional Analysis Journal*, 43: 296–310.

Landiache, N.M. (2014). Failure and shame in professional practice: The role of social pain, the haunting of loss. *Transactional Analysis Journal*, 44: 268–278.

Laplanche, J. (1995). Seduction, persecution, revelation. *The International Journal of Psycho-Analysis*, 76: 663–682.

Laplanche, J. (1997). The theory of seduction and the problem of the other. *The International Journal of Psycho-Analysis*, 78: 653–666.

Laplanche, J. (1999). *Essays on Otherness*. London: Routledge.

Laplanche, J., & Pontalis, J.-B. (1973). *The Language of Psychoanalysis*. New York: Norton.

Leader, D. (2008). *The New Black: Mourning, Melancholia and Depression*. London: Hamish Hamilton.

LeDoux, J. (1996). *The Emotional Brain*. New York: Simon & Schuster.

LeDoux, J. (2002). *Synaptic Self*. New York: Viking Press.

Levenson, R.W. (1999). The intrapersonal functions of emotions. *Cognition and Emotion*, 13: 481–504.

Levin, P. (1980). *Cycles of Power: A Guidebook for the Seven Stages of Life*. San Francisco: Trans Publishers.

Levin, P. (1985). *Becoming the Way We Are: A Transactional Guide to Personal Development*. Wenatchee, WA: Directed Media.

Levin-Landheer, P. (1982). The cycle of development. *Transactional Analysis Journal*, 12: 129–139.

Levine, S.B. (2003). The nature of sexual desire: A clinician's perspective. *Archives of Sexual Behavior*, 32: 279–285.

Lewin, M. (2000). "I'm not talking to you": Shunning as a form of violence. *Transactional Analysis Journal*, 30: 125–131.

Lichtenberg, J.D. (1989). *Psychoanalysis and Motivation*. Hillsdale, NJ: The Analytic Press.

Lifton, R.J. (1983a). *The Broken Connection: On Death and the Continuity of Life*. New York: Basic Books.

Lifton, R.J. (1983b). *The Life of the Self: Toward a New Psychology*. New York: Basic Books.

Ligabue, S. (1991). The somatic component of script in early development. *Transactional Analysis Journal*, 21: 21–29.

Lipgar, R.M., & Pines, M. (Eds.) (2003a). *Building on Bion: Branches*. London: Jessica Kingsley Publishers.

Lipgar, R.M., & Pines, M. (Eds.) (2003b). *Building on Bion: Roots*. London: Jessica Kingsley Publishers.

Little, R. (2012). The inevitability of unconscious engagements and the desire to avoid them: A commentary on Stuthridge. *Transactional Analysis Journal*, 42: 257–264.

Loevinger, J. (1976). *Ego Development*. San Francisco: Jossey-Bass.

Loewald, H.W. (1980). The waning of the Oedipus complex. In *Papers on Psychoanalysis* (pp. 384–404). New Haven, CT: Yale University Press.

Lucas, R. (2009). *The Psychotic Wavelength*. Hove, Sussex: Routledge.

Lyons-Ruth, K. (1998). Implicit relational knowing: Its role in development and psycho-analytic treatment. *Infant Mental Health Journal*, 19: 282–289.

Lyons-Ruth, K. (1999). The two-person unconscious: intersubjective dialogue, enactive relational representation and the emergence of new forms of relational organization. *Psychoanalytic Inquiry*, 19: 576–617.

Mahler, M., Pine, F., & Bergman, A. (1975). *The Psychological Birth of the Human Infant: Symbiosis and Individuation*. New York: Basic Books.

Mancia, M. (2007). *Feeling the Words: Neuropsychoanalytic Understanding of Memory and the Unconscious* (Trans. J. Baggott). London: Routledge.

Mann, D. (1997). *Psychotherapy: An Erotic Relationship*. London: Routledge.

Mann, D. (Ed.) (1999). *Erotic Transference and Countertransference: Clinical Practice in Psychotherapy*. London: Routledge.

Maquet, J. (2012). From the psychological contract to frame dynamics: Between light and shadow. *Transactional Analysis Journal*, 42: 17–27.

Marcher. L. (1996). Waking the body ego, Part 1: Core concepts and principles; Part 2: Psychomotor development and character structure. In I. Macnaughton (Ed.), *Embodying the Mind and Minding the Body* (pp. 94–137). North Vancouver, BC: Integral Press.

Marcuse, H. (1966). *One-Dimensional Man*. Boston: Beacon Press.

Maroda, K.J. (1991). *The Power of Countertransference*. Chichester: Wiley.

Maroda, K.J. (1999). *Seduction, Surrender, and Transformation*. Hillsdale, NJ: The Analytic Press.

Maslow, A. (1954). *Motivation and Personality*. New York: Harper and Row.

Maslow, A. (1962). *Toward a Psychology of Being*. Princeton, NJ: Van Nostrand.

Mazzetti, M. (2008). Trauma and migration: A transactional analytic approach toward refugees and torture victims. *Transactional Analysis Journal*, 38: 285–302.

McClelland, J.L. (1998). Complementary learning systems in the brain: A connectionist approach to explicit and implicit cognition and memory. *Annals of the New York Academy of Sciences*, 843: 153–178.

McLaughlin, J.T. (1993). Work with patients: The impetus for self-analysis. *Psycho-analytic Inquiry*, 13: 365–389.

McLaughlin, J.T. (1994). Analytic impasse: The interplay of dyadic transferences. Paper presented for the 41st Karen Horney Memorial Lecture Panel of the Karen Horney Psychoanalytic Institute and Center and the Association for the Advancement of Psychoanalysis.

McLaughlin, J.T. (2005). *The Healer's Bent: Solitude and Dialogue in the Clinical Encounter* (introduced and edited by W.F. Cornell). Hillsdale, NJ: The Analytic Press.

Mellacqua, Z. (2014). Beyond symbiosis: The role of primal exclusions in schizophrenic psychosis. *Transactional Analysis Journal*, 44: 8–30.

Mellor, K. (1980). Impasses: A developmental and structural understanding. *Transactional Analysis Journal*, 10: 213–220.

Milner, B., Squire, L.R., & Kandel, E.R. (1998). Cognitive neuroscience and the study of memory. *Neuron*, 20: 445–468.

Milner, M. (1987). *The Suppressed Madness of Sane Men: Forty-Four Years of Exploring Psychoanalysis* (Ed. D. . Tuckett). London: Tavistock Publications.

Mitchell, S.A. (1993). *Hope and Dread in Psychoanalysis*. New York: Basic Books.

Mitrani, J.L. (1996). *A Framework for the Imaginary: Clinical Explorations in Primitive States of Being*. Northvale, NJ: Jason Aronson.

Mitrani, J.L. (2001). *Ordinary People and Extra-Ordinary Protections: A Post-Kleinian Approach to the Treatment of Primitive Mental States*. Hove, Sussex: Routledge.

Moiso, C.M. (1985). Ego states and transference. *Transactional Analysis Journal*, 15: 194–201.

Moscovitch, M. (1994). *Neurological and Cognitive Bases of Memory*. Report to Harvard Medical School Conference on Memory. Cambridge, MA, May.

Moss, D. (Ed.) (2003). *HATING in the First Person Plural*. New York: Other Press.

Müller, U. (2000). Old roots revisited: Reassessing the architecture of transactional analysis. *Transactional Analysis Journal*, 30: 41–51.

Murphy, K. (2012). From a fumbled beginning: If you don't make a mistake, you don't make anything. *Transactional Analysis Journal*, 42: 28–33.

Nelson, K., & Gruendel, J. (1981). Generalized event representations: The basic building blocks of cognitive development. In M.E. Lamb & A.L. Browns (Eds.), *Advances in Developmental Psychology*, Vol. 1. Hillsdale, NJ: Lawrence Erlbaum Associates.

Nitsun, M. (1996). *The Anti-Group: Destructive Forces in the Group and Their Creative Potential*. London: Routledge.

Nitsun. M. (2015). *Beyond the Anti-Group: Survival and Transformation*. London: Routledge.

Novak, E. (2015). Are games, enactments, and reenactments similar? No, yes, it depends. *Transactional Analysis Journal*, 45: 117–127.

Novellino, M. (1984). Self-analysis of countertransference in integrative transactional analysis. *Transactional Analysis Journal*, 14: 63–67.

Novellino, M. (2005). Transactional psychoanalysis: Epistemological foundations. *Transactional Analysis Journal*, 35: 157–172.

Nussbaum, A. (2011). Changing the name of dementia during residency training: From medication management to CBT to psychodynamic psychotherapy. *Bulletin of the Menninger Clinic*, 75(3): 254–266.

Ogden, T.H. (1982). *Projective Identification and Psychotherapeutic Technique*. New York: Jason Aronson.

Ogden, T.H. (1989). *The Primitive Edge of Experience*. Northvale, NJ: Jason Aronson

Ogden, T.H. (2005). *This Art of Psychoanalysis: Dreaming Undreamt Dreams and Interrupted Cries*. London: Routledge.

Ogden, T.H. (2009). *Rediscovering Psychoanalysis: Thinking and Dreaming, Learning and Forgetting*. London: Routledge.

O'Hearne, J.J. (1981). Good grief. *Transactional Analysis Journal*, 11: 85–87.

Orr, G. (2004). *The Blessing*. Tulsa, OK: Council Oaks Books.

Pally, R. (2000). *The Mind–Brain Relationship*. London: Karnac.

Panksepp, J. (1993). Rough and tumble play: A fundamental brain process. In K. MacDonald (Ed.), *Parent–Child Play: Descriptions and Implications* (pp. 147–184). Albany, NY: State University of New York Press.

Panksepp, J. (2001). The long-term psychobiological consequences of infant emotions: Prescriptions for the twenty-first century. *Infant Mental Health Journal*, 22: 132–173.

Panksepp, J. (2009). Brain emotional systems and qualities of mental life: From animal models of affect to implications for psychotherapeutics. In D. Fosha, D.J. Siegel, & M.F. Solomon, (Eds.), *The Healing Power of Emotions: Affective Neuroscience, Development, and Practice* (pp. 1–26). New York: W.W. Norton.

Penfield, W. (1952). Memory mechanisms. *Archives of Neurology and Psychiatry*, 67: 178–198.

Pertegato, E.G., & Pertegato, G.O. (Eds.) (2013). *From Psychoanalysis to Group Analysis: The Pioneering Work of Trigant Burrow*. London: Karnac.

Petriglieri, G., & Wood, J.D. (2003). The invisible revealed: Collusion as an entry to the group unconscious. *Transactional Analysis Journal*, 33: 332–343.

Piaget, J. (1977). *Essential Piaget*. New York: Basic Books.

Piaget, J., & Inhelder, B. (1954). *The Construction of Reality in the Child*. New York: Basic Books.

Pierini, A. (2008). Has the unconscious moved house? *Transactional Analysis Journal*, 38: 110–118.

Pine, F. (1985). *Developmental Theory and Clinical Process*. New Haven, CT: Yale University Press.

Pines, M. (Ed.) (1983). *The Evolution of Group Analysis*. London: Routledge & Kegan Paul.

Pines, M. (Ed.) (1992). *Bion and Group Psychotherapy*. London: Tavistock/Routledge.

Pines, M. (2010). Learning peace: Here and now—the intercultural competence of groups. *Group Analysis*, 43: 465–475.

Pink, D.H. (2009). *Drive: The Surprising Truth about What Motivates Us*. New York: Riverhead Books.

Poland, W.S. (1996). *Melting the Darkness: The Dyad and Principles of Clinical Practice*. Northvale, NJ: Jason Aronson.

Poland, W.S. (2005). The analyst's fears. Paper presented at the conference Generativity: Honoring the Contributions of James T. McLaughlin. Pittsburgh, PA. October 15.

Poland, W.S. (2006). The analyst's fears. *American Imago*, 63: 201–217.

Poland, W.S. (2013). The analyst's witnessing and otherness. *Journal of the American Psychoanalytic Association*, 48: 17–36.

Poland, W.S. (2015). Personal communication, January 4.

Post, R.M., & Weiss, S.R.B. (1997). Emergent properties of neural systems: How focal molecular neurobiological alterations can effect behavior. *Development and Psychopathology*, 9: 907–930.

Quinodoz, D. (2010). *Growing Old: A Journey of Self-Discovery*. London: Routledge.

Rath, I. (1993). Developing a coherent map of transactional analysis theories. *Transactional Analysis Journal*, 23: 201–215.

Reich, W. (1970). *The Mass Psychology of Fascism*. New York: Farrar, Straus and Giroux.

Reich, W. (1972). *Sex-Pol: Essays 1929–1934* (Ed. L. Baxandall). New York: Random House.

Renik, O. (1993). Analytic interaction: Conceptualizing technique in the light of the analyst's irreducible subjectivity. *Psychoanalytic Quarterly*, 62: 553–571.

Renik, O. (1999). Playing one's cards face up in analysis. *Psychoanalytic Quarterly*, 68: 521–539.

Rich, A. (1979). *On Lies, Secrets, and Silence: Selected Prose 1966–1978*. New York: Norton.

Rogers, C. (1970). *Carl Rogers on Encounter Groups*. New York: Harper & Row.

Rogers, C., & Stevens, B. (1967). *Person to Person: The Problem of Being Human*. Moab, UT: Real People Press.

Rosenfeld, H. (1987). *Impasse and Interpretation: Therapeutic and Anti-Therapeutic Factors in the Psychoanalytic Treatment of Psychotic, Borderline, and Neurotic Patients*. London: Tavistock/Routledge, 1995.

Rothschild, B. (2000). *The Body Remembers: The Psychophysiology of Trauma and Trauma Treatment*. New York: Norton.

Salters, D. (2006). Simunye—sibaningi: We are one—we are many. *Transactional Analysis Journal*, 36, 152–158.

Schacter, D.L. (1992). Understanding implicit memory: A cognitive neuroscience approach. *American Psychologist*, 47(4): 559–569.

Schacter, D.L. (1996). *Searching for Memory: The Brain, the Mind, and the Past*. New York: Basic Books.

Schermer, V.L., & Pines, M. (Eds.) (1994). *Ring of Fire: Primitive Affects and Object Relations in Group Psychotherapy*. London: Routledge.

Schiff, J.L. et al. (1975). *Cathexis Reader: Transactional Analysis and Psychosis*. New York: Harper & Row.

Schore, A.N. (1994). *Affect Regulation and the Origin of the Self*. Hillsdale, NJ: Lawrence Erlbaum.

Schore, A.N. (2001). Contributions from the decade of the brain to infant health: An overview. *Infant Mental Health Journal*, 22: 1–6.

Schore, A.N. (2003). *Affect Regulation and the Repair of the Self*. New York: W. W. Norton.

Schutz, W.C. (1971). *Here Comes Everybody*. New York: Harper & Row.

Scorsese, M. (Director) (2005). *No Direction Home: Bob Dylan* [Motion picture]. United States: Paramount Pictures.

Searles, H. (1959). Oedipal love in the countertransference. *International Journal of Psychoanalysis*, 40: 180–190.

Searles, H. (1979). *Countertransference and Related Subjects*. New York: International Universities Press.

Searles, H. (1981). The informational value of the supervisor's emotional experiences. *Psychiatry*, 18: 135–146.

Shabad, P., & Selinger, S.S. (1995). Bracing for disappointment and the counterphobic leap into the future. In E.G. Corrigan & P.-E. Gordon (Eds.), *The Mind Object: Precocity and Pathology of Self-Sufficiency* (pp. 209–228). Northvale, NJ: Jason Aronson.

Shadbolt, C. (2012). The place of failure and rupture in psychotherapy. *Transactional Analysis Journal*, 42: 5–16.

Shapiro, S.A. (1996). The embodied analyst in the Victorian consulting room. *Gender and Psychoanalysis*, 1: 297–322.

Shahar-Levy, Y. (2001). The function of the human motor system in processes of storing and retrieving preverbal, primal experience. *Psychoanalytic Inquiry*, 21: 378–393.

Siegel, D.J. (1999). *The Developing Mind: How Relationships and the Brain Interact to Shape Who We Are*. New York: Guilford Press.

Siegel. D.J. (2001). Toward an interpersonal neurobiology of the developing mind: Attachment relationships, "mindsight," and neural integration. *Infant Mental Health Journal*, 22: 67–94.

Slavin, J. (2003). The innocence of sexuality. *Psychoanalytic Quarterly*, 72: 51–80.

Slavin, J. (2007). The imprisonment and liberation of love: The dangers and possibilities of love in the psychoanalytic relationship. *Psychoanalytic Inquiry*, 27: 197–218.

Slavin, M., & Kriegman, D. (1998). Why the analyst needs to change: Toward a theory of conflict, negotiation, and mutual influence in the therapeutic process. *Psychoanalytic Dialogues*, 8: 247–284.

Slochower, J. (2006). The psychoanalytic other: Commentary on paper by Helen K. Gediman. *Psychoanalytic Dialogues*, 16: 263–272.

Solomon, C. (2003). When intimate relationships end. *Transactional Analysis Journal*, 33: 58–67.

Sprietsma, L. (1978). A winner script apparatus. *Transactional Analysis Journal*, 8: 45–51.

Steere, D. (1981). Body movement in ego states. *Transactional Analysis Journal*, 11: 335–345.

Steere, D. (1985). Protocol. *Transactional Analysis Journal*, 15: 248–259.

Stein, R. (1998a). The poignant, the excessive and the enigmatic in sexuality. *International Journal of Psychoanalysis*, 79: 253–268.

Stein, R. (1998b). The enigmatic dimension of sexual experience: The "Otherness" of sexuality and primal seduction. *Psychoanalytic Quarterly*, 67: 594–625.

Stein, R. (2007). Moments in Laplanche's theory of sexuality. *Studies in Gender and Sexuality*, 8: 177–200.

Stein, R. (2008). The otherness of sexuality: Excess. *Journal of the American Psycho-analytic Association*, 56: 43–71.

Steinberg, R. (2010). Using redecision therapy to resolve postdivorce impasses and loss. *Transactional Analysis Journal*, 40: 130–143.

Steiner, C. (1971). *Games Alcoholics Play*. New York: Grove Press.

Steiner, C. (1974). *Scripts People Live*. New York: Grove Press.

Steiner, C. (2006). Personal communication, October 12.

Steiner, C., Wyckoff, H., et al. (1975). *Readings in Radical Psychiatry*. New York: Grove Press.

Stern, D.B. (1985). *The Interpersonal World of the Infant: A View from Psychoanalysis and Developmental Psychology*. New York: Basic Books.

Stern, D.B. (1997). *Unformulated Experience: From Dissociation to Imagination in Psychoanalysis*. Hillsdale, NJ: The Analytic Press.

Stern, D.B. (2003). The fusion of horizons: Dissociation, enactment, and understanding. *Psychoanalytic Dialogues*, 13: 843–873.

Stern, D.B. (2004). The eye sees itself: Dissociation, enactment, and the achievement of conflict. *Contemporary Psychoanalysis*, 40: 197–238.

Stuntz, E.C. (1971). *Review of Games: 1962–1970*. West Lafayette, IN: Wabash Valley TA Study Group.

Stuthridge, J. (2012). Traversing the fault lines: Trauma and enactment. *Transactional Analysis Journal*, 42: 238–251.

Stuthridge, J. (2015). All the world's a stage: Games, enactment, and countertransference. *Transactional Analysis Journal*, 45: 104–111.

Stuthridge, J., & Sills, C. (2016). Psychological games and intersubjective processes. In R. Erskine (Ed.), *Transactional Analysis in Contemporary Psychotherapy* (pp. 185–208). London: Karnac.

Thelan, E., & Fogel, A. (1989). Toward an action-based theory of infant development. In J.J. Lockman & N.L. Hazen (Eds.), *Action in Social Context: Perspectives on Early Development* (pp. 23–63). New York: Plenum Press.

Thelan, E., & Smith, L.B. (1994). *A Dynamic Systems Approach to the Development of Cognition and Action*. Cambridge, MA: The MIT Press.

Thomas, A., & Chess, S. (1980). *The Dynamics of Psychological Growth*. New York: Brunner/Mazel.

Torrey, E.F. (2014). *American Psychosis: How the Federal Government Destroyed the Mental Illness Treatment System*. New York: Oxford University Press.

Tosi, M.T. (2008). The many faces of the unconscious: A new unconscious for a phenomenological transactional analysis. *Transactional Analysis Journal*, 38: 119–127.

Tronick, E. (1998). Dyadically expended states of consciousness and the process of therapeutic change. *Infant Mental Health Journal*, 19: 290–299.

Tronick, E. (2001). Emotional connections and dyadic consciousness in infant–mother and patient–therapist interactions: Commentary on paper by Frank M. Lachmann. *Psychoanalytic Dialogues*, 11: 187–194.

Tulving, E., Kapur, S., Craik, F.I.M., Moscovitch, M., & Houle, S. (1994). Hemispheric encoding/retrieval asymmetry in episodic memory: Positron emission tomography findings. *Proceedings of the National Academy of Sciences*, 91: 2016–2020.

Vaillant, G. (1977). *Adaptation to Life: How the Best and the Brightest Came of Age*. Boston: Little, Brown & Co.

Vaillant, G., & Vaillant, C. (1981). Natural history of male psychological health, X: Work as a predictor of positive mental health. *American Journal of Psychiatry*, 138: 1433–1440.

Van Beekum, S. (2006). The relational consultant. *Transactional Analysis Journal*, 36: 318–329.

Van Beekum, S. (2009). Siblings, aggression, and sexuality: Adding the lateral. *Transactional Analysis Journal*, 39: 129–135.

Van Beekum, S. (2012). Connecting with the undertow: The methodology of the relational consultant. *Transactional Analysis Journal*, 42: 126–133.

Waldekranz-Piselli, K.C. (1999). What do we do before we say hello? The body as the stage setting for the script. *Transactional Analysis Journal*, 29: 31–48.

Weiner, T. (2015). *One Man against the World: The Tragedy of Richard Nixon*. New York: Henry Holt.

Williams, M. (1999). Compassion. In *Some Jazz a While: Collected Poems* (p. 254). Urbana, IL: University of Illinois Press.

Wilson, C. (1972). *New Pathways in Psychology: Maslow and the Post-Freudian Revolution*. New York: Taplinger Publishing.

Winer, R. (1994). *Close Encounters*. Northvale, NJ: Jason Aronson.

Winnicott, D.W. (1941). The observation of infants in a set situation. In D.W. Winnicott, *Collected Papers: Through Paediatrics to Psycho-Analysis* (pp. 52–69). London: Tavistock Publications, 1958.

Winnicott, D.W. (1949). Mind and its relation to the psyche-soma. In *Through Paediatrics to Psycho-Analysis* (pp. 243–252). London: Karnac, 1975.

Winnicott, D.W. (1950). Aggression in relation to emotional development. In D.W. Winnicott, *Collected Papers: Through Paediatrics to Psycho-Analysis* (pp. 204–218). London: Tavistock Publications, 1958.

Winnicott, D.W. (1960). Ego distortion in terms of true and false self. In *The Maturational Processes and the Facilitating Environment* (pp. 140–152). Madison, CT: International Universities Press, 1965.

Winnicott, D.W. (1968). The squiggle game. In D.W. Winnicott, *Psycho-Analytic Explorations* (Ed. C. Winnicott, R. Shepherd, & M. Davis; pp. 299–317). Cambridge, MA: Harvard University Press, 1989.

Winnicott, D.W. (1971). *Playing and Reality*. London: Tavistock Publications.

Winnicott, D.W. (1985). *Deprivation and Delinquency* (Ed. C. Winnicott, R. Shepherd, & M. Davis). London: Tavistock/Routledge.

Winnicott, D.W. (1989a). *Psychoanalytic Explorations* (Ed. C. Winnicott, R. Shepherd, & M. Davis). Cambridge, MA: Harvard University Press.

Winnicott, D.W. (1989b). Notes on play. In D.W. Winnicott, *Psycho-Analytic Explorations* (Ed. C. Winnicott, R. Shepherd, & M. Davis; pp. 59–63). Cambridge, MA: Harvard University Press, 59-63.

Wood, J.D., & Petriglieri, G. (2005). Transcending polarization: Beyond binary thinking. *Transactional Analysis Journal*, 35: 31–39.

Woods, K. (2003). The interface between Berne and Langs: Understanding unconscious communication. *Transactional Analysis Journal*, 33: 214–222

Index

101, 123; on hope 26; influence of 4, 5, 6, 46, 79, 108, 109, 170; on nonverbal behavior 109; on object usage 10, 15; *Playing and Reality* 23–4, 26–8; theory of play 23–4, 25, 28, 36; on the "true self" 183
Wood, J.D. 226

Woods, K. 151
working couple 146–8
World War I 200, 208–9, 216, 218, 220, 224
World War II 43, 195, 218, 220, 222, 223, 224
Wyckoff, Hogie 224

Taylor & Francis Group
an **informa** business

Taylor & Francis eBooks

www.taylorfrancis.com

A single destination for eBooks from Taylor & Francis
with increased functionality and an improved user
experience to meet the needs of our customers.

90,000+ eBooks of award-winning academic content in
Humanities, Social Science, Science, Technology, Engineering,
and Medical written by a global network of editors and authors.

TAYLOR & FRANCIS EBOOKS OFFERS:

A streamlined
experience for
our library
customers

A single point
of discovery
for all of our
eBook content

Improved
search and
discovery of
content at both
book and
chapter level

REQUEST A FREE TRIAL
support@taylorfrancis.com

 Routledge
Taylor & Francis Group

 CRC Press
Taylor & Francis Group